Language in Action

Language in Action

SFL Theory across Contexts

Edited by María Estela Brisk and

Mary J. Schleppegrell

SHEFFIELD UK   BRISTOL CT

Published by Equinox Publishing Ltd.

UK   Office 415, The Workstation, 15 Paternoster Row, Sheffield,
       South Yorkshire S1 2BX
USA   ISD, 70 Enterprise Drive, Bristol, CT 06010

www.equinoxpub.com

First published 2021

British Library Cataloguing-in-Publication Data

A catalogue record for this book is available from the British Library.

ISBN-13   978 1 80050 003 7   (hardback)
           978 1 80050 004 4   (paperback)
           978 1 80050 005 1   (ePDF)
           978 1 80050 043 3   (ePub)

Library of Congress Cataloging-in-Publication Data

Names: Brisk, María Estela, 1940- editor. | Schleppegrell, Mary, editor.
Title: Language in action : SFL theory across contexts / edited by María Estela Brisk and Mary J. Schleppegrell.
Description: Sheffield, South Yorkshire ; Bristol, CT : Equinox Publishing Ltd, 2021. | Includes bibliographical references and index. | Summary: "Language in Action: SFL Theory across Contexts brings together recent research in elementary and secondary education, higher education, and translation studies, informed by Systemic Functional Linguistics"-- Provided by publisher.
Identifiers: LCCN 2021000877 (print) | LCCN 2021000878 (ebook) | ISBN 9781800500037 (hardback) | ISBN 9781800500044 (paperback) | ISBN 9781800500051 (pdf) | ISBN 9781800500433 (epub)
Subjects: LCSH: Functionalism (Linguistics) | Systemic grammar. | Language and languages--Study and teaching.
Classification: LCC P147 .L38 2021 (print) | LCC P147 (ebook) | DDC 410.1/83--dc23
LC record available at https://lccn.loc.gov/2021000877
LC ebook record available at https://lccn.loc.gov/2021000878

Typeset by Sparks – www.sparkspublishing.com

Contents

Introduction   1

    Mary J. Schleppegrell and María Estela Brisk

Part I   Studies in elementary and secondary education   **11**

1 Theory inspired best practices: Elementary teachers appropriate
    SFL theory to inform their practice   13

    María Estela Brisk

2 The role of meaningful sentence-level metalanguage: Insights
    from children's thinking with functional grammar   33

    Mary Schleppegrell and Carrie Symons

3 From buttocks to seminal muscles: SFL-based physical education   55

    Ruth Mulvad

4 A geometry teacher's actions for engaging students in
    mathematizing from real-world contexts: A linguistic analysis   87

    Gloriana González

**Part II   Studies in student and faculty development
with respect to academic writing at the university level**   **117**

5 Exploring new perspectives and degrees of delicacy in *Appraisal*
    studies: An analysis of *Engagement* resources in academic
    discourse in Spanish   119

    Julio César Valerdi Zárate

6 A functional study of Transitivity and Attitude in student writing
    in Spanish across disciplines: Making connections   149

    *Natalia Ignatieva, Daniel Rodríguez-Vergara and Victoria
    Zamudio Jasso*

7   Scaffolding the wave: Supporting student teachers in professional
    academic writing through LCT and SFL   177
    Anna-Vera Meidell Sigsgaard and Susanne Karen Jacobsen

8   Scaffolding argument writing in history: The evolution of an
    interdisciplinary collaboration   207
    Silvia Pessoa, Thomas D. Mitchell and Aaron Jacobson

Part III   Studies in translation   **235**

9   Translation as re-instantiation: An investigation of verbal
    projection   237
    Hailing Yu and Canzhong Wu

10 Building and enhancing intercultural communication in museum
    spaces through SFL and translation studies   257
    Marina Manfredi

Index   285

Introduction

Mary J. Schleppegrell and María Estela Brisk

The title of this book, *Language in Action: SFL Theory across Contexts,* draws attention to the many ways Systemic Functional Linguistics (SFL) is informing not only researchers, but also applied linguists, educators, translators, and others interested in the ways language shapes and is shaped by the social contexts in which it acts as a powerful social semiotic. The ten chapters that make up this book exemplify the range of ways the theory and its powerful discourse analysis tools can be applied to better understand the role of language in social life. They also represent a key activity of systemic functional linguists in gathering internationally each year as a community of scholars.

The theme "(re)Imagining the Future: Expanding Resources and Making Connections" informed the 180 plenaries, colloquia, papers, roundtables, and posters presented at the 45th International Systemic Functional Congress. Researchers and educators from Asia, Europe, Africa, and South and North America gathered at Boston College in July 2018 to share their work that, in the spirit of the theme of the congress to make connections, represented several theoretical perspectives and various disciplines. Presenters were invited to submit papers for a full review process. This resulting volume of accepted chapters is divided into three sections. The congress also featured a "Teacher Researcher Day" where elementary and secondary teachers whose instruction is informed by SFL showed their work. Selected presentations are being featured in a separate volume (Gebhard & Accurso, forthcoming).

The first section, Studies in Elementary and Secondary Education, offers insights into curriculum and instructional issues in subjects including history, physical education, and mathematics, with a focus on development of students' reading, writing, and disciplinary literacy skills. A second section, Studies in Student and Faculty Development with Respect to Academic Writing at the University Level, reports on studies in teacher education and student learning in settings where Spanish, Danish, or English are the languages of instruction, with a focus on the development of advanced academic writing in these languages. The last section, Studies in Translation, offers new perspectives on translation from classical Chinese literature and Italian museum texts. Across the studies, the book offers readers a range of work informed by functional grammar, register theory, Appraisal, and Legitimation Code Theory. The volume aims to inspire and inform researchers and students interested in new approaches to systemic functional linguistics in action.

Contributions of the chapters

Each of the three sections of this book offers insightful and detailed presentations of the ways SFL can be used both in discourse analysis and in practical applications that improve the work of educators and translators.

Studies in elementary and secondary education

The studies in elementary and secondary education include a report on a decade-long school-based collaboration between researchers, teachers, and administrators to develop a genre-based pedagogy for multilingual learners, a report on bilingual children's use of functional grammar to read challenging texts, a curriculum development project that drew on register theory to create language-focused instruction in physical education (PE), and a discourse analysis of a secondary mathematics teacher's explanations. Each of these studies shows SFL at work to *expand resources and make connections,* addressing the theme of the conference by illustrating the power of the social semiotic theory in enabling students to engage with knowledge and learning with greater support for a focus on language.

Brisk (Chapter 1) describes a ten year collaboration between university researchers and an elementary school that brought about significant change in classroom writing instruction and improvement in bilingual students' performance. She traces the ways teachers took up SFL-informed pedagogical approaches based on the Sydney School genre approach and the Teaching and Learning Cycle (Rose & Martin, 2012) in a diverse urban school with a majority of bilingual pupils. She details the aspects of the language-based theory that teachers readily took up and those that required more support and practice, offering case studies of two fourth grade teachers' developmental pathways and connecting with educational research that shows teachers need time to take up new practices (Hargreaves & Fullan, 2012). Supported by the school administration, Brisk and her students collaborated with teachers and administrators to address the school's goals to improve student writing by engaging teacher agency and embracing the multilingual resources the children brought from their communities. These factors were key to the success Brisk reports, as the school moved from being among the lowest performing in the city to one of the top schools. Brisk shows how the collaboration supported teachers' growth and leadership and created a learning context where children, teachers, and researchers all learned together.

Schleppegrell and Symons (Chapter 2) report on a different kind of research in an elementary school context where teachers were engaging children learning English as an additional language in exploring language and meaning with functional grammar as they read and wrote challenging texts. The chapter reports on think-aloud interviews with the children that explored their understanding about how the SFL metalanguage of *Process, Participant, Circumstance* helped them deconstruct the language of challenging texts. The children also reflect on the ways functional grammar metalanguage can support them in reading with greater understanding. The chapter presents evidence that the SFL metalanguage offers these bilingual learners a valuable resource for exploring meaning in the texts they read.

Ruth Mulvad (Chapter 3) reports on a project where linguists collaborated with Physical Education (PE) instructors to create model materials following a Danish educational reform that called for more focus on language in each subject. Following an analysis of PE pedagogy, the group developed model lessons for teacher education in how to infuse a language focus into PE instruction. They drew on the notion of *Register* to analyze the Field, Tenor, and Mode of language use in PE and then developed lessons that would move students across the mode continuum, building from their everyday language toward more expert language. The chapter describes lessons that guide children in adopting increasingly abstract language for construing the activity of creating an acrobatic sequence, with Derewianka's (1990) "snail" model providing a framework for moving from action (doing the acrobatics) toward reflection (writing a report about the acrobatics). Mulvad then describes how teachers were introduced to this new approach through vignettes that first engaged them in teaching the sequence, and then supported them in understanding the theoretical perspective underlying the approach. This chapter offers a valuable framework for anyone doing curriculum development to consider how to prepare teachers to build on students' everyday language and enable them to take up the more challenging disciplinary and technical language they need to use to display their new knowledge.

Gloriana Gonzalez (Chapter 4) shifts our focus to the secondary mathematics classroom and to SFL as a tool for discourse analysis. She shows how the particular language choices of a geometry teacher enable students to draw on their everyday language, connect with real-world contexts, and use learning in other subjects to begin to engage with a challenging new concept that involves reading and working with diagrams. In addition, the analysis of the teacher's language shows how he supports students in making reasoned conjectures during problem-solving activities; a key focus of new mathematics standards for secondary school. Gonzalez argues that such detailed analysis can inform professional development for mathematics teachers by identifying specific actions they take to engage and support students in developing mathematical understanding. She also characterizes these teacher moves as literacy practices that promote problem-solving and student learning.

Studies in student and faculty development with respect to academic writing at the university level

The studies in this section include reports from Spanish, Danish, and English language contexts. They include two analyses of Mexican university students' writing. In the first, Valerdi argues for bringing insights from outside of SFL into conversation with the SFL analysis in studying students' argument writing. Ingatieva, Rodríguez-Vergara, and Zamudio Jasso explore the interaction between ideational and interpersonal meaning in students' language choices and contribute to contrastive studies across languages. Then Meidell Sigsgaard and Jacobsen, working in a Danish teacher education context, show how discourse analysis of students' texts, using Legitimation Code Theory (LCT), can be used to raise students' awareness about the ways they bring theory and data into conversation with each other in their writing. Finally, Pessoa, Mitchell, and Jacobson describe how collaboration with a history professor helped applied linguists sharpen the ways they were supporting Middle Eastern students to write arguments. These studies highlight various kinds of *connections* the work with SFL has stimulated, addressing the theme of the conference by showing the value of engaging with commensurate theories, contributing to cross-lingual comparisons, and collaborating with disciplinary experts.

Valerdi (Chapter 5) presents an analysis of graduate student academic writing in Spanish at a Mexican university as he explores the ways their MA theses in applied linguistics use the resources of *Engagement* to introduce their work. In this study of Spanish academic writing, the author incorporates constructs from Toulmin (2003) to enhance his discussion of the role of Engagement and dialogic contraction and expansion. Building from other analyses of Engagement in Spanish, Chinese, and English academic discourse, the author shows how the Toulminian constructs of *Claim, Data, Warrant,* and the various ways *Warrants* can be established, offer new insights into how Engagement subsystems are deployed. He argues that this approach offers specific insights both for pedagogy in Spanish academic writing and for research on argumentation more generally, as it reveals how authors open or close dialogic space at the level of the argumentative move. This adds a dimension to research that has typically reported the distribution of Engagement resources more globally.

Ignatieva, Rodríguez-Vergara, and Zamudio Jasso (Chapter 6) report on an ongoing study at the National Autonomous University of Mexico (UNAM), which is part of the international *Systemics Across Languages* project (Scotta Cabral & Barbara, 2018). They present analysis of academic texts written in Spanish by university students in history, geography, and literature to explore the interaction of experiential and interpersonal meanings through a focus on students' choices from systems of Transitivity and Appraisal. They show how writers exploit different process types to represent outer and inner worlds and how these language choices are related to expression of attitudes. They argue that texts called "essays" actually realize different genres related to the different purposes of the texts in each discipline. They suggest that the higher rate of expressions of judgment that they find in geography and literature and of affect in history, for example, point towards differences in the kinds of values expressed by students in different fields. At the same time, they argue that the higher presence of inscribed attitude in texts written by freshmen students (as compared to the senior students of literature) can signal the development of students' evaluative resources. This study contributes to contrastive studies across disciplines.

Meidell Sigsgaard and Jacobsen (Chapter 7) report on a teacher education context in Denmark where pre-service teachers often exhibit difficulty writing about practice in a theoretically informed way. They use SFL's functional grammar and the analytical tools of LCT to analyze research papers that require students to use theoretical knowledge to write about an aspect of pedagogical practice. They offer case studies of the writing of a good and a poor writer, and show that the lower performing student's text presented generalizations without reference to either theory or data. They argue that the poorer writer could improve through explicit attention to the semantic waves of varying gravity that are created as writers connect theory and practice.

In the last chapter of this section (Chapter 8), Pessoa, Mitchell and Jacobson report on a study at a US university in the Middle East where students are learning to write in a second language in the context of a history course.

The researchers had previously worked in this context to support writers with Dreyfus, Humphrey, Mahboob, and Martin's (2016) 3×3 model; and the focus of this chapter is on the ways collaboration between the researchers and a new history professor brought into focus additional issues in the scaffolding of argument writing in history. The authors show how the history professor's understanding of the language resources of history arguments developed, and how his flexibility and feedback facilitated the refinement of the applied linguists' workshop materials and the development of a new assessment rubric. This chapter, like others, speaks to the role of collaboration with disciplinary experts in the efforts to bring a language focus to education.

Studies in translation

The chapters in the two sections above all focus on applications of SFL in contexts of education. The two chapters in this section show how SFL analysis can be done in another applied context: translation. Here again the authors show how SFL helps *expand resources and make connections* as they work in the area of instantiation of meaning across languages.

Hailing Yu and Canzhong Wu (Chapter 9) use SFL's functional grammar to understand the differences in translation of the same literary Chinese text by different translators at different times. They investigate how verbal projection in a Buddhist text written in literary Chinese in 1291 is re-instantiated in four English translations written in 1930, 1977, 1998 and 2011. The system of projection is more rigid in Literary Chinese than in English, and they describe the decisions translators have made, as English offers a greater variety of resources for projection of saying and thinking. The chapter argues that the choices translators make relate to the contexts of translation and the backgrounds of the different translators.

Finally, Maria Manfredi (Chapter 10) reports on a study of museum translations in Bologna, Italy that demonstrates how SFL, with its metafunctional perspective, has much to offer museum translators. She identifies issues in translating for the public and proposes specific ways that knowledge of SFL might be drawn on to further develop the understanding of museum translators and to make translations clearer and more accessible to museum visitors.

SFL analytic approaches used

Table 0.1 offers a snapshot of the different ways the authors of this book draw on SFL's systems and tools to analyze language in action.

Table 0.1 Key SFL themes by chapter

Linguistic or Pedagogical Construct from SFL	*Chapters where this is in focus*									
	1	2	3	4	5	6	7	8	9	10
Register	x	x	x			x	x	x		x
Field, Tenor, Mode	x		x				x			
Metafunctions		x				x	x	x		x
Transitivity resources	x	x		x		x	x		x	x
Nuclear Relations				x						
Process, Participant, Circumstance Configurations		x				x	x			x
Process types						x	x			
Verbal Projection									x	
Nominalization/Complex Noun Groups	x						x			x
Appraisal resources					x	x	x	x		x
Attitude						x	x			
Engagement					x		x	x		
Graduation							x			
Modality										x
Texturing resources	x	x		x			x			x
Lexical Strings/Cohesion				x						x
Conjunction		x		x						
Theme/New	x						x			x
Resources for pedagogy	x		x				x	x		
Legitimation Code Theory							x			
Genre Pedagogy	x		x					x		
Teaching and Learning Cycle	x		x							

A key tenet of Systemic Functional Linguistics is that language itself is a key actor in social life. These studies show *Language in Action* through the work of educators, students, curriculum developers, discourse analysts, and translators. They demonstrate the spread of the theory across global and multilingual contexts, informing and supporting advances in pedagogy, research, and cultural life. We hope they will inspire new contributions by readers.

About the authors

Mary Schleppegrell is Professor of Education at the University of Michigan. She uses systemic functional linguistics to study the linguistic challenges of learning and children's language development. With literacy scholar Annemarie Palincsar, she led the *Language and Meaning* project to support bilingual children's literacy development across subject areas, and is currently collaborating with Chauncey Monte-Sano to study teacher learning to support emergent bilinguals in social studies. She is the author of *The Language of Schooling* (Erlbaum, 2004), *Developing Advanced Literacy in First and Second Languages* (with Cecilia Colombi, Erlbaum, 2002), *Reading in Secondary Content Areas (*with Zhihui Fang, University of Michigan Press, 2008)*, and *Focus on Grammar and Meaning* (with Luciana de Oliveira, Oxford University Press, 2015).

Maria Estela Brisk is Professor of Education at Boston College. Her research and teaching address writing instruction, genre pedagogy, bilingual education, bilingual language and literacy acquisition, and preparation of mainstream teachers to work with bilingual learners. She is the author of numerous articles and six books: *Bilingual Education: From Compensatory to Quality Schooling*; *Literacy and Bilingualism: A Handbook for ALL Teachers*; *Situational Context of Education: A Window into the World of Bilingual Learners*; *Language Development and Education: Children with Varying Language Experiences* (with P. Menyuk); *Language, Culture, and Community in Teacher Education*; and *Engaging Students in Academic Literacies: Genre-based Pedagogy for K-5 Classrooms*. Professor Brisk is a native of Argentina.

References

Accurso, K. & Gebhard, M. (2020) SFL praxis in U.S. teacher education: a critical literature review, *Language and Education*, https://doi.org/10.1080/09500782.2020.1781880

Derewianka, B. (1990). Rocks in the head: Children and the language of geology. In Carter, R. (ed.) *Knowledge About Language and the Curriculum.* London: Hodder & Stoughton, 197–215.

Dreyfus, S., Humphrey, S., Mahboob, A., & Martin, J. M. (2016). *Genre Pedagogy in Higher Education. The SLATE project.* London: Palgrave Macmillan.

Gebhard, M. & Accurso, K. (forthcoming). *Teacher Action Research Across the Curriculum: An SFL Approach to Supporting Diverse Learners' Disciplinary Literacies in Hard Times.* Routledge.

Hargreaves A. & Fullan, M. (2012). *Professional Capital: Transforming Teaching in Every School.* New York: Teachers College Press.

Rose, D., & Martin, J. R. (2012). *Learning to Write, Reading to Learn: Genre, Knowledge and Pedagogy in the Sydney School.* Sheffield: Equinox.

Scotta, S. R. & Barbara, L. (eds.) (2018). *Estudos Sistêmico-Funcionais no* Âmbito *do Projeto SAL.* Santa Maria: PPGL Editores.

Toulmin, S. (2003). *The Use of Argument* (updated edition). New York: Cambridge University Press.

Part I
Studies in elementary and secondary education

1 Theory inspired best practices: Elementary teachers appropriate SFL theory to inform their practice

María Estela Brisk
Boston College

Since writing is considered the most neglected language skill in schools (Graham & Harris, 2013), it is recommended that writing assumes a more prominent role in school curricula, and that teachers provide more writing instruction to students while also having access themselves to quality pre- and in-service training (National Commission on Writing, 2003).

In response to the need to improve the teaching of writing, a number of researchers and teacher educators employ systemic functional linguistics (SFL) to inform writing instruction. An effort to improve the teaching of writing was launched by Australian linguists and educators in the 1980s. Their motivation emerged from their observations of how limited writing instruction was, especially for bilingual students (Martin, 2009). The *Writing Project* and *Language and Social Power* project brought to elementary schools genre pedagogy informed by SFL theory. In the 1990s the work was extended to secondary schools in the project called *Write it Right,* and finally *Reading to Learn* integrated reading and writing (Rose & Martin, 2012).

A number of educators and linguists in the U.S.A., especially those working with bilingual populations, brought to the schools what they had learned from the Australian colleagues (Aguirre-Muñoz, Park, Amabisca, & Boscardin, 2008; Brisk, 2015; Brisk & Ossa-Parra, 2018, de Olivera & Dodds, 2010; Gebhard, Chen, & Britton, 2014; Schleppegrell & Go, 2007, to name a few). One such project took place at a multilingual urban elementary school in Boston, Massachusetts (Brisk, 2015). This chapter traces the changes in instructional content and pedagogy of two teachers who participated in a ten-year collaboration between this urban school and Boston College. The purpose of the collaboration was to improve writing instruction informed by SFL and the teaching and learning cycle (TLC).

Systemic functional linguistics and the teaching and learning cycle

SFL is rooted in Halliday's (1985) scholarship on social semiotics, which emphasized the relationship between text and context. SFL is "a very useful descriptive and interpretive framework for viewing language as a strategic, meaning-making resource" (Eggins, 2004, p. 2). SFL also helps teachers by giving them concrete information on aspects of the discourse, sentence, and word level features of various genres.

An essential premise of SFL is that language is conceived as whole text rather than isolated words or sentences. These texts exist in the immediate context of the situation, which in turn is nested in the larger context of culture (Butt, Fahey, Feez, & Spinks, 2012). The writing practices of a culture are characterized by recurrent forms of texts used for specific purposes, each characterized by specific discourse organization and language features. These are called *genres* (Martin & Rose, 2008). The most common writing genres in elementary school include different types of recounts, fictional narratives, procedures, reports, explanations, and expositions or arguments. Each genre differs and is achieved through the stages or text structure and language used.

In addition to the context of culture, texts exist within the context of situations where language choices vary with respect to three variables: field, tenor, and mode. These variables constitute the *register* and correspond with three metafunctions of language (Eggins, 2004; Halliday & Matthiessen, 2004; Thompson, 2004). Language reflects the *field* or content of the text (experiential function) through clauses formed by processes, participants, and circumstances. When clauses combine in clause complexes, the logical function serves to express relationships, often signaled by conjunctions. The *tenor* of a text reflects the relationship between language users. In writing, language choices depend on the author's awareness of the intended audience as well as the writer's voice or identity. Language resources used to create a cohesive text constitute the *mode*. Language choices will differ depending on whether the text is oral, written, or multimodal.

Successful schools develop all these language resources to give students choices when writing in different academic contexts. Teachers build these resources through instruction using the TLC, an approach to writing instruction that apprentices students to writing through four stages: negotiation of field or developing content knowledge, deconstruction of text, joint construction of text, and independent construction of text (Rothery, 1996).

During the negotiation of field, students develop the content knowledge of the particular discipline and topic they will be writing about and the language needed to express that knowledge. This particular aspect of the TLC actually takes place in anticipation of writing and during the other stages as well (Rose & Martin, 2012). Teachers guide students through deconstruction (a close analysis of mentor texts to learn about the stages and the language features of the particular genre). Teachers collaborate with students in their class to construct texts jointly based on what they have learned through the deconstruction of mentor texts. With all of the knowledge and experience acquired through deconstruction and joint construction of a text, students can then create their own independent writing.

Teacher change

Educational change is difficult to achieve and sustain. Rincon-Gallardo (2016) argues that the knowledge cannot easily be transmitted from educator to learner but requires to be co-constructed in collaboration and negotiation between researchers bringing the change and teachers enacting it. Because teachers bring different backgrounds their transformation will differ and result in hybrid practices (Viesca, Strom, Hammer, Masterson, Linzell, Mitchell-McCollough, & Flynn, 2019). Collegiality and collaboration are also needed among the teachers themselves (Fullan, 1991). Collaborations take time because they require building trust and relationships. To be effective they have to be structured and the participants need to show commitment. They cannot be either forced or hurried (Hargreaves & Fullan, 2012).

Sustainability of change is achieved when teachers are supported beyond initial implementation. Hogdson-Drysdale's (2016) study showed that extent of professional development (PD) support and level of intensity of interactions among researchers and teachers impacted the level of engagement and depth of knowledge acquisition among teachers participating in a long-term PD. This support needs to be embedded in the teachers' practice and present in the whole school (Brancard & Quinnwilliams, 2012). Research on educational leadership shows that support from principals is essential in reforming schools (Scanlan & López, 2012). Principals support teachers by participating in PD sessions, providing teachers with resources and creating a supportive school environment (Aguirre-Muñoz, 2008; Fullan, 2007).

A story of change

In 2007, the mayor of Boston asked five private universities to support ten of the district's worst performing schools. One of the two schools assigned to Boston College (BC) was the Russell Elementary School, a multilingual community where the student population is 52% Latino, 30.3% Black (including Cape Verdeans and Haitians), 11.2% Asian, 4.4% Native American, Hawaiian or Pacific Islander and 2% White. Fifty six percent of the students are considered English language learners (ELLs) with varying degrees of proficiency.

The approach to the partnership that Boston College developed with the Russell School was to introduce a genre-based approach to teaching writing (Derewianka & Jones, 2016; Martin & Rose, 2008) informed by SFL theory (Halliday & Matthiessen, 2004). When the project started, teachers at Russell were unfamiliar with SFL and the TLC, the basis of the professional development and the force behind the change in the approach to teaching writing. Initially upper elementary classrooms participated but by the end of the second year, at the direction of the principal, all classroom teachers and specialists participated in the project. In the sixth year of the program, given the teachers' developed expertise on language instruction, the principal decided to enroll bilingual students with beginning and intermediate levels of English proficiency in the mainstream upper elementary classrooms rather than have them in specialized classrooms. She argued that the work informed by SFL theory had turned mainstream teachers into knowledgeable language teachers capable of educating emergent bilinguals (Brisk & Ossa Parra, 2018).

Over the ten-year period my graduate students and I documented the work by observing and audio or video recording classroom instruction. We collected sample student work from two students in each class and for each genre taught, and periodically interviewed teachers. In addition, the school monitored students' performance in state administered tests in English Language Arts. Students' performance improved over time and within each genre. Standardized testing results showed a steady progress over the years. Based on the results in the standardized test, the district classified schools by levels. The school had scored a 5, i.e. the lowest possible level, when the project started. Four years later, the school earned a top rating (Level 1) for meeting achievement gap narrowing goals for the whole student population, as well as for all subgroups (e.g. high needs students, low-income students, and ELLs and former ELLs). The performance of bilingual students still in the process of acquiring English showed consistent improvement in English proficiency (listening, speaking, reading, and writing) as measured by the ACCESS test (scale of 1–6), which began to be administered in 2013 (see Table 1.1).

Table 1.1 Overall ACCESS for the Russell School: Mean composite score by cohort of ELLs

	2013	*2014*	*2015*	*2016**
Kindergarten	248.93	243.12	234.94	246.55
1st Grade	295.11	295.16	297.91	288.25
2nd Grade	310.06	314.41	321.24	321.90
3rd Grade	343.73	347.48	355.86	358.52
4th Grade	364.45	353.23	359.05	372.15
5th Grade	370.45	374.43	369.20	374.89

Note: * in 2017 WIDA changed the way the ACCESS test was scored so that results are not comparable to previous scores but the results continued to improve.

This ten-year partnership illustrates how genre pedagogy informed by SFL and using and adapting the TLC brought positive change to a multilingual urban school in the way teachers teach and students learn. Four factors supported this change:

- The school-initiated focus on writing.
- Long-term, collaborative, and responsive professional development (PD).
- Collaborative and responsive classroom instruction that embraced the background of multicultural students.
- A strong and deeply involved principal.

When the partnership started, Boston College was informed that the school plan for improvement identified writing as one of the priorities for the coming year. At the first meeting of the collaboration I explained to the teachers and principal the genre-based approach to writing instruction informed by SFL. Enthusiastic teachers embraced the project from its initiation.

The PD activities included whole day workshops before the start of the school year, monthly grade level meetings with me during the school day, and informal consultation during classroom observations by the research team. Over time other activities emerged, such as co-teaching at the university with me, presentations by teachers and members of the research team at professional conferences, as well as collaboration to write articles and book chapters on various aspects of the project.

The long-term nature of the PD helped teachers acquire the knowledge, try new things in small chunks, and develop trust in the research team.

Knowledge acquisition happened in the collaborative interaction between teachers and researchers. I presented the theory to grade level teams and, in collaboration with teachers, created genre units of instruction. The goal of the PD was to make teachers confident contributors to the new knowledge rather than seek absolute fidelity to a prescribed instructional approach brought by an outsider. The content of the PD was achieved through a combination of material on genre-based pedagogy and features of the TLC contributed by myself, and materials that addressed concerns expressed by the principal and teachers. In a survey, teachers spoke highly of the PD. They found the content valuable, and activities useful and transferrable to their instruction. Some teachers described the content as intellectually stimulating (Daniello, 2012). The materials prepared for the PD combined with observations of classroom implementation resulted in a volume Brisk (2015) that became a resource for teachers and teacher educators.

This collaborative approach to instruction was mirrored by the way teachers apprenticed students in their writing. Teachers involved students in manipulating text, either published or student generated, to learn the discourse and language demands of genres. Teachers constantly adjusted their agenda for instruction based on their students' needs. For example, the inclusion of Spanish-speaking newcomers who had emergent proficiency in English into upper grade classrooms resulted in creating classroom contexts that embraced bilingualism and the use of the newcomers' language as a resource, avoiding marginalization of these students. All students helped each other. "It's amazing how those cooperative groups [work], it's just amazing what happens inside those classrooms," Linda, the ESL teacher, commented.

In this project, teachers co-constructed with me knowledge that succeeded in having theory influence practice. In turn, teachers and students co-constructed knowledge in highly collaborative classrooms (Figure 1.1).

None of the changes would have happened if it weren't for the strong support of the principal. The principal became knowledgeable of the content by participating in all PD activities over the ten years of collaboration. She encouraged teachers to implement the co-constructed ideas and protected the project from interference of district mandates. For example, when the district imposed a new curriculum for reading and writing, teachers used it for reading but not for writing. She also brought stability to the school with many of the teachers staying in the school. Given the success of the project, the district encouraged dissemination of the approach to other schools.

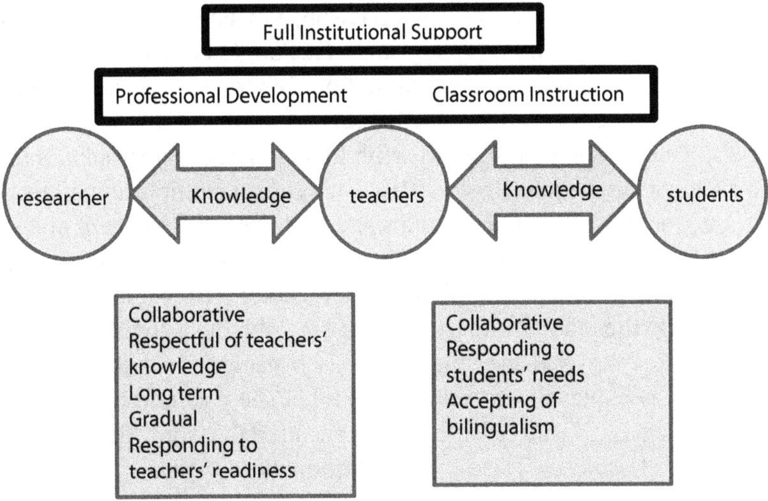

Figure 1.1 SFL informed educational change

Cheryl's and Pat's practice changes over time

Cheryl and Pat were members of the collaboration for all ten years, and they are still in the school and still in touch with me. When the project started they were part of the fourth grade team. After the third year, the principal assigned them to two different teams of teachers who stayed with their students for two years in fourth and fifth grades. With new teachers on board they became leaders of their teams.

Cheryl's practice

Cheryl implemented units in a number of different genres over the years. Her first one was an argument unit where she had the students choose a topic from a list. She then taught them the stages: thesis statement, reasons and evidence. The students wrote the thesis as a question and Cheryl called it a "hook" to attract their audience. For a final piece, students wrote letters to a general audience persuading them to visit their country of origin. The letters included use of first and second person, making them very informal.

Since the fourth grade was reading *Charlotte's Web*, Cheryl and the fourth grade team decided to try fictional narratives. At my suggestion, the teachers had students research an animal of their choice and make it the main character of their narratives (Brisk, Nelson, O'Connor, 2016). The next genre attempted was reports. Cheryl was reluctant to implement reports because she did not believe students would be able to write good paragraphs. At my suggestion, the students created reports in the form of posters about animals. This avoided the need to write long coherent paragraphs. Images with captions did the job (Brisk, 2016). Cheryl read multiple animal reports to deconstruct with her students the stages, i.e. general statement and subtopics. After agreeing on subtopics, the students went on to do their research to find information about the animal of their choice. Eventually, Cheryl had her students write reports with paragraphs, teaching them about the "theme" of the whole essay and the "theme" of each paragraph. Although it was clear from the explanations and activities that she was referring to macro and hyperthemes (Martin & Rose, 2007), she used the word "theme" for all, including for lessons on Theme – New Information/Rheme.

In her later argument units, Cheryl introduced aspects of the SFL appraisal framework, such as modality, evaluative language, and graduation (Martin & Rose, 2007). To help students with the language, she downloaded a list of "persuasive" words from the internet, which included examples of all three features without distinguishing them. She also discussed with students when it would be appropriate to use first and third person in their arguments. The main emphasis, however, was still on thesis, reasons, and evidence. She deconstructed texts by asking students to identify these genre stages and she conferenced with students once they prepared their graphic organizers to see if their thesis, reasons, and evidence were coherent.

Cheryl's first attempt at teaching empathetic autobiographies (EA) (Christie & Derewianka, 2008) came in connection to a visit to Plimoth Plantation, an outdoor museum that replicates the village of the first colonizers and an adjacent Indian village. Having read a series of books written as if the narrator were a Wampanoag Indian boy, a pilgrim boy, and a pilgrim girl, students wrote their own "A day in the life of…" Their writing reflects the emphasis on the stages, with an orientation and a sequence of events. For example, one of the fifth grade students started his EA, *Good morrow. I am Emmanuel Jencon. I live with my mom, father, and two sisters. We are now on a voyage to new land…*[1] Then he wrote events, each in a short, underdeveloped paragraph. The students imitated the language of the time, which they experienced through the mentor texts and the interpreters in the museum who make a point of speaking as in the 17th century.

In later report units, in addition to working on subtopics, Cheryl taught that reports are written in the third person and mostly about generalized participants. She continued to help students express what their paragraph was about and how they could create topic sentences that indicated it. She introduced the notion of "linking words," such as *however*, *therefore*, *for example*, *such as*, and so on. She downloaded a list from the internet, gave a copy to the students and encouraged them to use language from the list. However, these sorts of words are not common in texts for fourth or fifth grade students. They are more frequently found in reports for earlier grades.

When Spanish-speaking newcomers were assigned to her class, Cheryl worked hard to make sure they felt integrated into the class. During class discussions she would encourage them to speak Spanish, "digalo en español" (say it in Spanish), she paired them with bilingual colleagues, and even purchased the Spanish version of the book the class was reading at the time. Cheryl used hybrid practices to ensure participation of newcomers (Brisk & Ossa-Parra, 2018; Kaveh, 2020).

She continued to focus her teaching mainly on arguments, reports, and fictional narratives. In the tenth year of the project, she decided again to do a unit on EAs. The focus of the unit was to teach students how to do research on their chosen historical figure, and how to use language to reveal the personality and state of mind of that person, i.e. focus on the "empathy," which Cheryl considered very difficult for her students. After an initial discussion of the purpose of EAs, the difference with biographies, which students had written in earlier grades, and the need for the writer to get inside the head of their person, Cheryl read aloud examples of EAs. Together with the students they identified the language that revealed personality features of the person. For example, Cheryl gave the word "pacifist" after they read *I am Martin Luther King*. The students identified the clause "fight with words" as the example of the action that showed he was a pacifist.

To further reinforce how to do research and identify ways of showing personality, Cheryl jointly constructed with the class an empathetic autobiography of George Washington. Together they researched information about the life of Washington, to create a timeline. They also discussed what Washington's actions revealed about his character. Cheryl wrote on the side of the timeline the person's features such as *brave, smart, helpful, independent, strong, hardworking*. They had to identify precisely the language that helped create the image of the personality. Cheryl connected this feature of EAs with what they had learned in the past about character development in fictional narratives. They together took the information from the graphic organizer and wrote the EA on George Washington, including in the events what he did, thought, and felt as evidence of the personality features they had established. For example, instead of writing "I was motivated" the students suggested they should write "Even though I wasn't in school,

I didn't stop learning. I taught myself at home at night after working in the fields" (Classroom observation transcription 3/15/18). Finally, the students, confident of their task, went on to write their own EAs about their chosen historical figure. They repeated the process of researching, creating a time-line with important events, isolating personality features of their historical figure, and writing a full essay. Cheryl gave students much feedback by conferencing and jointly revising student work, especially those students that would have the most trouble to revise their own work. The students' writing reflected the efforts Cheryl had put into the unit. One student wrote as if she were Anne Frank. The events were written in a clear flow. They included technical language but it was obviously written by the student and not copied from the source. The student made an effort to show through language the situation faced by Anne and her family: *I was born during an era of terror and political chaos… My family and I moved to Amsterdam for safety because Hitler hated Jews*. She also used language to reflect Anne's feelings, *It was like being imprisoned… I have been separated from vater and I feel so alone… I felt my heart sink*. (MV final paper 4/10/18).

Cheryl's journey implementing genre pedagogy went through tentative lessons on stages that became more grounded with practice. Over time she moved to incorporate more language. However, she sometimes drew ideas from materials from the internet that were not informed by SFL. The presence of bilingual learners made the language needs of learners more salient. In the last recorded project, empathetic autobiographies, Cheryl's instruction reflects her awareness of the need of students to learn how to do research to master the field and the importance of teaching the function of the language features that were the focus in the particular genre.

Pat's practice

After a few years of trying different genres, Pat settled on teaching either reports or arguments at the beginning of the year, followed by the other genre. The topics of the reports changed following curricular changes. He had students write reports on states in the United States, following the social studies curriculum, and on animals, connected to the unit on animal adaptation in the reading curriculum adopted later by the school. One year, as a result of a field trip, they wrote about the Wampanoag tribe in Massachusetts. In 2016, they switched to writing reports on the positions of the two presidential candidates.

As was the case with Cheryl, Pat asked students to create posters in his first attempt at teaching reports. Pat deconstructed multiple texts and showed students how to fill the information for the subtopics in a graphic organizer. Then he helped students plan the layout for their posters. Finally, students added images.

Once the fourth grade teachers gained confidence in teaching the genre and working with students who had experienced genre-based pedagogy in earlier grades, they assigned students to write their reports with separate paragraphs for each subtopic. Pat liked to have his students work in pairs, creating books with a subtopic on each page and some illustrations drawn by the students or downloaded from the internet.

Pat's content and approach to teaching how to write reports evolved over four years. Pat always started the unit with making the purpose of reports clear and reading several examples. In the initial years, the stages (general statement and subtopics) guided the organization of the lessons. Through deconstruction of multiple texts, students learned that they had to plan their reports by establishing the subtopics and finding information in resources about these subtopics. With the whole class, Pat planned the subtopics they were to include in their animal reports. Then, choosing one animal, he asked students in groups to research a variety of sources and write on Post-it notes information related to the various subtopics, which the students then attached to a large graphic organizer he had placed in the front of the room. The class discussed the content and the process of the organizer. Then students, working in pairs, began to collect data on their chosen animal using the same type of graphic organizer.

After a few years of giving priority to the stages, Pat focused on some aspect of language for each genre. He affirmed that "the way we teach here is that language is incorporated into kind of everything that we do" (interview 3/16/17). At a PD meeting, I showed Pat that a very challenging aspect of report writing for elementary grades is the use of complex noun groups. Noun groups are important because they hold most of the information. For example, almost 70% of the words in a paragraph from a book about snakes, often used by the teachers as a mentor text, were part of a noun group. Therefore, Pat chose noun groups as the language focus of his lessons. On chart paper, Pat wrote sentences from mentor texts, underlining the modifiers. For example, *Many spiders are <u>black, brown,</u> or <u>gray</u>. Some spiders have <u>furry</u> bodies.* He talked about "exaggerating the use of describing words" since students tended not to use any. After working together on a few sentences, he had the students, working in groups, find describing words in mentor texts or propose adding descriptive words to a noun without one. He encouraged students to use describing words when writing their drafts.

In the last three years of the project, Pat and the other fourth and fifth grade teachers, including Cheryl, decided to increase the scaffolds for building the field. Teaching how to conduct research and learning the language to express ideas within the framework of the stages of reports became the organizer for their genre units. Pat moved on to teach how to find resources that were at the reading level of students. Then the class deconstructed paragraphs from the texts, underlining words they did not know, looking for meaning in dictionaries and synonyms in a Thesaurus. When researching the webpages of the presidential candidates for the 2016 election, students learned how to replace words to make their text more comprehensible to other students their age (*childcare costs* for *childcare expenses*). At the same time, they identified terms that they needed to learn and use in their writing (*income tax, tax code*). Pat spent considerable time making sure the students took notes that were not full sentences copied from the texts but just the key ideas that included the content language of the texts. He made sure that students understood the meaning of the notes they took, and the language they "collected" to make their writing look "professional." Students were told that their writing should reflect their expertise on the topic.

The following year, when writing a report on presidential candidates, Pat and his students jointly researched the internet sites for each candidate, listing the topics of the various positions of each candidate as potential choices for subtopics in their reports. Pat created a graphic organizer to be used for every subtopic in the report, with space to take bullet point notes and for content language. He demonstrated how to produce a paragraph by choosing one of the subtopics, and then modeled for them how to take notes and identify content language to write on the topic, such as *promote, clean energy, increase, natural resources* and so on.

Pat jointly wrote the paragraph with the students, insisting that they incorporate the language listed in the graphic organizer. Students went on to choose the subtopics they were going to cover in their own reports, using the same type of organizer to take notes and identify language, followed by writing the paragraphs on each chosen subtopic. Students wrote two to four full paragraphs. If the students took notes on something and asked Pat what it meant, he told them to check on a video or another source to try to figure out what it meant and then check back with him. He stressed understanding whatever was included in their notes.

At a meeting with me, the notion of informative noun groups (as opposed to content words) as essential in reports, discussed in earlier PDs, was reinforced. Pat began to point out noun groups in the research sources. But frustrated that students in their own drafts were still using nouns without modifiers, Pat developed additional lessons. On chart paper he had two columns: *Noun* and *Noun groups*. He listed several nouns that students were using and together with the class they filled in the noun group columns by adding modifiers for the nouns that they found in their research resources. Students went back to their drafts and added modifiers to further specify the nouns; for example, changing *soldiers* to *active duty soldiers* (Brisk, Alvarado, Timothy & Scialoia, 2018, p. 95). In his interview, Pat commented on the lack of teaching "parts of speech" in schools. He recalled how when he started teaching he was told to use a grammar book to teach 30-minute grammar lesson every day. Currently all teachers teach language within the genre units completely embedded in the unit content (Interview 3/16/17). Pat appreciates how noun groups help develop the field of a particular topic. He tells the students that he should be able to tell what they are writing about by the noun groups they have listed in their graphic organizers in connection to each individual topic.

This focus on language also supported teachers in helping their students understand how they could structure their sentences in new ways. For several years I had done theme/new information analysis of students' paragraphs during PD sessions. This analysis showed that the students' writing looked more like oral language, with just a noun or a pronoun in the theme, while most of the information was included in the new information (rheme). The year students worked on the presidential candidates, Pat tried two things to improve control of the theme. He had the students vary the way they wrote when naming the candidate at the start of their sentences, such as Hillary, Clinton, she, the presidential candidate. He also taught the students to "flip sentences" by placing the second part of the sentence first. For example, one student switched from "Hillary wants to increase opportunities for disabled people" to *Increasing oppertunities for disabled people in america is what Hillary will do* (NK final report 10/13/16). Some students did not like this strategy and chose not to use it. Pat accepted these students' decision, consistent with the SFL notion that language is about choice and not about rules (Halliday & Matthiessen, 2004).

The year after the election students wrote reports about animals connected to a curricular unit on animal adaptation. This time, instead of just one subtopic, Pat jointly constructed a complete report with the whole class. They researched, planned, and wrote about one animal. Not only did he jointly constructed text on chart paper for the whole class to see, but also had the students in pairs working on their own notebooks, sharing ideas. Then the students individually, using the same process, wrote a report on

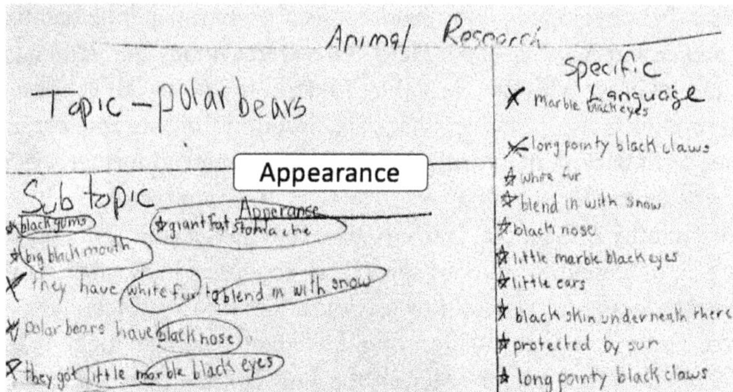

Figure 1.2 Section of a subtopic graphic organizer

their own chosen animal. Pat has continued to use this process of jointly constructing a report fully before asking the students do their own.

He demonstrated how to create a graphic organizer with each subtopic on a separate page (see Fig. 1.2). The page had two columns. On the left side he wrote important information in notes without copying whole sentences from the sources. In the right column, he showed how to isolate the noun groups in these notes and then copy them on that column, stressing the need to use these noun groups in their writing.

After writing, students shared some of the sentences they had written. Pat complimented students for using precise modifiers by contrasting with a sentence without those modifiers. For example, one student read aloud, *They can climb the tallest trees*. Pat chimed in, "Not just trees, tallest trees." Another student read, *There are 2500 different types of snakes.* Pat said, "She didn't say 'There are a lot of snakes.'" (Classroom observation transcripts, 9/25/17).

As Cheryl did, Pat incorporated changes in his practice, guided by the needs of the students and discussions with me during PD sessions. Pat's instruction changed from tentative attempts at teaching a variety of genres, to stressing the stages of specific genres that best fitted the curricular content, to emphasis on language instruction. His approach to teaching increasingly emphasized aspects of the TLC with initial emphasis on deconstruction, followed by partial joint construction of text, to full joint construction of text stressing the development of the field.

Initially, Pat went through a similar change process as Cheryl because he taught the same grade and planned together. Later, working on a different grade level, he developed a style of his own but continued to collaborate with Cheryl. In the last phase, he also focused on the development of the field and language to have students sound "professional" in their writing. He too jointly constructed with the class one piece to model the process for the students and develop their confidence in writing.

From learners to teachers

The nature of PDs in the last year has changed from an agenda planned by me to conversations where teachers reported new things they had tried. Initially teachers' practices followed the lead of what was discussed at the PD meetings. Over time, however, their instructional decisions were guided by students' needs, as the teachers worked to apply their new knowledge to better meet these needs. Teachers kept trying and modifying practices based on their experience implementing genre pedagogy and shared any new practices with me. When the project started, the teaching was stronger from me to the teachers. In recent years the tide has turned, with the teaching becoming stronger from the teachers to me. Initially the professional development introduced the notion of genres focusing on the purpose and the stages, which teachers promptly adopted. They introduced the stages to the students through deconstruction of mentor texts and the use of graphic organizers, with the stages that I had developed. Their teaching included hybrid practices. For example, Cheryl initially had students choose a topic from a list and start essays with a "hook," an approach she had already been using. Once teachers felt grounded with the genres, I introduced genre-specific rubrics to evaluate the purpose, stages, and essential language features (Brisk, 2015). These rubrics were used both to discuss what was important to teach as well as a tool to analyze student work. The inclusion of language features in these rubrics spurred the attention to language. Pat and Cheryl selected specific language features to teach with the genres, increasing the use of SFL metalanguage as they also continued to draw on their original metalanguage. For example, they taught modality, and the use of noun groups with descriptive words, but they also presented "persuasive language" and "content words." They used their own adaptation of the SFL metalanguage when talking about "positive" and "negative" words for evaluative language. Once teachers felt confident teaching purpose and stages of the genres, PD sessions focused more intensely on language. This delay on emphasizing language was intentional on my part because teachers find language more difficult to understand and teach. With the influx of emergent bilinguals in their classrooms, however, Cheryl and Pat started incorporating language lessons earlier in their unit. They concluded that it was essential to teach a few key language features from the very beginning. As a result, I have started to recommend to all teachers to start language lessons simultaneously with the introduction of the purpose and stages of the genre.

The next focus of attention on the part of these teachers was the development of the field. They found that students had difficulty doing research and learning from sources with information about what they were going to write. Students would often copy long chunks of text without comprehending what they were writing. Observing this led teachers to consider and create new ways of helping students develop the field and the language needed to present the information and ideas they would include in their written texts. The teachers started to read the research sources jointly with the students to identify useful content and language. They developed new ways of collecting information through note-taking, following the organization of the stages as well as preparing language in advance of writing.

Currently, together with the whole class, Cheryl, Pat and their teams jointly construct a report, argument, empathetic autobiography or whatever genre they are teaching. Together, they do the research, take notes, isolate examples of the particular language feature in focus, and organize the notes according to the stages of the genre. They take the time to do this activity until they feel that their students understand what needs to be done and have the language to do it. Then the students do their own writing individually or in groups, collaborating all along.

I have begun to disseminate Pat's and Cheryl's new approach to teaching genre units through online courses focusing on genre pedagogy. I encourage other teachers to embed teaching of content into genre units that include deep development of the field and selected aspects of language, as well as to jointly construct with the whole class one piece from research to final product.

Conclusion

Teaching writing rather than telling students to write is a much needed practice in schools, not only for the sake of literacy development but for learning in general. Because written language, especially that encountered by students in the context of schools, is different from oral language, students need a scaffolded approach to acquiring this language. Genre pedagogy informed by SFL greatly supports teachers and students in this process.

Long-term, collaborative, and theory-based PD is essential for producing needed and sustainable change in schools. Teachers develop a way of teaching writing and an understanding of the function of language in making meaning for themselves as well as their students. This knowledge becomes part of their professional expertise and may develop differently in different settings and for different students, but still has a positive impact on students' writing development. Sustainable educational change takes time and requires support from individuals and their institutions.

About the author

María Estela Brisk is Professor of Education at Boston College. Her research and teaching address writing instruction, genre pedagogy, bilingual education, bilingual language and literacy acquisition, and preparation of mainstream teachers to work with bilingual learners. She is the author of numerous articles and six books: *Bilingual Education: From Compensatory to Quality Schooling*; *Literacy and Bilingualism: A Handbook for ALL Teachers*; *Situational Context of Education: A Window into the World of Bilingual Learners*; *Language Development and Education: Children with Varying Language Experiences* (with P. Menyuk); *Language, Culture, and Community in Teacher Education*; and *Engaging Students in Academic Literacies: Genre-based Pedagogy for K-5 Classrooms*. Professor Brisk is a native of Argentina.

Note

1   Here, and throughout, spelling and grammar as written by the children.

References

Aguirre-Muñoz, Z., Park, J-E., Amabisca, A., & Boscardin, C. K. (2008). Developing teacher capacity for serving ells' writing instructional needs: A case for systemic functional linguistics. *Bilingual Research Journal, 31*, 295–322. https://doi.org/10.1080/15235880802640755

Alvarado, J., Kim S. L., Tian, Z., Drueding, L., O'Connor, C., Peterson, R., Scialoia, P., & Timothy, B. (forthcoming). Uncovering "the story" behind meaningful texts: Understanding the impact of an elementary school team's sfl theory-based curriculum and instruction. M. Gebhard & K. Accurso (eds.), *Teachers as SFL Practitioners*.

Brancard, R. & Quinnwilliams, J. (2012). Learning labs: Collaborations for transformative teacher learning. *TESOL Journal, 3*, pp. 320–349. https://doi.org/10.1002/tesj.22

Brisk, M. (2015). *Engaging Students in Academic Literacies: Genre-based Pedagogy for K-5 Classrooms*. New York: Routledge. https://doi.org/10.4324/9781317816164

Brisk, M. E. (2016). Multimodal reports in elementary school classrooms. In M. F. Alexandre & C. A. M. Gouveia (eds.), *Theory, Application, Analysis: Studies in Systemic Functional Linguistics* (pp. 281–304). Lisbon, Portugal: CELGA-ILTEC.

Brisk, M. E., Nelson, D., & O'Connor, C. (2016). Bilingual fourth graders develop a central character for their narratives. In L. de Oliveira & T. Silva (eds.), *L2 Writing in Elementary Classrooms* (pp.88–105). New York: Palgrave/MacMillan. https://doi.org/10.1057/9781137530981_6

Brisk, M. E., Alvarado, J., Timothy, B., & Scialoia, P. (2018). Breaking the linguistic ceiling: Bilingual students appropriate academic English. In J. Sharkey (ed.), *Transforming Practices for the Elementary Classroom* (pp.85–98). Alexandria, VA: TESOL International Organization.

Brisk, M. E. & Ossa-Parra, M. (2018). Mainstream classrooms as engaging spaces for emergent bilinguals: SFL theory, catalyst for change. In R. Harman (ed.), *Bilingual Learners and Social Equity: Critical Approaches to Systemic Functional Linguistics* (pp. 127–151). N.Y.: Springer. https://doi.org/10.1007/978-3-319-60953-9_7

Butt, D., Fahey, R., Feez, S., & Spinks, S. (2012). *Using Functional Grammar: An Explorer's Guide*. (3rd ed.) South Yarra, Victoria, Australia: Palgrave Macmillan.

Christie, F. & Derewianka, B. (2008). *School Discourse: Learning to Write Across the Years of Schooling*. London: Continuum.

De Oliveira, L. C. & Dodds, K. (2010). Beyond general strategies for English language learners: Language dissection in science. *Electronic Journal of Literacy Through Science, 9*. Retrieved from http://ejlts.ucdavis.edu, pp. 1–14.

Daniello, F. (2012). Systemic functional linguistics theory in practice: A longitudinal study of a school-university partnership reforming writing instruction in an urban elementary school (Doctoral dissertation, Boston College).

Derewianka, B. M., & Jones, P. T. (2016). *Teaching Language in Context*. (2nd ed.). Melbourne: Oxford University Press.

Eggins, S. (2004). *An Introduction to Systemic Functional Linguistics* (2nd ed.). London,   England: Continuum.

Fullan, M. (1991). *The New Meaning of Educational Change* (2nd ed.). New York: Teachers College Press.

Fullan, M. (2007). *The New Meaning of Educational Change* (4th ed.) New York: Teachers College Press.

Gebhard, M., Chen, I-An, & Britton, L. (2014). "Miss, nominalization is a nominalization:" English language learners' use of SFL metalanguage and their literacy practices. *Linguistics and Education, 26*, 106–125. https://doi.org/10.1016/j.linged.2014.01.003

Graham S., & Harris, K. R. (2013). Designing an effective writing program. In M. Johnson, S. Graham, C. A. MacArthur, & J. Fitzgerald (eds.). *Best Practice in Writing Instruction* (pp. 3–25). New York: Guilford Press.

Halliday, M. A. K. (1985). *An Introduction to Functional Grammar*. London: Edward Arnold.

Halliday, M. A. K., & Matthiessen, C. M. I. M. (2004). *An Introduction to Functional Grammar* (3rd ed.). London: Hodder Arnold.

Hargreaves A., & Fullan, M. (2012). *Professional Capital: Transforming Teaching in Every School*. New York: Teachers College Press.

Hogdson-Drysdale, T. (2016). Teaching writing through genres and language. In L. C. de Oliveira & T. Silva (eds.). *Second Language Writing in Elementary Classrooms: Instructional Issues, Content-area Writing and Teacher Education* (pp. 69–87). New York: Palgrave Macmillan. https://doi.org/10.1002/tesj.330

Kaveh, Y. M. (2020). Unspoken dialogues between educational and family language policies: Language policy beyond legislations. *Linguistics and Education, 60*, [page range not available]. https://doi.org/10.1016/j.linged.2020.100876

Martin, J. (2009). Genre and language learning: A social semiotic perspective. *Linguistics and*

Education, 20, 10–21.

Martin, J. R., & Rose, D. (2008). *Genre Relations: Mapping Culture*. London: Equinox.

Martin, J. R., & Rose, D. (2007). *Working with Discourse: Meaning Beyond the Clause* (2nd ed.). London: Continuum.

National Commission on Writing. (2003). *The Neglected R: The Need for a Writing Revolution.* Retrieved from www.collegeboard.com

Rincón-Gallardo, S. (2016). Large scale pedagogical transformation as widespread cultural change in Mexican public schools. *Journal of Educational Change, 17*, 411–436. https://doi.org/10.1007/s10833-016-9286-4

Rose, D., & Martin, J. R. (2012). *Learning to Write, Reading to Learn: Genre, Knowledge and*

Pedagogy in the Sydney School. Sheffield: Equinox.

Rothery, J. (1996) Making changes: Developing an educational linguistics. In R. Hasan & G. Williams (eds.), *Literacy in Society* (pp. 86–123). New York: Longman.

Scanlan, M., & López, F. (2012). ¡Vamos! How school leaders promote equity and excellence for bilingual students. *Educational Administration Quarterly*, **48**(4), 583–625. https://doi.org/10.1177/0013161x11436270

Schleppegrell, M., & Go, A. L. (2007). Analyzing the writing of English learners: A functional approach. *Language Arts,* **84**, 529–538.

Thompson, G. (2004). *Introducing Functional Grammar* (2nd ed.). London: Routledge.

Viesca, K. M., Strom, K., Hammer,S., Masterson, J., Linzell, C. H., Mitchell-McCollough, J., & Flynn, N. (2019). Developing a complex portrait of content teaching for multilingual learners via nonlinear theoretical understandings. *Review of Research in Education,* **43**, 304–335. https://doi.org/10.3102/0091732x18820910

2 The role of meaningful sentence-level metalanguage: Insights from children's thinking with functional grammar

Mary Schleppegrell
University of Michigan, Ann Arbor, MI

Carrie Symons
Michigan State University, Lansing, MI

Introduction

Metalanguage refers to language for talking about language, supporting both the naming of linguistic features of texts and talk about how particular language choices mean what they do. In this chapter we review research in education that has used the metalanguage of systemic functional linguistics (SFL) to support talk about language and meaning as students read. We illustrate the use of meaningful metalanguage in action in a primary school classroom, showing how students and the teacher used SFL metalanguage to understand challenging texts, and we report on interaction with children from the class that revealed how they are using functional grammar in their own reading.

The children we report on are emergent bilinguals, speakers of Arabic at home and learners of English as an additional language at school. Second language development research tells us that engaging in meaningful interaction about language and meaning in contexts of shared experience, with a focus on form-meaning connections, raises students' consciousness about how language works (e.g., Ellis & Larsen-Freeman, 2006). Here we illustrate these processes in action in a fourth grade classroom, showing how use of SFL's meaning-oriented functional metalanguage can also play an important role in learning school subjects. It supports children's noticing of language and attention to meaning in the texts they read, offering a resource for talk about how a text means what it does.

Research on metalanguage in pedagogical contexts

One of Michael Halliday's goals in developing systemic functional linguistics was to create a theory of language that could be used in educational applications (Halliday, 1985). SFL is a functional theory of language, focused on accounting for how language is used in social contexts. It takes meaning as the starting point for exploration of grammar in the different linguistic systems through which we share our experience and enact social relationships. Many SFL researchers have shown how use of linguistic metalanguage can support curricular learning through talk about language and meaning in various classroom contexts (e.g., Brisk, 2015; French, 2010; Gebhard, Chen, & Britton, 2014; Moore & Schleppegrell, 2014; Schleppegrell, 2013; Simmons, 2018; Symons, 2017; Williams, 2004); at the same time it supports students' critical language awareness (e.g., Gebhard & Graham, 2018; Schleppegrell & Moore, 2018).

SFL's grammar recognizes three *metafunctions* of language: that every meaningful use of language in context, realized in spoken or written text, simultaneously presents three strands of meaning that can be traced and analyzed as the text evolves. The *ideational* metafunction creates a strand of *experiential* and *logical* meanings that constitute representations of the world and of human experience, while the *interpersonal* metafunction enables us to enact relationships, and the *textual* strand of meanings creates cohesive messages. Our focus on metalanguage in this chapter draws primarily on work that has explored how experiential meanings are presented in the system of *transitivity* through choice of processes, participants, and circumstances. These are the meaningful constituents of a clause that present "happenings" and the social actors and circumstances related to those happenings. Several research studies have reported on the ways this sentence-level metalanguage has been introduced to children and made a focus of classroom activity. Here we review those studies, and then report on our own work that drew on these constructs and gathered information from children about how this metalanguage supports their reading.

Geoff Williams's work has been groundbreaking in this area. Williams (1998) illustrates how six-year-old children use functional grammar metalanguage to identify *saying processes* and enact dialogue with appropriate expression; he shows how this is not just "labelling what they already in some sense know," but instead is "attending to new, complex phenomena through the use of the metalanguage in the discussion of text in context" (p. 36). In other words, the metalanguage helps students notice what language is doing and name those meanings and concepts, raising their consciousness about the resources available to them for making their own meanings. Williams (2000) describes how sixth grade students analyze process types in the children's book *Piggybook* and then focus on the participant roles of Actor and Goal in material processes. This focus on participants who are agentive enables students to critically analyze the roles of different characters and recognize how the linguistic patterning in the story positioned Mrs. Piggott in relation to the other family members, thus also raising students' critical awareness about gender roles. From her work with Williams, French (2010) shows how talk with children about processes, participants, and circumstances, among other SFL constructs, helped young children develop conscious control of their writing, a critical understanding of stories as "crafted" by an author (p. 224), and improved expression in speaking aloud as well as improved punctuation of direct speech.

Williams (2004) argues that metalanguage that links language and meaning (rather than metlanguage that offers only word class labels such as *noun, verb*) is crucial to supporting children in constructing relationships "between the grammatical descriptions and practical literacy activities *from children's point of view*" (p. 242, emphasis in original). He suggests that the ability to draw on grammatical constructs in meaningful ways depends on the nature of the constructs and the school literacy tasks children are asked to engage in, using the constructs. He cites research showing that children happily engage in play with language and suggests that meaningful ways of drawing their attention to language connect with this "natural interest" (p. 243) in how language works. He describes how the metalanguage of *process* was introduced as children were learning to read and write procedures, a genre where the processes present the instruction to act and where identifying the processes helps students understand what they are to do. Williams points out that the multifunctionality of processes presented in the context of the imperatives that typically structure a procedure enabled the teacher to draw attention to the ways processes also function as Theme in this context. Theme is an SFL construct for recognizing how information flows across a text, so attention to co-patterning of Theme and Process supported students in attending to the ways texts of different types are structured and the meanings they present.

Williams points out that as students engage in these activities to explore how language works, they are also learning to think in new ways. Citing

Vygotsky's theoretical perspective on the ways linguistic signs function in the development of voluntary attention, Williams (2004) argues that the metalanguage serves as a resource that becomes "the means with which to think" (p. 244). He reports on interviews with children where they reflect on their own language choices, using the functional grammar constructs (see Williams, 2005, for other reports on interviews with children about their knowledge and use of functional grammar). The metalanguage offers students new constructs (e.g., there are different process types through which we represent our experience; texts are structured by Themes to build on what has been said and introduce new ideas; participants in texts may be agentive or not have agency) and explicit ways of developing new conceptual understandings. This makes the metalanguage helpful across subject areas for considering the different kinds of disciplinary meanings presented in texts and practices.

Research in the U.S. context has also shown how SFL metalanguage can support talk about language and meaning in different disciplinary contexts and grade levels. Schleppegrell, Greer, and Taylor (2008), for example, used the SFL transitivity metalanguage in professional development with secondary history teachers, who then used it with their students to deconstruct sentences for deeper discussion to achieve important historical learning goals. Gebhard, Chen, Graham, and Gunawan (2013) describe how teacher candidates learn to use the constructs *process*, *participant*, and *circumstance* to talk to their students about the texts they are writing. The authors suggest that this, and other SFL metalanguage, offers developing teachers new ways of conceptualizing grammar and seeing links between grammar and meaning. The teacher candidates learned to talk about how different types of processes help students make arguments more authoritative, how using circumstances helps add details, and how abstract and concrete participants are used in different genres.

Gebhard, et al. (2014) report on a unit of study that introduced talk about processes and participants to support reading in a third grade reading classroom with students who were beginning to learn English. They show how students began to notice that words such as *name* and *stamp* can function as either participant or process. As Menyuk and Brisk (2005) point out, bilingual students typically have high levels of metalinguistic awareness, and teachers can take advantage of that awareness to engage students in talk about what they notice as they learn English. In Gebhard et al.'s study, this metalanguage became part of the classroom culture, as students began to notice the different process types that they encountered in reading stories, compared with reading science. They also began to see that some processes in science texts (e.g., *to melt,* in *Polar ice caps are <u>melting</u>*) were followed by a sentence where the same meaning was now presented as a participant (e.g., *<u>This melting</u> is causing the sea level to rise.*) In this case, as in Williams' work, the teacher linked this to SFL's notion of Theme and text organization.

Moore, Schleppegrell, and Palincsar (2018) caution that the focus on process, participant, and circumstance needs to be in service of meaning-making. They illustrate how an activity that involves students in identifying processes of different types but that doesn't then connect that analysis to the meaning in the text, while functioning to promote noticing and focused attention and support vocabulary learning, does not result in attention to language that is meaningful in supporting larger disciplinary learning goals. They report that this realization helped them shift their focus, in their design-based research, to the disciplinary goals of instruction and adapt the use of metalanguage to that end (see also Schleppegrell, 2016). One example of this is their work in a primary school English Language Arts (ELA) classroom (Moore & Schleppegrell, 2014), where they describe how identifying processes of different types helped students recognize the ways authors use *doing* and *saying* processes to "show" characters' attitudes, and *being* and *sensing* processes to "tell" what characters' attitudes are, helping students think about what needs to be interpreted when quoting from a story as they write a character analysis.

This brief review shows that SFL metalanguage can support concept development and curricular learning through discussion of meaning in language. It offers a means of linking a particular instance to a broader linguistic system, making language awareness purposeful in context, and enabling reflection on language choices and discovery of patterns. Using metalanguage raises students' consciousness about how language works and offers ways into disciplinary learning for emergent bilinguals.

Beyond this work with the curriculum, however, we were interested in other affordances of the SFL metalanguage. We wanted to go beyond research on metalanguage in contexts of pedagogy to also explore the ways metalanguage from SFL might help learners parse and understand what they read and to tap into students' metacognition about how the metalanguage supports their reading and relates to other reading strategies they are using. Thus, this study explores the following research questions through analysis of classroom interaction, think-aloud, and interview data:

- How does use of functional grammar metalanguage shed light on children's metacognition while reading?

- What do children say about how functional grammar supports their reading for understanding?

Methods

The context of this research

The *Language & Meaning* project was a three-year design-based research project whose purpose was to explore the ways SFL theory and concepts can support the language and literacy development of emergent bilingual students. The project was carried out in 23 second- through fifth-grade classrooms (students ages 7–10), in six elementary schools in an urban immigrant community. The children in these classrooms were learning English as an additional language (more than 90% spoke Arabic). An overview of findings from this research is available in Moore, et al., (2018).

Throughout the project, we engaged teachers in professional development that introduced them to functional grammar as a metalanguage for talking about meaning in the texts they read with students, as well as in support of the children's writing development. We collected data in the form of video records of classroom enactment of the strategies and activities we introduced, as well as through teachers' reflection logs and interviews with teachers and children. In this chapter, our focus is on how fourth grade students who had experience using the SFL metalanguage of *process, participant, circumstance,* and *connector* while reading in their classrooms were also able to use it to think aloud about new texts they encountered. We report on what their use of the metalanguage reveals about how they understood a text and on what they said about how functional grammar can help them as they read. Before describing our data collection methods and discussing the findings from our analysis of students' talk, we provide an illustrative classroom example of how teachers and children used the metalanguage of process, participant, and connector to explore meaning in complex text.

Metalanguage in classroom interaction

In the classroom episode transcribed below, students are reading a text about electricity. The teacher, Ms. Youssef, and her students have read through the text already once, talking about what it says, but now they are looking at it more closely, with the text projected on the board. They are moving through it sentence by sentence and are now exploring this sentence: *The acid allowed the electrons in the metals to travel even more freely*. Ms. Youssef asks:

Ms. Y:	Who[1] are the participants? Who is doing the work? Who is involved?
Amina:	Acid.
Ms. Y:	The acid is a participant. Who else?
Samir:	The electrons.
Ms. Y:	The electrons. Who else?
Ahmed:	The metal?
Ms. Y:	The metal. Anything else? Okay. What is the process here?
Nadia:	Allow.
Multiple Ss:	Allowed.
Ms. Y:	Allow… so, let's read… The acid is doing what?
Multiple Ss:	Allowing.
Ms. Y:	Allowing WHO?
Multiple Ss:	Electrons!
Abdul:	– in the metals to travel even more freely.
Ms. Y & Ss:	– to travel even more freely.

In this episode, Ms. Youssef's use of the metalanguage *participants* and *processes* served multiple purposes simultaneously: it helped distinguish the actors and the action in a scientific process, drew attention to the meaningful constituents in the sentence, and reinforced discipline-specific vocabulary. When reflecting on this curricular unit, Ms. Youssef said:

Identifying the participants helped the students rethink and focus on who is doing what. Even though I had to stop sometimes and ask the same question in different ways, towards the end of the unit, the children have become better in pulling out the participants in other subjects.

Ms. Youssef's use of the metalanguage in other subjects speaks to how functional grammar analysis can be used as a strategy for comprehending text across content areas.

In addition to process, participant, and circumstance (*circumstance* not illustrated above), the class also used the metalanguage of *connectors* (e.g., to refer to *and, but, since*) to talk about meaning in conjunctions and linking phrases. Later, while reading a different section in the same text, Ms. Youssef focuses on connectors to help students see where the author of this text is pointing out something surprising. She asks the students to read the section of the text below on their own, identify the connectors, and discuss them with the other students at their tables. This movement back and forth between whole group, individual, and pair activities, using the metalanguage, was an important aspect of supporting students to look for meaning in the texts they read. Ms. Youssef instructed them in this activity with these words:

> Read this paragraph and find any connectors. And I want you to find the important ones. I am not looking for *and* in this paragraph. So start reading. And once you signal those connectors, discuss at your tables. Just this paragraph, *Inventing the Light Bulb.*
> *... Many people think Thomas Edison invented the light bulb. But, in fact, a Canadian scientist named Henry Woodward was the first to develop the light bulb. Unfortunately, he did not have the money to make light bulbs after inventing them. He sold his idea to Thomas Edison, who was the first to figure out how to make large numbers of light bulbs available to the public.*

Students discuss, and Ms. Youssef circulates to listen to groups, reminding them to discuss *why* the author used those connectors. She then engages them in this interaction:

Ms.Y:	Alright, we have been talking about meanings in connectors. And we said connectors tell me what? What do they tell me, connectors in general?
Salma:	They tell you what's an important fact.
Nadia:	To connect the sentences with each other.
Ms. Y:	To connect or?
Kamil:	Or to read the sentence.
Hadiya:	To give more information.
Ms. Y:	To give more information or what did we say in our objective?
Ms. Y & Ss:	(Reading the objective displayed on the whiteboard) *Understand how authors use connectors to explain or signal unexpected information.*

Ms. Y:	Unexpected information or surprise information. So where is the connector in this paragraph that is surprising you? That the author chose to surprise you with some information.
Mariam:	*But, in fact.*
Ms. Y:	*But, in fact.* Why is this the connector here? What is the author trying to tell me?
Salma:	It wants to give people more information like to get their attention.
Ms. Y:	Okay, what else? Let's read.
Ms. Y & Ss:	(Reading from the text displayed on the whiteboard) *Many people think Thomas Edison invented the light bulb.*
Ms. Y:	So what do people think?
Multiple Ss:	Thomas Edison invented the light bulb.
Ms. Y:	Then the author says, (reading) *But, in fact –*
Ms. Y & Ss:	*a Canadian scientist named Henry Woodward was the first to develop the light bulb.*
Ms. Y:	What kind of attitude is the author trying to bring me here? Jafar.
Jafar:	He's trying to tell that Henry Woodward was the first to develop the light bulb.
Ms. Y:	Did he surprise me –
Students:	Yes.
Ms. Y:	– with that information?
Multiple Ss:	Yes.
Ms. Y:	So the author did surprise me by correcting what? (pointing to the text)
Multiple Ss:	What people think.

When Ms. Youssef initially introduced *connectors*, she used the word *and* as an example. In the episode above, she gave the direction to look for words other than *and*, which created the opportunity for students to realize that *connectors* communicate particular relationships among ideas (e.g., additive, temporal, consequential, contrastive). In her reflection log, Ms. Youssef wrote, "It is very useful to teach 'connectors' to make children ask questions about what they read. Connectors also show students how and why the author chooses a particular word." By drawing students' attention to connectors and discussing why the author chose to use a particular word or phrase to signal unexpected or surprising information, Ms. Youssef made the deliberateness of an author's word choice explicit. Used this way, meta-language can mediate students' awareness of language and the purposes it serves in a given context, which in turn supports their reading comprehension and writing.

Data sources

To explore the sense-making of students who had experienced SFL-informed instruction like that illustrated above, we conducted think-alouds and interviews with a subset of Ms. Youssef's students at the end of the academic year. In collaboration with Ms. Youssef, we identified students with basic to intermediate levels of English proficiency to participate in this activity (for further details about the data collection see Symons, Palincsar, & Schleppegrell, 2017). We report on interaction with seven of the students here. The children represent different levels of reading proficiency. At the time of data collection, Salma, Nadia, and Kamil read above grade level, Ahmed read on grade level, Hadiya read slightly below grade level, and Samir and Mariam read below grade level.

The task asked students to read an unfamiliar text to the interviewer, stopping at designated points to "think aloud" about what they understood. One of the texts is an excerpt from *Dragonfly Explanations* from *The Seeds and Roots* science series (Loper, 2011). This text is at the fifth-grade level and was unfamiliar to these end-of-year fourth-grade students. The section students read began with the following sentences (asterisks indicate places students were asked to stop and think aloud):

Zip. A flash of red zooms through the air. The red flash dives and darts. When it rests on a stem it holds open two pairs of wings. * They are shiny and clear as glass with veins like the ones on a leaf. Two huge red eyes gaze in all directions. This amazing insect is a dragonfly. *

If students did not pause at the marker, the interviewer encouraged them to stop and share their thinking. Otherwise, she just gave encouragement to continue, not commenting on or identifying any misunderstandings. This gave the children opportunities to talk about the ways they understood the text without feedback or prompting. In one instance, however, which we report below, the interviewer did respond to a student's question as she began to read; their interaction at this point further illustrates the value of metalanguage for supporting students' understanding.

Following the think-alouds, we asked students to identify features of the text they had read, using the functional grammar metalanguage that they had learned (e.g., asking them to identify processes or participants). We also asked them to tell us how they use functional grammar as they read and how they would advise other students to use functional grammar to better understand challenging texts. Each think-aloud and interview session was recorded and transcribed.

Findings

We report here on how one participant responded to the interviewer's use of functional grammar to help her see meaning in the text and on the challenges other students faced in recognizing meaning in the same textual context. We suggest some reasons that they struggled. We then share the children's perspectives on functional grammar strategies they recommend using to read difficult text. We found that children readily took up the meaning-based metalanguage and that their comments offer insights into what they found difficult and how they use functional grammar to support their reading.

Using the metalanguage to make sense of text

As we saw in the transcripts above, children had learned to use the functional grammar metalanguage to make sense of challenging text through classroom interactions. This was exemplified during one of the think-aloud interviews. This episode, reported more fully in Symons, et al. (2017), was an exception to the interviewer refraining from intervening during the think-aloud session. After Mariam, a "below grade level reader," read the first sentence, she asked the interviewer what a *red zooms* meant. The researcher told her that *zooms* means *flies*. When Mariam then said *it's the name of a fly*, the researcher responded that *zooms* is a *doing process*. Being able to label *zooms* in this way shifted Mariam's understanding about the meaning being presented here. In subsequent exchanges, Mariam concludes that *flash of red is the name*. The interviewer confirms that *flash of red* is the participant. This moment of interaction during the think-aloud explicitly addresses a comprehension problem that many of the students encountered but that their fluent oral reading of the sentence did not reveal. However, the questions the interviewer asked others after the think-aloud task showed that Mariam's misunderstanding was widely shared. We discuss this in the next section.

The challenge of recognizing the meaningful sentence constituents in an unfamiliar text

After students had read and thought aloud about the text, the interviewer suggested that "how the author begins this, this is kind of interesting" and asked each student to find the processes and participants in the first two sentences of the text: *Zip. A flash of red zooms through the air.* Analysis of these interactions helps us see how the students parse the text into meaningful segments and where challenges to understanding emerge.

All of the students identified *Zip* as a process, but the second sentence presented challenges. The dialogue that ensued revealed misunderstandings in recognizing these constituents but also showed how the meaningful metalanguage aided students in talking about what they did understand from the text.

Using the SFL metalanguage, the three constituents of the second sentence can be analyzed as:

A flash of red	*zooms*	*through the air.*
Participant	Process	Circumstance of place
(who/what)	(doing/action)	(where)

As they worked to identify the process in this sentence, the children looked for words that indicate *action,* as they recognized that something was happening here. But there are several words in the sentence that could be seen as construing action. For example, from the point of view of meaning, besides the verb *zoom, flash* and *through the air* are both sentence constituents that evoke meanings of action. Four of the students included *flash* as they identified the processes in these sentences, and two of them named *through the air* as a process. None thought *zooms* was the sole process in the second sentence.

Kamil, a strategic reader who first thought the text was about a bird but then acknowledged the mistake when he encountered the reference to the dragonfly, correctly identified participants in the sentence as *flash, red,* and *air.* When asked to find the processes in the sentence, he also identified *flash* as a process, as well as *zooms.* Nadia, a strong reader, identified *red zooms* both as process and participant.

Hadiya, reading slightly "below grade level," adjusted her understanding of the meaning of *flash of red* while thinking aloud, from her initial thought that it had to do with electricity to understanding that the text is about a firefly. When asked about the second sentence after the think-aloud activity, she readily identified *red, flash of red* as a participant. But then she also identified *flash* as the process in the sentence. When the interviewer said that she had it right, that *a flash of red* was the participant, Hadiya said "the process is it flashed through the air zooms."

There are two perspectives on meaning in English grammar that can help us understand the children's potential confusion about the functional roles of these constituents. As Halliday points out, SFL offers a *functional* grammar, where the grammar offers a means of expression of semantic systems in the language. While words typically present either a process or participant, the principle of *grammatical metaphor* enables meanings to be "represented by categories other than those that evolved to represent them" (Halliday, 1985, p. xviii). The children recognize in this sentence that the meaning of *flash* is simultaneously both *process* and *thing;* both aspects of the semantics of *flash* in *a flash of red* are acknowledged in the children's comments. Indeed, *flash* can be either a process or participant. That *through the air* is also named as a process can be explained in the ways Halliday and Matthiessen (2004) characterize prepositions, from a functional perspective, as "minor processes" (p. 277). They point out that the relationship between a preposition and the noun group participant that follows it is similar to the relationship between a verb and a noun that follows it. A preposition/noun structure such as *through the air* is not an extended verb phrase nor an extended noun phrase, but a combination of two different kinds of structures. From this perspective, although *through the air* is a circumstance of place (where the flash of red zooms), it is understandable that several of the children recognize the action presented through this minor process and characterize the whole phrase as a process.

Other challenges are also revealed by Ahmed's response, as he says that "red zooms are the participant and the process is the flash." As noted above, *flash* can be either a verb that constructs a process or a noun that presents a participant. Relatedly, *red* is more typically an adjective than the noun it presents in this sentence. Since both the word *flash* and the word *red* typically serve as different word classes than those they present in this text, the identification of *A flash of red* as a participant is challenging. In addition, since *red* is often followed by a noun, seeing *red zooms* as a participant makes sense, especially if the meaning of *zooms* is not clear.

These examples show how asking students to identify meaningful constituents in the sentences they read can reveal the parsing challenges they encounter – parsing challenges that speakers of English who are fluent readers might not recognize as problematic. It's likely that many reading comprehension problems that result from misidentification of sentence constituents are not revealed in talking about texts in ways that do not draw on meaningful metalanguage.

Children's perspectives on how functional grammar supports reading challenging text

After asking students to read aloud and then identify the processes, participants, and circumstances in the first two sentences, the researcher also asked them to reflect on how they might use functional grammar constructs while reading. Her question was: "If readers found this text to be difficult, how might you use functional grammar or suggest that they use functional grammar to help them make sense of this text?" Here we see how children are able to use this metalanguage as a strategy for reading and understanding.

For example, Salma's response shows that she uses a "process first" approach to a challenging sentence (*R* is the interviewer):

Salma: They should stop on every period and they should look which one is a process, which one is a word that it's doing, saying, or describing.

R: Okay, can you give me an example of where you might do that?

Salma: Right here (pointing and rereading). *One dragonfly may eat hundreds of predators every day.* They may EAT hundreds of small predators, insects every day.

R: Okay, so what do you notice about that? Why would you point that out and what functional grammar might you use to help somebody understand that?

Salma: I would use go back and reread because you can look at the process, what they're doing, how they're eating, what they eat and how much they eat.

"Go back and reread" is a common strategy promoted by the teacher; here we see that Salma uses the functional grammar metalanguage as a strategy for looking for the process when rereading.

Hadiya's response is more complicated in what it reveals about her understanding of the metalanguage. Here, she first identifies *more than* as a connector but then sees that it functions in a different way in this text:

R: Okay so if readers found this text to be confusing, how might you use functional grammar to help them understand it?

Hadiya: You may use functional grammar is when you look at the connecting words. The most common connecting words I see almost every time I read are the words *but* and *if*. They, some connectors tell us *but* – that there's something unexpected.

R: Uh huh. Are there any connectors in here?

Hadiya: *More than.*

R: Interesting, say more about that.

Hadiya: (reading) *More than two feet across. They had wings more than two feet across. More than* is … I get mixed up. I get mixed up with the math.

R: Oh ok. Oh *more than, less than*. Is that what you're thinking? Well that's helping you make sense of this text, right? Whether or not it's a connector, what does that tell you?

Hadiya: It tells me that it used to be greater but these years they shrink.

R: Okay. Alright, can you find the circumstance of time that helped you figure that out?

Hadiya: *Long, long ago.*

Other students also identified the circumstance *long ago* and were able to talk about its meaning, as in this example from Mariam:

R: Can you find a circumstance of time in this text? [pause] Remember talking about that, yeah.

Mariam: *Long ago?*

R: Yes, how might that help somebody understand the text.

Mariam: That it would- it's not like now it was like a long time ago in the past

R: Very good.

Mariam: They're saying here they are talking about it from a long time ago.

Summary

We have shown here that in addition to the ways research has reported on how children use functional grammar to get meaning from text, we can learn from the ways students use functional grammar metalanguage to talk about and parse sentence constituents. They are also able to use the functional grammar metalanguage to suggest strategies for how the metalanguage can help a student read challenging texts.

Discussion

SFL metalanguage gives children and teachers useful ways of talking about meaningful constituents and exploring meaning in text. In this chapter, we have presented evidence from think-aloud research that offers insights into how readers understand what they are reading, showing the importance of accurately recognizing meaningful sentence constituents in the texts they read. We have also reported on what the children themselves say about the ways functional grammar supports them in reading with greater understanding.

Use of meaningful metalanguage in dialogue about text enables children's greater understanding. In addition, use of the metalanguage through the process of talking about how they are making sense of the text with an interlocutor reveals linguistic demands that might otherwise be overlooked. As Ms. Youssef said in an interview about teaching with the text on electricity, "It's a complex text; it is not easy. Even though when you read it for the first time you think 'Oh, a beautiful story,' when you dissect it, it is a tough text." With a meaningful linguistic perspective on text complexity, teachers can better understand why students construct the meanings they do and support students in engaging with meaning as they read and write.

The important point, however, as Williams's work argues, is that the functional metalanguage is more than a resource for labeling concepts that already exist for children; it actually provides a means of offering new "consciousness about language in social life" (Williams, 2005, p. 289). Drawing on Vygotskian theory, Williams argues that the "meaning first" focus of the SFL metalanguage offers opportunities for *semiotic mediation* of the kind we have illustrated here as the teacher and students in this study use the grammatical concepts to recognize the relationship between "actors" and "action," or to identify what is "surprising" in a text. The notion that language choices are meaningful and that they connect to larger concepts that can be presented in text can be developed through talk about how specific wordings make the meanings they do, and about how particular meanings can be presented in different language choices. We have also shown how using the metalanguage can reveal how a reader understands a challenging text and where intervention to support understanding can be usefully offered, and it gives students new strategies for rereading and exploring text, as we have seen in this study.

There are barriers, though, to persuading teachers to take up new linguistic metalanguage. One issue that teachers may raise in being introduced to functional metalanguage is the value of the functional metalanguage in relation to traditional metalanguage (e.g., *verb, noun, prepositional phrase, conjunction*). This concern is also raised in other research using functional grammar. Carpenter, Achugar, Walter, & Earhart (2015), for example, used the metalanguage of *Process* and *Participant* in the work they report in a teacher education context but then found that teachers "translated" *process* into the word class term *verb*. Carpenter et al. reflect on this, recognizing that the history teacher they report on is bringing his own understanding and prior knowledge to the task. While they see the value of this, they also show that the traditional metalanguage does not connect to meaning in the ways the functional metalanguage does, and so it can be problematic when, as they report, the teacher says that "verbs [give] you that idea of what their intentions are," in referring to thinking/feeling processes during an interview with the researchers (Carpenter et al., 2015, p. 89). As the authors reflect on this, they suggest that it is important for the development of critical language awareness that teachers have a meaning-focused metalanguage and that the metalanguage not be transformed in ways that lose its conceptual integrity and meaning as a scientific concept. They suggest that "to ensure that the metalanguage fulfills its purpose there needs to be an explicit and sustained focus on the meaning and use of these concepts as tools that serve particular functions. The challenge lies in how to make it accessible and useful while not diluting its power" (p. 95). They also point out that metalanguage has to be contextualized in classroom discourse and pedagogical practices that support students' development of multilingual repertoires as well as construction, not just reproduction, of knowledge.

Developing knowledge about and using metalanguage as a pedagogical tool requires, for most teachers, learning a new way of thinking about language comprehension and writing instruction. In teacher education programs, if pre-service teachers are introduced to an SFL-approach in the context of literacy and language instruction, this can be a starting point for developing greater understanding of *how language means* and its power in social life. Adopting a functional linguistics perspective calls for teachers' engagement in learning alongside their students as they explore how authors use language to construct texts and how readers can use (meta)language to construct meanings with text. Using a functional grammar metalanguage to have meaningful conversations about texts holds promise as an instructional practice teachers can use to learn more about how their students understand what they read.

About the authors

Mary Schleppegrell is Professor of Education at the University of Michigan. She uses systemic functional linguistics to study the linguistic challenges of learning and children's language development. With literacy scholar Annemarie Palincsar, she led the *Language and Meaning* project to support bilingual children's literacy development across subject areas, and is currently collaborating with Chauncey Monte-Sano to study teacher learning to support emergent bilinguals in social studies. She is the author of *The Language of Schooling* (Erlbaum, 2004), *Developing Advanced Literacy in First and Second Languages* (with Cecilia Colombi, Erlbaum, 2002), *Reading in Secondary Content Areas (*with Zhihui Fang, University of Michigan Press, 2008*)*, and *Focus on Grammar and Meaning* (with Luciana de Oliveira, Oxford University Press, 2015).

Carrie Symons is Assistant Professor in the Department of Teacher Education at Michigan State University, U.S.A. Her research explores the relationship between classroom teachers' instructional practices and immigrant-origin youth's literacy and language development in multilingual contexts. Formerly an elementary classroom teacher of ten years, Dr. Symons prioritizes the building of long-term, mutualistic, research-practice partnerships with local community organizations, schools, and teachers. In collaboration with these critical partners, she aims to identify *what* teachers need to know to effectively facilitate immigrant-origin youth's learning across content areas and *how* this culturally and linguistically responsive pedagogical knowledge is best developed.

Note

1   Ms. Youssef is a native speaker of Arabic who refers to herself as an "English learner." She consistently referred to non-human participants in this informational text as "who" rather than "what." In Arabic, these pronouns do not take different forms based on the human/non-human distinction.

References

Brisk, M. E. (2015). *Engaging Students in Academic Literacies: Genre-based Pedagogy in K-5 Classrooms*. New York and London: Routledge.

Carpenter, B., Achugar, M., Walter, D., & Earhart, M. (2015). Developing teachers' critical language awareness: A case study of guided participation. *Linguistics and Education, 32*, 82–97.

Ellis, N., & Larsen-Freeman, D. (2006). Language emergence: Implications for applied linguistics. Introduction to the special issue. *Applied Linguistics, 27*(4), 558–589.

French, R. (2010). Primary school children learning grammar: Rethinking the possibilities. In T. Locke (ed.), *Beyond the Grammar Wars: A Resource for Teachers and Students on Developing Language Knowledge in the English/ literacy Classroom* (pp. 206–229). New York: Routledge.

Gebhard, M., Chen, I.-A., Graham, H., & Gunawan, W. (2013). Teaching to mean, writing to mean: SFL, L2 literacy, and teacher education. *Journal of Second Language Writing, 22*, 107–124. https://doi.org/10.1016/j.jslw.2013.03.005

Gebhard, M., Chen, I.-A., & Britton, L. (2014). "Miss, nominalization is a nominalization:" English language learners' use of SFL metalanguage and their literacy practices. *Linguistics and Education, 26*, 106–125.

Gebhard, M., & Graham, H. (2018). Bats and grammar: developing critical language awareness in the context of school reform. *English Teaching: Practice & Critique, 17*(4), 281–297. doi:10.1108/ETPC-12–2017–0183

Halliday, M. A. K. (1985). Introduction. *An Introduction to Functional Grammar,* pp. xiii–xxxv. London: Edward Arnold.

Halliday, M. A. K., & Matthiessen, C. M. I. M. (2004). *An Introduction to Functional Grammar* (3rd ed.). London: Hodder Arnold.

Loper, S. (2011). *Dragonfly Explanations*. Nashua, NH: Delta Education.

Macken-Horarik, M., Sandiford, C., Love, K., & Unsworth, L. (2015). New ways of working "with grammar in mind" in School English: Insights from systemic functional grammatics. *Linguistics and Education*, **31**, 145–158. https://doi.org/10.1016/j.linged.2015.07.004

Menyuk, P., & Brisk, M. E. (2005). *Language Development and Education*. Houndmills, Basingstoke, Hampshire, and New York: Palgrave Macmillan.

Moore, J., & Schleppegrell, M. J. (2014). Using a functional linguistics metalanguage to support academic language development in the English Language Arts. *Linguistics and Education*, **26**, 92–105. https://doi.org/10.1016/j.linged.2014.01.002

Moore, J., Schleppegrell, M. J., & Palincsar, A. S. (2018). Discovering disciplinary linguistic knowledge with English learners and their teachers: Applying SFL concepts through design-based research. *TESOL Quarterly*, **52**(4), 1022–1049. doi:org/10.1002/tesq.472.

Schleppegrell, M. J. (2013). The role of metalanguage in supporting academic language development. *Language Learning*, **63** (Suppl 1), 153–170. https://doi.org/10.1111/j.1467-9922.2012.00742.x

Schleppegrell, M. J. (2016). Content-based language teaching with functional grammar in the elementary school. *Language Teaching*, **49**, 116–128. doi: 10.1017/S0261444814000093.

Schleppegrell, M. J., Greer, S., & Taylor, S. (2008). Literacy in history: Language and meaning. *Australian Journal of Language and Literacy*, **31**(2), 174–187.

Schleppegrell, M., & Moore, J. (2018). Linguistic tools for supporting emergent critical language awareness in the elementary school. In R. Harman (ed.), *Bilingual Learners and Social Equity: Critical Approaches to Systemic Functional Linguistics* (pp. 23–43). New York: Springer.

Simmons, A. (2018). Student use of SFL resources on fantasy, canonical, and non-fiction texts: Critical literacy in the high school ELA classroom. In R. Harman (ed.), *Bilingual Learners and Social Equity: Critical Approaches to Systemic Functional Linguistics* (pp. 71–90). New York: Springer.

Symons, C. (2017). Supporting emergent bilinguals' argumentation: Evaluating evidence in informational science texts. *Linguistics and Education*, **38**, 79–91. https://doi.org/10.1016/j.linged.2017.02.006

Symons, C., Palincsar, A. S., & Schleppegrell, M. J. (2017). Fourth-grade emergent bilinguals' uses of functional grammar analysis to talk about text. *Learning and Instruction*, **52**, 102–111. doi:http://dx.doi.org/10.1016/j.learninstruc.2017.05.003.

Williams, G. (1998). Children entering literate worlds: Perspectives from the study of textual practices. In F. Christie & R. Misson (eds.), *Literacy and Schooling* (pp. 18–46). London: Routledge.

Williams, G. (2000). Children's literature, children and uses of language description. In L. Unsworth (ed.), *Researching Language in Schools and*

Communities: Functional Linguistic Perspectives (pp. 111–129). London: Cassell.

Williams, G. (2004), Ontogenesis and grammatics: functions of metalanguage in pedagogical discourse. In G. Williams & A. Lukin (eds.), *The Development of Language*, pp. 241–267. Continuum, London.

Williams, G. (2005). Grammatics in schools. In R. Hasan, C. M. I. M. Matthiessen, & J. Webster (eds.), *Continuing Discourse on Language* (Vol. 1, pp. 281–310). London: Equinox.

3 From buttocks to seminal muscles: SFL-based physical education

Ruth Mulvad
Formerly Associate Professor, University College Copenhagen

Introduction: Language in PE

As a rule, language is not often considered a significant part of the school subject physical education (PE). PE in a Danish context is considered a practical subject, just like subjects such as art, music and home economics. However, even though these subjects primarily focus on the practical dimension, i.e., what the learners do with their bodies and hands, and not on written texts, it is impossible to think about any subject without thinking about the language that constitutes it: learners are instructed, they communicate, evaluate and are evaluated through language. Thus, PE – like any other subject – is based on language. Without language, students cannot develop their professionalism in PE learning.

This chapter presents a curriculum plan for PE developed in close collaboration between teacher-educators and PE teachers. It shows how such a plan can incorporate disciplinary language learning within PE lessons, and how teachers can develop their knowledge about language. Through a series of lessons planned for 4th grade, and vignettes with explicit language use by teachers and students, the chapter illustrates disciplinary language instruction for teachers who do not have the experience of incorporating disciplinary language.

Unfortunately, PE has not been subjected to language analyses, neither internationally, nor nationally to the extent that traditional "academic" subjects such as science, history or languages have. Within SFL-based educational research, two studies are worth highlighting: Slater & Butler (2015) and Forey & Cheung (2019).

Slater & Butler (2015) show that the subject of PE has common denominators with science in what is referred to as knowledge framework. PE, like science, is organized around three theory–practical dimensions: classification/description (theory), principles/sequence (sequencing actions or ideas) and evaluation/choice (evaluating student choices). Each of these three aspects has its specific language structures, which Slater & Butler show have PE-specific challenges while maintaining general similarities with science. In this perspective, PE is not just a recreational subject excluded from other academic subjects. Organized around school-related social practices, PE plays a role along with other school subjects as a socialization factor for the learners.

Forey & Cheung (2019) focus on the language requirements, especially of students' written work within the theoretical part of the subject and in an exam context. The study criticizes CLIL (content and language integrated learning) approaches for putting an extra burden on students, as it becomes an extra dimension to have their attention directed onto the language patterns, particularly because linguistic skills are trained separately from content. With their point of departure in a number of SFL studies, Forey & Cheung argue that SFL metalanguage in school subjects promotes learning. They developed language-based teaching of students' written text production in the theoretical part of PE and, consequently, students' exam results improved dramatically (Forey & Cheung, 2019, p. 91).

Education and language – and PE

The Danish public school aims to provide students with knowledge and skills to understand other countries and cultures and prepare them to become Danish citizens and world citizens in our globalized society; this also applies to PE[1]. The school subject PE has changed with a significant school reform of 2014[2]. PE is still characterized by physical activity and lessons challenge and develop students' physical ability. However, with the reform, new demands have been made, introducing a theory- and practice-integrated exam where students must design, construct, demonstrate and explain a sequence. This means that students must learn to understand and explain what they do physically, socially and academically within the context of PE. Therefore, teachers have to anchor instruction in relevant theory, using expert concepts that benefit all pupils' learning processes. In other words, with the school reform, PE is now clearly an actual school subject which also entails learning language.

An unintentional consequence of the increased language requirements in PE may be that linguistically challenged students become lost, as tends to happen in other more "academic" subjects. A significant part of the group of students participating in this study is made up of learners of Danish as a second language. Despite yearslong attention to the problem, studies show that these students tend to underperform in more traditionally academic subjects (e.g. Pisa Etnisk, 2015; 2017).

The language in subjects' project

As a consequence of the 2014 school reform, the Danish Ministry of Education (2016) launched a project on language in a number of academic school subjects, such as Math, Danish, History, Science and PE. The expected outcome of the project was three teaching sequences for beginners (grades 1–3), intermediate (grades 4–6) and advanced (grades 7–9) levels for each subject, each with an associated teacher guide. A requirement was that all teaching sequences must have a language focus, in order to accommodate Danish as a second language learners' linguistic development in Danish. Additionally, the sequences needed to be concrete enough for teachers to be able to use them straight off the website, www.emu.dk. Within each of the chosen subjects, expert groups were formed to develop these teaching sequences. The expert groups consisted of teacher educators and educational researchers.

In the following part of this chapter I shall present the theoretical background of the PE project, guiding questions for exploring the context, as well as methods and our main findings. This part will be rounded off by a presentation of the pedagogical model, the so-called "snail," developed on the basis of Derewianka (1990). The "snail" model has been the point of departure for the three teaching sequences developed within PE. The last part of the chapter presents the intermediate level teaching sequence in the way we presented it for PE teachers.

Exploring language in PE – a functional approach: *Register*

In a social semiotic way of thinking, subject and language are completely integrated; they are two sides of the same coin. The overarching purpose for the students is to develop their PE capabilities and knowledge. The Hallidayan metalanguage of *systemic functional linguistics (SFL)* (Halliday & Matthiessen, 2014) offers tools for students and teachers which enable them to talk about and understand the subject: they can discuss the role of the language in the educational process in a way that makes the subject visible and enables students to reach their maximum potential (Christie & Derewianka, 2008, Forey & Cheung, 2019; Schleppegrell, 2004).

From the concept of *Register* (Halliday & Hasan, 1976) the subject PE was analyzed as a *sub-system* (Christie & Macken-Horarik, 2011), understood as ways of using the language in various contexts, configured by *Mode, Field* and *Tenor* (Andersen & Holsting, 2015; Eggins, 2004; Martin, 1992). Through the perspective of *Mode*, we can thus describe a continuum of ways of using language in classroom talk between teacher and students (Gibbons, 2006): Is it primarily spoken-like or written-like? With SFL we can describe this continuum more precisely as a movement from *language as action* to *language as reflection.* Along the *Mode*-continuum from left to right, language can be described as *Language accompanying action,* as *Language as reconstruction,* as *Language as construction* and as *Language as reflection* (Martin, 1992; Mulvad, 2012a). From the perspective of *Field*, we can visualize which *Arena* (Andersen & Holsting, 2015; Leckie-Tarry, 1995) students and teachers are placing themselves in within the teaching context. *Arena* shows how organization affects *Field*, whether the content is more everyday-like or more expert-like. Through *Tenor* we can analyze student and teacher roles, and the position of the actors and their mutual relations (Polias, 2016).

Three questions for exploring the context

Before developing new language-based teaching sequences in PE, the expert group determined what characterized typical PE teaching sequences. Based on the combined expertise of the research group's members and initial analyses of the subject PE, three overarching questions arose:

1   What is the interplay between language and subject in PE?
2   Are there any recurrent typical activities, and do they have a typical structure and sequence?
3   How is the student positioned in the learning process?

Answers to these questions give an account of what is typical within PE teaching sequences (Table 3.1).

Table 3.1 shows some initial observations about typical PE teaching sequences. Typical for language use in PE is the predominance of oral language: teachers tend to use expert or academic language, while students rely mainly on everyday language. Written language is uncommon, and teachers tend not to use texts, posters, blackboards, etc. On the other hand, students are expected to use academic, expert language for their final exam in PE and are expected to be able to read and speak using appropriately

Table 3.1 Features of typical PE teaching sequences

Questions for exploring the context	*Initial observations*
1 What is the interplay between language and subject in PE?	• Everybody talks a lot, i.e. the oral language is dominant, but does not get much attention, apart from when the students speak too much – or too little (as in when not answering the teacher's questions). • Within the teaching space, academic language is used. This includes use of specialized PE expressions, difficult concepts and possibly lesson aims. • Many activities are carried out without students' using language. The teacher instructs with body and language, while students almost exclusively use their bodies, without verbalizing their actions. • Instructions may include written texts such as illustrations with adherent text, rules for ball games, etc. However, if used, these are not taught explicitly. • Students may produce written texts themselves, e.g., rules for self-invented ball games. • No writing in the teaching space: We seldom see blackboards, smartboards, space for posters, etc. • As in other subjects, texts exist (in the curriculum, in textbooks, etc.) These are included when needed and with varying frequency. Many of these texts are multimodal, representing many different genres. • For their exam, students are required to use academic language (reading and speaking in particular).
2 Are there any recurrent typical activities, and do they have a typical structure and sequence?	• In PE, teaching is organized around activities: students, teachers, materials and props are organized in many different ways, requiring many different ways of using language. • A typical teaching sequence is constructed with a point of departure in an introductory teacher instruction and a warm-up, followed by activities which are combined into, e.g., a ball game, an acrobatic figure, a somersault, a dance, etc. at the end of the teaching sequence. This follows the so-called PPP model: presentation, practice, production (e.g. Anderson, 2017).
3 How is the student positioned in the learning process?	• Typical for student–teacher interaction, especially in the beginning and the end of the teaching sequence, is the so-called IRF pattern (Sinclair & Coulthard, 1975). In this type of interaction, students are positioned as responders. When used as an overarching conversation structure, students are provided with very limited opportunities for linguistic expression or language development. • A widespread phenomenon is the occasional segregation of some learner groups, which risks passive participation or even truancy. Often, these include second language learners.

academic language. A typical way of organizing a PE teaching sequence is to rely on the PPP model: presentation, practice, production (e.g. Anderson, 2017). Consequently, students are positioned as recipients, often engaging in IRF sequences, where the teacher initiates by asking (closed) questions and students respond with often brief answers, followed up by an acknowledgement from the teacher (Sinclair & Coulthard, 1975). Often certain groups of students are marginalized, second language learners in particular.

Language-based PE teaching sequences: Using *Register* as a planning tool

The students' learning process is at the core of the so-called "snail" model (Fig. 3.1) which we used. The students' learning process is here seen from a social-semiotic perspective through the concept of *Register*, as configured by *Field*, *Tenor* and *Mode* (Derewianka, 1990). Thus, it is not just the target text, e.g., a report of an acrobatic figure and the students' way towards mastery of it, which is the object of our planning. The overall principle in the model is to shape the pedagogical discourse, taking account of all the actors and necessary processes, materials and equipment, organizing the teaching sequence as a linguistic development process with the SFL concept of *Register* as a basis. This model naturally includes a variety of genres and ways of working with them.

The "snail" in Figure 3.1 is a graphic model for a linguistically informed way of planning teaching sequences. It is a generic model and can be used as a basis for all subject areas. The labels of the sections of the "snail" in Danish can be translated to English as follows: *handling* is *action*, *rekonstruktion* is *reconstruction*, *transformation* is *transformation*, *konstruktion* is *construction*, *refleksion* is *reflection*. *Felt*, *Relation* and *Måde* are *Field*, *Tenor* and *Mode* respectively, in English. From the perspective of the variable *Mode*, we can describe the general principle of planning teaching sequences: instruction moves from the language the students bring, their common-sense or everyday language, corresponding to *action* in the snail model, via *reconstruction* towards the specialized, expert language of the subject (*construction* and *reflection*). *Tenor* concerns student and teacher roles and their interrelational positioning. *Field* relates to how the classroom is organized and consequently how students and teachers are placing themselves within the teaching context. In the following section the snail model will be elaborated within the context of a particular 4th grade teaching sequence about acrobatic figures.

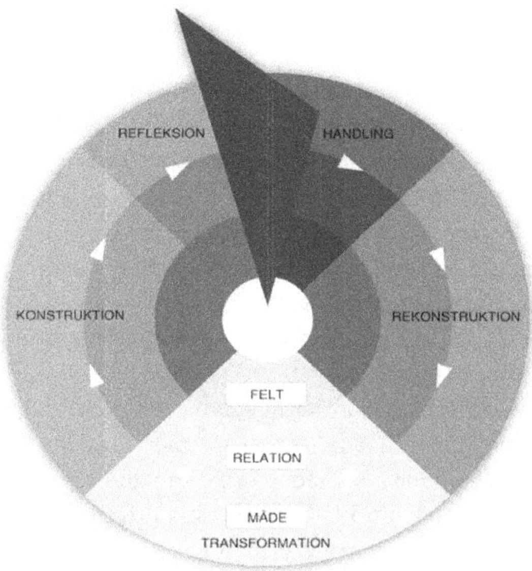

Figure 3.1 Derewianka's "snail" model, National Centre for Literacy and Utterslev School, modified from Derewianka, 1990.

In learning processes, repetitions in new constellations are important. This is why we added a section called *transformation* in the "snail." This term, *transformation*, is not a linguistic term such as the terms, *action*, *reconstruction*, *construction* and *reflection*. We added this element because our experience shows that it is essential to make the transformation from more congruent to more incongruent meaning-making clearly visible. In this way it resembles the child's early language development (Halliday, 1975; Painter, 1984) which, in SFL-based teaching, is a main basis for the understanding of scaffolding in pedagogical contexts (Rose & Martin, 2012; Østergaard, 2017).

The snail model illustrates the linguistic development and development of students' PE-understanding. This development can also be described as a chain of linguistic activities, where output from one activity acts as input for the next activity in the chain (Mulvad, 2012b). Planning teaching sequences using a chain of linguistic activities reduces the gap between what the students can do on their own, and what the students are expected to do next, ensuring their ability to participate. In this progression there is also a training perspective: students are continuously given the opportunity to repeat what they have learned, but continually in new contexts and with new perspectives.

Principles for changing PE to language-based teaching

From the above mapping of typical PE teaching sequences (Table 3.1), we identified which elements to maintain and expand, and what needed changing to develop the three exemplary and ready to use teaching sequences to be published on the Ministry website. From the perspective of *Register* we were able to determine how a typical PE teaching sequence could be changed into an SFL-based sequence. This could be done, for example, by swapping the sequence of activities, changing the organization of activities, modifying student roles and position, adjusting interaction patterns and making language use visible.

We took our point of departure in a typical structure of a teaching sequence by adding the following criteria: every student must be able to participate, and everybody should profit from the teaching. We focused on developing students' oral PE language and directed our attention to the various activities: how they were organized, in what ways language was used, and students' academic language use. Writing also ended up playing a more prominent role toward the end of the developed sequences as well. We did not, however, include textbooks or written instructions for reading academic texts to a very large degree. The focus in the developed sequences was, nonetheless, towards meeting the requirements for the exam, where the students are expected to be able to explain and describe their self-composed PE series of movements in an academic way.

Finally, we were highly sensitive towards how students were positioned in the learning process, including the teacher–student dialogue in the classroom. A social-semiotic approach could have had a focus on other "signs" in the room which contribute to meaning-making processes within PE where body, movement and equipment are dominant. However, our focus here was on the verbal language within PE, and how working with this could leverage students' development of participating in PE more "academically."

The exemplary teaching sequence developed for 4th grade PE: *acrobatic figures* and *making each other good*

The teaching sequence presented here combines two areas from the PE curriculum: the topic *acrobatic figures* and the theme *making each other good,* which is a key social aim of the PE curriculum. Teachers use this expression, as we will see below, to encourage students to support and help each other do well. The teaching sequence was developed for a 4th grade with a diverse student group in terms of gender, language backgrounds, ethnicity and cultural backgrounds. Through the teaching sequence, students learn to perform, guide others, and explain in an expert way so as to help and support each other in their individual and mutual development. Table 3.2 shows the structure of the developed PE-sequence.

Table 3.2 shows a description of the teaching sequence with both a PE focus (e.g., warming up, presentation and testing of acrobatic figure, etc.) and a language focus (e.g., adding language, stretching the language, approaching generalizations). Because of the class schedule, lessons were delivered back-to-back, two on the same day: the first and second lesson, the third and fourth lesson, and the fifth and sixth lesson. The third column in the table shows the lessons' correlation with the *Mode*-continuum sections in the snail model, and the theoretical underpinnings of the teaching sequence. The third column thus demonstrates the language development of the teaching sequence as a progression in the variable *Mode,* from *Language accompanying action* to *Language as reflection.*

Table 3.2 The six lessons of the developed teaching sequence for 4th grade PE

	Teaching practice *The six lessons*	*Corresponding sections* *from the snail model*
First lesson	1. The first experiences Introduction and warm-up	*Action* Language accompanying action
Second lesson	2. Adding language Presenting and testing an acrobatic figure and summarizing the first lesson	*Reconstruction* Language as reconstruction
Third lesson	3. Stretching the language Introduction and warm-up	*Action* Language accompanying action
Fourth lesson	4. Approaching generalizations Experiment with acrobatic figures	*Transformation* From situation-dependent to situation-independent language use
Fifth lesson	5. Professional knowledge 1 Summary of the whole study	*Construction* Language as construction and reflection
Sixth lesson	6. Professional knowledge 2 Written summary	*Reflection* Language as construction and reflection

Pedagogical considerations when presenting the 4th grade teaching sequence to PE teachers

In many ways, this teaching sequence (Table 3.2, second column) resembles other (more typical) sequences in PE, which any PE teacher could have prepared. The crucial difference, however, is seen in two details: the clear language dimension added in the lesson headlines, and the final, sixth lesson, where students participate in joint-construction of a text.

The approach in the teaching sequence is predictably new and somewhat strange to teachers in the target group (PE teachers without any specific linguistic knowledge). Consequently, we (in the expert group), wanted to introduce it to teachers in a way that minimized the gap between what PE teachers typically do and what the developed teaching sequence prescribes. Accordingly, the teachers were introduced to the teaching sequence and the theoretical underpinnings little by little, making the new way of teaching more comprehensible and accessible.

The first steps towards the theoretical underpinnings of the teaching sequence

Each lesson was first described using case-like presentations of how each lesson could look in practice. This was done to demonstrate for teachers how the teaching in each lesson is organized, inviting them in to "observe" a PE lesson.

After each vignette, the language perspective is added by commenting on what happened. This encompasses a reconstruction and moves (the teachers) along the variable *Mode* in the snail model.

Table 3.3 shows how the three perspectives in the comments: *learning objectives and roles*, *language use*, and *progression of content knowledge and language* correspond to *Tenor*, *Mode* and *Field* in the snail model.

The comments reconstruct the lesson, adding a new (language) dimension for the teachers. While commenting on the cases, the teaching context is highlighted through three headings as a first step to understanding each of the three variables: *Tenor, Mode* and *Field.* The lessons of the teaching sequence are thus linked to elements of the snail model. Only after that are the selected SFL terms introduced, and always while also providing clear references to the previous lessons and the comments. In this way, teachers are introduced to the exemplary teaching sequence for the 4th grade while themselves progressing along the *Register* continuum: from concrete, practice-oriented understandings to ultimately a more abstract, theoretically

Table 3.3 Three perspectives for commenting on the vignettes

Teaching practice **The three perspectives in the** **comments**	*Register* **The snail model:** *Tenor*, *Mode* **and** *Field*
Learning objectives and roles Which activities support the learning objectives, and what is the intended relation between teacher and learner?	*Tenor* Relations between the participants
Language use In what way are the students expected to use the language (about PE)?	*Mode* Ways of using language
Progression of content knowledge and language What is the progression of the learners' academic and linguistic development?	*Field* The arena in which something happens

informed understanding of each lesson in the 4th grade PE teaching sequence. These three perspectives are the point of departure for our comments on lessons 1, 2, 4 and 5 in the teaching sequence presented below.

Presenting the 4th grade teaching sequence to PE teachers

In the following, the elaboration of the developed 4th grade teaching sequence mirrors the way in which the teachers were introduced to it.[3]

First lesson. The first experiences. Introduction and warm-up

Introduction and warming up. The 4th grade is gathered at the back wall of the gym hall. The teachers have hung up a poster with the learning goals, a picture of the acrobatic figure students will be learning, a poster with relevant vocabulary, targets of assessment and examples of sentences which students can use when instructing and guiding each other or when asking questions and summarizing from group work activities.

The teacher tells the students that during this unit of study they will learn to keep their balance and do acrobatic exercises by tightening muscles in the right places in their body: they will learn muscular tension and balance. She tightens her abdominal muscles and holds both hands on her stomach.

She encourages students to do the same and feel the tightening of their own muscles."What happens when you let go of the tightening?" she asks."It gets soft," says one student."Mine is loose," another says.The teacher also says it is important that they help each other and work together to do the exercises so that everyone can *"make each other good."* She points to the words *body tension* and *balance* and points out that the learning objective is also learning to use the language of the subject, PE. This is why they must use the language in different ways throughout the process. Among other things, they will ask questions (see Table 3.4), guide each other (see Table 3.5) and tell each other what they have done during group work. Finally, she points to the posters on the wall and encourages students to get help from them and from each other throughout the lesson.

During the warm-up, in pairs, the students perform different fighting games which challenge their balance. These are designed to make them aware of relaxed and tightened muscles. Between the individual exercises, students talk together about the muscles they feel, whether they are tightened, soft or relaxed and how it affects their balance.

While students talk about their experience, the teacher scaffolds from everyday, common-sense language to more specialized language: "So when your buttocks are hard, it means that you are tightening them, right?" The students take up the term "tightening," using it themselves: "Yeah, when I tighten my buttocks, then …" The warm-up ends with a series of swing, stretch, strength and balance exercises which students and teachers perform together. During the exercises, the teacher includes the words *swing, stretch, bend, tighten* and *balance* in her talk, and encourages students to use the words while performing the movements as well.

Comments on the first lesson: The first experiences. Introduction and warm-up

Learning objectives and roles. The warm-up exercises are carefully selected to fit into subsequent lessons of the entire teaching sequence, both in terms of PE and in language. Students feel body tension, experience working together and use the language they already have in order to do so. The teacher uses PE-relevant terms so that students hear them and through repetition become familiar with them, possibly trying them out themselves (though this is not a requirement yet). The terminology is subject-specific vocabulary which students later will be given the opportunity to apply in new contexts, deepening their understanding. Hence, the role of the students is actively to follow the teacher's instructions, bodily and linguistically.

Language use. In the situations where students work together, they use what could be called here-and-now language, for example: "Hey, do this here …" "Try and feel …" "Cool! I couldn't throw you off balance 'cause you didn't tighten!" "And when I make my butt hard, then …"

Coming from the outside and reading these bits of text, it is difficult to understand what is happening. The role of the language here is to be a "social lubricant" to get things done, i.e., to help students and teacher succeed in their actions. The content and meanings lie in what they are doing. Everyone in this phase of the unit of study can concentrate on what he or she does without thinking about how to say it.

Professional and linguistic progression. The point of this initial lesson is that the students both build understanding and motivation, and develop knowledge based on an immediate experience closely related to what they do. Here the teacher uses an everyday way of developing knowledge while using language as an effective support for the learners (in future) to enter the academic and expert world.

Second lesson: Adding language. Presentating and testing an acrobatic figure and summarizing the two first lessons

In the second lesson, students are divided into groups of four. With the help of one of the groups, the teacher shows the balance exercise 'the figurehead' and demonstrates how body tension and cooperation are important for the performance.

Students study the image of "the figurehead" on the poster and make suggestions about where in the body they expect muscle-tension to occur when

Figure 3.2 The acrobatic figure the "figurehead."

performing this figure:"It's here in the stomach it's tensing … otherwise you fall.""It's also here," says another student and points."Yes," the teacher says, "the *base* of the figure also tightens in the thighs."Two students, Aisha and Dan, demonstrate the balance exercise. The teacher asks Aisha, who is at the top, to release the tension a little in her thighs, which nearly makes them lose their balance. The figure is about to collapse, but the teacher quickly moves herself and Benjamin under Aisha to support the figure and prevent them from falling. She explains that Benjamin's role is to support and assist Aisha and Dan with the balance exercise. She also asks Heitsam to instruct and guide Aisha and Dan so they can regain their balance. To guide the students, the teacher asks questions such as:"What should they do to keep their balance?""How can they make their balance be as stable as possible?"

"Which muscles should they tighten?" "Should they lean more backwards or should they bend their legs …?" Heitsam in the role of *guide* grabs Dan's arm: "You have to go this way," he says. The teacher asks Heitsam to move away from the figure, forcing him to use the appropriate PE language while instructing orally. In this way the teacher illustrates how being able to touch the figure or being forced to move away has an impact on their language use: "You need the language to instruct," she explains.

Everyone in the group tries out all the roles in the balance exercise: two students to perform the figure (*the base,* and *the top*), one to guide (*the guide*) and one to support (*the support*). They take a picture of their best figure. To facilitate students' oral participation, the teacher hands out a list of prompts for instructing and for guiding each other (shown in Tables 3.4 and 3.5).

Testing the figures. While the students are working with the figure, asking questions and guiding each other, the teacher gives feedback. In her conversation with the groups, she clarifies the order of the movements:

Lærer:	"Prøv at forklare hvad der er det første *toppen* og *bunden* skal gøre." (Teacher: "Try to explain what the first thing is that the *top* person and *base* need to do.")
Guide:	"De skal … sådan her …" (The *guide*: "They are going to … like this … ')
Lærer:	"Ja først skal *bunden* bøje i benene …' (Teacher: Yes, first, the *base* should bend the legs …")
Guide:	"Og tage *toppen* i hænderne." (The *guide*: "And hold hands with the top.")

Table 3.4 Student handout: To support students in asking questions

In Danish	In English
Sådan kan du stille spørgsmål	**How to ask questions**
Brug hv-spørgeord, for eksempel:	Use wh-questions, for example:
– *Hvad vil det sige at ...?*	– *What does it mean to...?*
– *Hvordan forstår du ...?*	– *How do you understand...?*
– *Hvorfor gør du sådan ...?*	– *Why do you do that?*
– *Hvornår vil du mene at ...?*	– *When do you want to...?*
– *Hvilke muskler er spændte, når ...?*	– *What muscles are tensed when...?*
– *Hvordan fik vi gode råd?*	– *How did we get good advice?*
Eller start med et udsagnsord (verbum, proces), fx:	Or start with a verb (process), such as:
– *Betyder det ...?*	– *Does it mean...?*
– *Kommer man så til at ...?*	– *Are you going to...?*
– *Kunne man også gøre sådan her?*	– *Could you also do this here?*
– *Gør det noget at ...?*	– *Does it matter if you...?*
– *Er det en god måde at gøre det på?*	– *Is this a good way to do it?*

Table 3.5 Student handout: To support students in instructing and guiding

In Danish	In English
Sådan kan du instruere og guide, for eksempel:	**To instruct and guide, you can say:**
– *Hvis du ... så ...*	– *If you... then*
– *Prøv at ...*	– *Try to...*
– *Har du selv et forslag til ...*	– *Do you have a suggestion for...?*
– *Først ... du sådan her ... så sådan her ... derefter ... til sidst ...*	– *First ... you do like this ... then like this ... then ... finally...*
– *Hvor er det godt! Kom igen!*	– *Well done! Try again!*
– *Nu fungerer det!*	– *Now it works!*
– *Du er bare så dygtig/god/fantastisk!*	– *You are so good/great/amazing*

Lærer: "Ja, så skal de tage hinanden i hænderne ... og bagefter?" (Teacher: "Yes, then they have to hold each other's hands ... and afterwards?)

Top: "Så sætter jeg mit ene ben op på hans lår." (The *top*: "Then I put my one leg up on his thighs.")

Lærer: "Men inden du gør det, hvad gør I så?" (Teacher: "But before you do this, what are you doing?")

> *Guide*: "Så læner de sig bagud." (The *guide*: "Then they are leaning backwards.")
>
> Lærer: "Ja, de læner sig bagud, ellers kan de ikke holde balancen." (Teacher: "Yes, they are leaning backwards, otherwise they can't keep the balance.")

Using the student handouts and the teacher's scaffolding, students challenge and *stretch* their oral language, which helps them to see and understand what they observe and do, and to communicate, instruct and help each other.

Summing up. After the group work, the teacher reassembles the groups in front of the posters. She points to the words on the poster *body tension, balance, cooperation* and *responsibility* and asks the students, first in groups, then, with the whole class, to say what they can about the words. While talking, students use many words, both everyday words and the vocabulary from the posters. In order to further challenge students' language while allowing them to reflect on what they have learned, the teacher asks students to show their parents the pictures they took, telling them what they worked on that day in PE: "Explain what you did, and how you guided and helped each other." In this way, students are asked to actively use the language they have just worked with in the classroom again in another context.

Comment on second lesson: Adding language. Presentating and testing acrobatic figures and summarizing the two first lessons

Learning objectives and roles. In this second lesson the teacher shows and verbalizes all actions along the way. The role of the students is to contribute both bodily and orally with the knowledge they have gained from the introduction and warm-up. The posters help to support all students, giving access to the required knowledge. The teacher involves the students by asking questions about their actions. In this way, the teacher guides the students' development and knowledge. Throughout this lesson, students are given an increasingly active role, culminating in their controlling the entire recount of their work when they describe the acrobatic figure of the "figurehead" to their parents in the homework.

Language use. The language in this lesson does more work than in the first lesson. In this lesson, students must say *who* must do something (e.g., the *base, the top*), what they are doing (e.g., *tighten, relax, fall, move*) and *where and how* they are doing it (e.g., *in the stomach, to regain the balance, backwards*). This means that from the language alone, you can understand what is going on without having to point (compared to the language used in the first lesson, where students only needed "here-and-now" language).

The teacher uses the expressions *first, then, next* and *finally* from the poster on the wall. This helps both teacher and students to build knowledge of how to structure the *sequence of actions* in the construction of the figure, the "figurehead," and when reporting at the end of the lessons. These *sequencing words* must be made explicit and used in the activities so that students too can actively use them.

When teachers and students talk in this sequence, the students are developing their academic PE-language. The teacher shunts between everyday and academic language and vocabulary, such as *buttocks* and *gluteal muscles, doesn't fall* and *keeps the balance* so that the new vocabulary is constantly linked to what the students already know. Students are thus encouraged to use the new expressions and stretch their everyday language towards the more expert PE language. In this way, the gap that some students experience between their existing everyday knowledge and the knowledge presented in class is reduced to manageable steps.

Professional and linguistic progression. The aim of this lesson in the teaching sequence is for students to build up knowledge that enables them to distance themselves from their concrete experience. To do this, students must use language which is moved a little further away from the concrete situation. This is for example when students say, *"We knew we tightened the muscles when we wanted to keep from falling."* The teacher encourages students to use more generalizing statements such as "W*hen you tighten your muscles, it's easier to keep your balance."* In this way, students are helped to construct their knowledge more generally and expertly. After the first lesson, the students are on their way, moving from the arena of everyday experience towards a more specialized PE-field, building a good foundation to progress further into the expert field.

Third lesson. Stretching the language. Introduction and warm-up

Using the posters of the unit of study's learning goals, the figure of the "figurehead," the vocabulary and the examples of language use from the previous lessons, the teacher activates the students' memory and experience from the first two lessons. She points to the posters and says to the students:

"Tell me what you did and how you did it." When she talks, she focuses on the words *did*, *what* and *how*:

Teacher: "How did you make the 'figurehead'? What did you do first? What happened then? What happened afterwards? And what did you do last?"
Louise: "First we took each other's hands."
Nouri: "Then … we bent our legs."
Tom: "Afterwards, we leaned backwards."
Aiya: "Last, we got up and stood on our thighs … and leaned backwards."
Teacher: "How did you work out keeping the balance?"
Benny: "We tightened the muscles in the stomach and back."
Amina: "And our butts."
Louise: "It's called the gluteal muscles."
Teacher: "Exactly. What happens if you do not tighten the muscles in your stomach, back and spinal muscles?"
Tom: "Then we collapse."
Teacher: "Yes, the muscles help us keep our balance."
Teacher: "What did you do to make each other good?"
Amina: "We told them what to do."
Aiya: "We said what they should do first and then afterwards."

After this knowledge sharing, teacher and students repeat the warm-up from the first lesson. The sound of different voices in the gym hall this time includes words like *swing, stretch, bend, span* and *tighten* while students swivel, tighten and stretch.

Comment on the third lesson: Stretch the language. Introduction and warm-up

The introduction consists solely of repetition from the first two lessons. The teacher involves all the students in the conversation about the shared experiences with the "figurehead." The teacher deliberately avoids asking questions of the type: "What do you know about …?," as such "display" questions typically are answered only by a few students, often using single words. By asking more openly for students to recount experiences from the previous lessons, she increases their linguistic participation, all the while providing support from the posters on the wall. This is presumably also made easier after having introduced their parents to the "figurehead" as assigned for homework previously. In this way, the teacher both obtains insight into what the students know, while continuing to focus on the students' language development.

In the dialogue, the teacher again supports students in stretching their language (Gibbons, 2014). She offers vocabulary to replace students' everyday language choices. She provides sequencing words such as *first, then, after that.* She reminds them that they should not only say what they did, but also how they did it, having experienced that students often leave out the *how* if not encouraged otherwise. Interestingly, the students themselves begin to help each other to stretch their language. The role of the students during this lesson is an active partner in a dialogic exchange. They are provided a role in which they can actively initiate exchanges, rather than being constrained to the role of responders.

Fourth lesson. Approaching generalizations. Experiment with acrobatic figures

Initiation. In this lesson, the students themselves experiment with creating a new acrobatic figure using their experiences from the previous lessons. With the help of three other students, the teacher shows how students can develop their acrobatic figure, using the words *the base, the top* and *the support* and the different kinds of muscle-tension help to them talk about the figure they are developing.

Experimentation. All four students in the group test all positions in the figure, taking a picture of each of their figures. Finally, the group selects one of their figures to present to the rest of the class in a following plenary discussion. Prior to the plenary, the teacher hands out laminated strips with the following sentence prompts:*When you're the top in this figure, you have to ... When you're the base in this figure, you have to ... When you support this figure, you should ... We make each other good in this figure by ...* Each sentence is a prompt for talking about one of the four roles. Each student in the group, *the top, the base, the support* and *the guide,* must complete a sentence that applies to their role in the group. The sentences form the basis for and scaffold the *guide*'s oral presentation, while the rest of the group performs the figure.

Presentation. The groups take turns, each presenting their new figure to the class in the plenary discussion. The teacher asks the *guide* to stand away from the figure while presenting. "This way, you will talk a bit differently," she explains. "Imagine, for example, the commentator of a bicycle race. He is not a part of the race but describes what is happening for others."

Amina's group chooses to make a figure where the *base* is on the floor with bent legs, and the *top* rests with the back and thighs on the base's arms and knees. The *support* is close to the figure, ready to intervene if the *top* loses his balance. The *guide*, Amina, has placed herself slightly away. She holds the laminated strips in one hand and looks at the group occasionally. The strips help her keep the planned order of events and use the unfamiliar language. Amina: "When you're the *base* in this figure, keep your shoulders on the floor and tighten up your muscles."

> Teacher: "Yes, you have to tighten your stomach."
> Amina: "When you're the *top* in this figure, you have to tighten
>   your body. When you're *supporting* this figure, stand close
>   to the figure. We make each other good in this figure by
>   telling each other what we can do better."

Comment on the fourth lesson. Approaching generalizations. Experiment with acrobatic figures

In this part of the fourth lesson, students begin to understand the general and specialized aspects of the activities in which they have participated. They learn a more specialized language that expresses general knowledge. The prerequisite for doing this is that the students are familiar with the content and can deal with it using the specialized vocabulary and language.

The students now become builders and co-developers of the expert knowledge. Therefore, they are not provided with a handout of different acrobatic figures to imitate, as these can be imitated without deeper academic understanding. Instead, the students must use what they bring along, in their minds, bodies and language-use in an active process, creating the new figures together.

Learning objectives and roles. In this lesson, the teacher's role is to guide the students in the process, and the students are knowledgeable contributors. Students are getting more and more space to manage their presentation.

Language use. Initially, the students use language in a concrete way and closely related to their experiences, but at the end of this part of the fourth lesson, the students have developed more generalized language, using their written sentence prompts. The professional and linguistic development now goes from concrete to more generalized PE knowledge: from situation-dependent, here-and-now language towards more situation-independent language use.

Professional and linguistic progression. The aim of this part of the teaching sequence is that students begin to generalize their knowledge. The more everyday knowledge and language constitutes a solid foundation for the students' first steps into a general, more specialized way of knowing about PE and using language, and is appropriate at the start of the teaching sequence. This far into the teaching sequence, however, students are now ready to move from an everyday arena to a more expert field.

Fifth lesson. Professional knowledge 1. Summary of the whole teaching sequence

In this lesson, the teacher assembles the students in front of the whiteboard, where a mind map has been drawn with a center labeled: *Making each other good – acrobatic figures*. Around the center four circles have been drawn with the words *top*, *base*, *support* and *guide*. The four circles are connected to the center. Students provide suggestions for the mind map, drawing on the content and examples of the previous conversations about making each other good, such as:*The whole figure must tighten ... It's easier if the top is lighter than the base ... The base and the top must not laugh ... You need to shift the weight to avoid falling ...*

The teacher discusses with the students which statements fit into a summary of what it means to make each other good. "It's true that the *base* and the *top* mustn't laugh. That's important," she says, "but how can you say it more expertly?" There are different suggestions, i.e.: "The *base* and the *top* should concentrate on tightening their muscles, and the whole figure must tighten ..." Together, teachers and students continue to jointly construct the expert language of PE, and soon, the mind map is spelled out with words like *tension, body tension, tighten, balance, weight shift, support, precision, feeling safe, hold, carry, hard gluteal muscles*. Figure 3.3 shows the completed mind map.

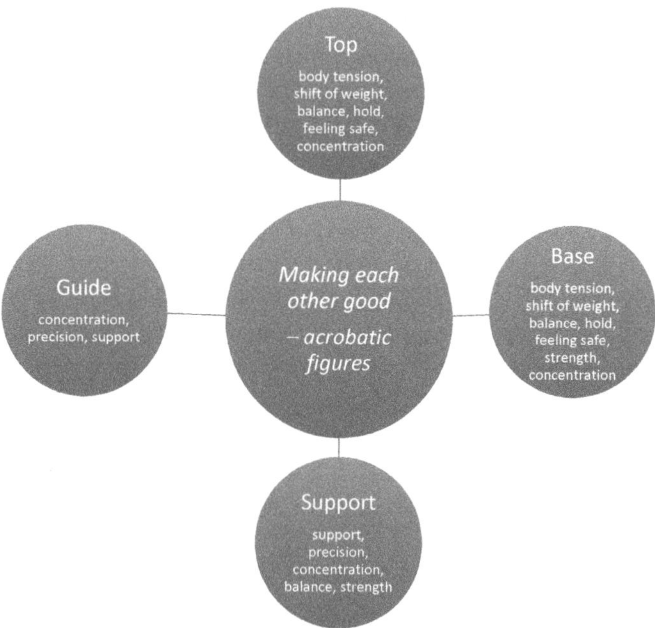

Figure 3.3 Making each other good – acrobatic figures. Mind map, made in joint construction

Comment on the fifth lesson. Professional knowledge. Summary of the whole teaching sequence. Learning objectives and roles

The teacher's role throughout this part of the lesson has been to control the dialogue, while building the taxonomic knowledge through the headings of the mind map. Students have much knowledge to offer and are active and knowledgeable contributors to the mind map.

Language use. It is a difficult matter to separate language and action, whether in a native language or in an additional language. The mind map activity is a summary of the entire teaching sequence so far. The focus in the summary is on understanding that *the top*, *the base*, *the support* and *the guide* are not only people who do something particular in the group's experiments. They are at the same time abstract concepts from within the field of acrobatic figures. While producing the mind map, students and teacher collaborate on how to make the language more generalized, referring to the roles of these concepts in developing or performing an acrobatic figure. In this way, the mind map activity focuses on the concepts as the organizing principle for the knowledge developed by the students in the previous activities, within a concrete framework provided by the teacher.

Professional and linguistic progression. The aim of this part of the teaching sequence is for the students to build up knowledge that is distanced from their concrete experiences, now constructed in generalized, abstracted language. At the end of the lesson, the students are much closer to a specialist expert field which provides a good foundation for their further development of independent, professional knowledge and language in PE.

Sixth lesson. Professional knowledge 2. Joint construction of a report

In the sixth lesson students and teachers jointly construct an expert text titled, *Making each other good – acrobatic figures*. In a report genre (Martin, 1992; Martin & Rose, 2008; Mulvad 2012a) they describe what it takes to make each other good when constructing acrobatic figures. Students reuse what they have written in the four circles in the mind map in the fifth lesson, organizing the text in four sections with the headings *the top*, *the base*, *the support* and *the guide*. Students make their suggestions based on their previous work with body and language, drawing on their written sentences and the posters provided by the teacher. Together they remove recounting features in the language, e.g., words and phrases that point to the specific persons and their actions, thus constructing an example using more expert language, independent of time and place.

In joint negotiation with the teacher, who acts as the writer who thinks aloud, they co-write the four sections on *the top*, *the bottom*, *the support*, and *the guide*. The class then summarizes the four sections (see Table 3.6) into an introduction to what the text is about: *Making each other good at creating acrobatic figures is about concentration, helping and supporting each other, having eye contact and speaking clearly.*

Comments on the sixth lesson. Professional knowledge 2

Structuring the text is a way of organizing students' knowledge. Where the students previously organized their knowledge in participants involved in concrete processes under certain circumstances, now any trace of a specific time has been eliminated. It is thus both the linguistic patterns, i.e., using the phrase *creating good tension*, and the way of organizing their knowledge of concepts that characterizes the specialized language usage in this lesson.

Table 3.6a Informerende beskrivelse: *At gøre hinanden gode – akrobatiske figurer*. Fælles konstruktion. Danish version.

Informerende beskrivelse Teksttrin	Overskrift	Tekst
1. teksttrin: **Afgrænsning** **- klassifikation**	*At gøre hinanden gode – akrobatiske figurer.*	*At gøre hinanden gode til at lave akrobatiske figurer handler om at være koncentreret, at hjælpe og støtte hinanden, at have øjenkontakt og tale tydeligt.*
2. teksttrin: **Beskrivelse af delene**		
1. del	*Top*	*At være en god top handler om* — *at kunne spænde i kroppens store muskler, for eksempel sædemuskel, ryg og mave* — *at kunne vægtforskyde kroppens tyngdepunkt for at holde balancen i samarbejde med "bunden"* — *at kunne samarbejde om øvelsen trygt og med fuld koncentration.*
2. del	*Bund*	*At være en god bund handler om* — *at være en stærk og solid støtte* — *at kunne bære "toppen"* — *i samarbejde med "toppen" kunne vægtforskyde det fælles tyngdepunkt så der skabes balance og god spænding i figuren/øvelsen.*
3. del	*Støtte*	*At være en god støtte handler om* — *at kunne arbejde koncentreret og hjælpe "bunden" med at bære/balancere "toppen"* — *at arbejde præcist og koncentreret* — *at være stærk* — *at spænde musklerne der hvor det er nødvendigt.*
4. del	*Guide*	*At være en god guide handler om at være koncentreret og arbejde opmærksomt og hjælpe "toppen," "bunden" og "støtten." Det handler om at hjælpe til at fastholde gruppens koncentrerede arbejde.*

Table 6b Report: *Making each other good – acrobatic figures*. Joint construction. English version.

Report Stages	Heading	Text
Stage 1: **Classification**	***Making each other good – acrobatic figures***	*Making each other good at creating acrobatic figures is about concentration, helping and supporting each other, having eye contact and speaking clearly.*
Stage 2: **Description of the parts** **1st description**	*Top*	*Being a good top is* — *being able to tighten the large muscle groups of the body, for example gluteus, back and stomach,* — *shifting the body's center of gravity to keep the balance in collaboration with "the base"* — *being able to collaborate on the exercise safely and with full concentration.*
2nd description	*Base*	*Being a good base is about* — *being strong and being a solid support* — *being able to support "the top"* — *Collaborating with the top to shift the weight of the combined center of gravity creating a balance and good tension in the figure.*
3rd description	*Support*	*Being a good support is about* — *being able to work with concentration to help "the bottom" support and balance "the top"* — *working precisely and with concentration* — *being strong* — *tightening muscles in the body where necessary.*
4th description	*Guide*	*Being a good guide is about concentrating and working attentively to help "the top," "the base" and "the support." It is all about maintaining the concentration of the group.*

The six lessons in relation to the sections in the snail model language

In the following, the six lessons of the 4th grade teaching sequence are correlated to the snail model. In this way, the practical examples expanded upon above are connected clearly to the language and pedagogical theory behind the model.

In the first lesson the focus is on the students' actions. The function of the language here is to support and accompany students' actions. In language theory terms, it is labeled *Language accompanying action;* in the snail: *handling (action).* Students are not challenged linguistically but can use the language they already have.

In the second and third lesson the figure, the "figurehead" is repeated, and the language is used to reconstruct what happened. The language used in these lessons is referred to as *Language as reconstruction*, and corresponds to the section of the snail model titled *rekonstruktion (reconstruction)*. The language used in this part of the teaching sequence is close to language-usage situations in everyday life, for example, students telling their parents what they did at school, what a movie was about, etc. This way of using language is commonly supported in PE, especially in physical activities: students can see what they have to say, doing what is said. Activities that support this kind of language use are situations where you recount an experience or a course of action, such as the presentation of the figure the "figurehead," class experiences reported to parents, etc. Reconstructive language usage is more context-independent than *Language accompanying action*, making the language requirements more demanding here, thus affording a (minimal) shift along the *Register*–continuum towards the academic language use.

Most of the fourth lesson lies within the language usage situation in the snail model element entitled *transformation (transformation)*. Here the students' experiences enacting the figure "the figurehead" are transformed into new figures through experiments, trial and error. This requires students to have a general level of PE-knowledge, and to use more generalized language in their communication with each other.

Scaffolding activities are crucial for students to be able to make this transformation from situational, context-dependent language use (characterized by concrete experiences) to more general academic knowledge (characterized by situationally independent ways of using language). In the 4th grade PE teaching sequence described here, the following two scaffolding activities were particularly important in supporting this transformation:

1   Scaffolding the students so that they can draw general knowledge from their initial work and use it in new constellations. In the example, the teacher shows this in her presentation of experimentation with the figure, the "figurehead" by emphasizing the general language usage. The specialized vocabulary, e.g. *the top, the base, the support* and *tension* are used clearly, repeatedly, and in dialogue with the students. The teacher shows examples of different constellations while using these terms to describe them.

2   Scaffolding students' development towards more generalized language use. In the above example, the teacher does this by letting students write the sentences on the laminated slips, shifting the mode and pushing the language use even further towards a more formal language use.

The fifth lesson, the oral summary in the mind map, correlates to *konstruktion (construction)* in the snail model. In the mind map, students and the teacher jointly construct a general knowledge of *Making each other good – acrobatic figures.* The language usage does not follow what specific people did in a particular order under certain circumstances but represents the knowledge as completely independent of the actual events in which students have participated. Furthermore, the students' contributed knowledge is organized according to a professional logic, based on the constituents of the figures. This is continued in the sixth lesson where students and teachers jointly construct a report on the basis of the mind map.

The language use required for the sixth lesson exhibits characteristics of *Language as reflection,* corresponding to the *reflection* section of the snail model. In an SFL-perspective, the term *reflection* means that it is the language which represents the social process, as the text can stand on its own over time and space, just like the jointly constructed text should be able to do.

Progression in the teaching sequence: A chain of linguistic activities

The PE teaching sequence explored here provides a logical order of both learning and progression through different sections, following the white arrows around the snail model. This does not, however, mean that all elements of the snail must be enacted in every activity. Nor does it mean that you cannot go back and forth between the elements as needed, shunting back and forth to ensure students' abilities and knowledge. It depends on the specific situation, the grade and the level of the learners. In primary school, it may be advisable to focus primarily on *action* and *reconstruction* in the development of student proficiency and language. The section known as *construction* and *reflection* might be more relevant and expanded upon in secondary grade levels. The teaching sequence described above is aimed at middle-school ages (4th grade) and focuses on *reconstruction* and *transformation*. *Reconstruction* plays an important part in the teaching sequence, providing a recurrent learning, supporting students' development of being able to construe an expert position.

In this principled way of planning a teaching sequence, it is paramount that the teacher ensures that the chain of linguistic activities is intact: at no time are students exposed to activities and language which they do not already have the prerequisites to master. Each activity's output provides the linguistic input necessary for the subsequent activity. This level of support ensures that students' self-esteem and commitment are encouraged and amplified by the teacher. At the same time, students are provided with adequate scaffolding to take on positions of knowledgeable contributors, participating actively in the development of new knowledge.

Rounding off

PE is a subject like any other subject in the school. It takes its place in the socialization of students alongside the school's academic as well as practical subjects, construing knowledge linguistically and with similar linguistic patterns (Slater & Butler, 2015). And as is the case in other school subjects, students' learning can be consolidated in PE through a focus on language and on metalanguage with SFL (Forey & Cheung, 2019). In trying out the developed teaching sequences described here, it became clear that students' activity was intensified. All students were actively participating, and everybody could explain the figure, support each other and develop new figures. And as an extra bonus, the classroom was buzzing with engagement and joy of learning: all students were able to participate, and all students were successful to some degree. We have no direct test results from this sequence, but from other subjects with a similar intervention we have significant improvement of students' academic achievement (Jacobsen & Mulvad, in progress). Forey and Cheung (2019) too have shown direct improvement in academic tests.

The specific in PE – and what arguably delineates PE from other academic school subjects – is that it does not have texts as a point of departure. This may be a case of blindness to the fact that PE is a subject with high demands, not only of physical skills, but also of the specialized knowledge and linguistic development. Just like other subjects.

The reason for focusing on PE as an academic subject in this chapter was the introduction of the final PE-exam at the end of grade 9, enacted by the Danish Ministry of Education. In making PE a so-called exam subject, the state legitimized PE in a similar way to other exam subjects, changing the requirements of how PE must be taught.

In SFL-based literature about PE, it is a recurrent theme that through a social-semiotic SFL analysis, PE is raised into the ranks of academic subjects from an isolated marginalized position as a kind of a recreational subject. It could, however, be interesting to go the other way: to see the (other) academic subjects in the light of the study of PE done by the expert group reported on here. To develop a language-based teaching sequence in PE, we had to focus on the entire teaching space with all its actors and requisites as a social-semiotic meaning making process. As texts are not the foundation of PE, we are able to see the complete picture. In this way the researcher is forced to uncover the teaching discourse rather than relying on typical (written) texts. It becomes necessary to examine the teaching discourse from the perspective of the *Context of situation* as configured by *Field*, *Tenor* and *Mode* (French, 2019). In other words, an explicit realization of what an SFL-based pedagogy contains must be completed: Learning is to learn language, through language and about language.

About the author

Ruth Mulvad, mag.art et cand.mag., is Associate Professor emerita, National Centre for Literacy, Denmark, previously also employed in teacher education in Denmark and Finland. She is a member of the board of the Nordic Association of SFL and Social Semiotics and Chair of the Danish Association for SFL in Education. Her research addresses SFL-based teaching and learning across the curriculum in primary and secondary schools and in teacher education. She has written an introduction to SFL in education, *Sprog i skole (Language in school),* articles and books about SFL in education, teaching materials and theoretical texts, in Danish and Nordic publications.

Notes

1   In a Danish context, in addition to the physical expression, physical education also includes musical, aesthetic, creative and social dimensions. Therefore, the subject is called physical education, and not sport as in many other countries. https://arkiv.emu.dk/sites/default/files/Idr%C3%A6t%20-%20januar%202016.pdf

2   Folkeskolereformen, 2014. https://www.retsinformation.dk/Forms/r0710.aspx?id=196651

3   The presentation of the developed PE-sequence for PE teachers is an extended and modified version of Kofoed, Mulvad & Regnarsson (2021).

References

Andersen, T. H. & Holsting, A. E. M. (2015). *Teksten i Grammatikken*. Odense: Syddansk Universitetsforlag.

Anderson, J. (2017): A potted history of PPP with the help of *ELT Journal*. *ELT Journal*, **71**(2), 218–227. https://doi.org/10.1093/elt/ccw055

Christie, F. & Derewianka, B. (2008). *School Discourse: Learning to Write Across the Years of Schooling*. Continuum Discourse series. London, New York: Continuum.

Christie, F. & Macken-Horarik, M. (2011). Disciplinarity and school subject English. In F. Christie, & K. Maton (eds.). *Disciplinarity. Functional Linguistic and Sociological Perspectives*. London, New York: Continuum, 175–196.

Derewianka, B. (1990). Rocks in the head: Children and the language of geology. In R. Carter (ed.). *Knowledge About Language and the Curriculum.* London: Hodder & Stoughton, 197–215.

Eggins, S. (2004). *An Introduction to Systemic Functional Linguistics* (2nd ed.). London: Continuum.

Forey, G., & Cheung, L. M. E. (2019). The benefits of explicit teaching of language for curriculum learning in the Physical Education classroom. *English for Specific Purposes*, **54**, 91–109. https://doi.org/10.1016/j.esp.2019.01.001

French, Ruth (2019): Reflection literacy. Purpose, practice and possibilities. *Language, Context and Text*, **1**(2), 260–287. https://doi.org/10.1075/langct.00011.fre

Gibbons, P. (2006). *Bridging Discourses in the ESL Classroom: Students, Teachers and Researchers.* London, New York: Continuum. https://doi. org/10.5040/9781474212137.ch-001

Gibbons, P. (2014). *Scaffolding Language, Scaffolding Learning. Teaching English Language Learners in the Mainstream Classroom* (2nd ed.). Portsmouth, NH: Heinemann.

Halliday, M. A. K. (1975). *Learning How to Mean – Explorations in the Development of Language.* London: Arnold.

Halliday, M. A. K. & Hasan, R. (1976): *Cohesion in English.* London: Routledge.

Halliday, M. A. K. (1978). *Language as a Social Semiotic.* London: Arnold.

Halliday, M. A. K. (1993). Towards a language-based theory of learning. *Linguistics and Education,* **5**(2), 93–116. https://doi. org/10.1016/0898-5898(93)90026-7

Halliday, M. A. K. & C. M. I. M. Matthiessen (2014). *An Introduction to Functional Grammar* (4th ed.). London: Routledge.

Jacobsen, G. K. & Mulvad, R. (in progress): *Sprog i naturfag.* København: Akademisk.

Kofoed, U., Mulvad, R. & Regnarsson, I. (2021). Fra baller til sædemuskler. – sprogbaseret fagundervisning. In S. K. Knudsen & L. Wulff (eds.). *Kom ind i sproget. Flersprogede elever i fagundervisningen* (2nd ed.). København: Akademisk Forlag, 263–295.

Leckie-Tarry, Helen (1995): *Language and Context: A Functional Linguistic Theory of Register.* London: Pinter.

Martin, J. R. (1992). *English Text: System and Structure.* Philadelphia, Amsterdam: Benjamins.

Martin, J. R. & Rose, D. (2008): *Genre Relations. Mapping Culture.* London, Oakville: Equinox.

Mulvad, R. (2012a). *Sprog i skole. Læseudviklende undervisning i alle fag.* København: Akademisk Forlag.

Mulvad, R. (2012b). Sprog i skole – om at integrere arbejde med sprog i fagenes didaktik. *Sproget i skolen. Tidsskriftet KvaN,* **94**, 7–18.

Painter, C. (1984). *Into the Mother Tongue: A Case Study in Early Language Development.* London: Frances Pinter.

Polias, J. (2016). *Apprenticing Students into Science. Doing, Talking and Writing Scientifically.* Melbourne: Lexis Education.

Rose, D. & Martin, J. R. (2012). *Learning to Write/Reading to Learn Genre, Knowledge and Pedagogy in the Sydney School.* London, Oakville: Equinox.

Slater, T., & Butler, J. I. (2015). Examining connections between the physical and the mental in education: A linguistic analysis of PE teaching and learning. *Linguistics and Education*, **30**, 12–25. https://doi.org/10.1016/j.linged.2015.03.006

Schleppegrell, Mary J. (2004). *The Language of Schooling: A Functional Linguistic Perspective*. Mahwah, NJ: Lawrence: Erlbaum.

Undervisningsministeriet (2014). *Idrætsfagets formålsparagraf.* www.uvm.dk

Undervisningsministeriet (2016). *Inspirations – og vejledningsmaterialer.* UCC & VIA. www.emu.dk

Undervisningsministeriet (2017). *PISA Etnisk 2015 – Hvordan elever med indvandrerbaggrund klarer sig i PISA-testen og deres holdninger og forventninger til naturvidenskab.* København: Kora.

Østergaard, W. (2017). Registerkontinuum – et værktøj til planlægning og refleksion. In S. K. Knudsen & L. Wulff (eds.). *Kom ind i sproget. Flersprogede elever i fagundervisningen.* København: Akademisk Forlag, 63–85.

4 A geometry teacher's actions for engaging students in mathematizing from real-world contexts: A linguistic analysis

Gloriana González
University of Illinois at Urbana-Champaign

Mathematics discourse is multisemiotic. People communicate mathematical ideas through mathematical language, symbols, and visual images (O'Halloran, 2005). Moreover, *doing* mathematics requires using language, symbols, and visual images simultaneously. In mathematics classrooms, students need to appreciate shifts in meaning when relying on different semiotic systems (O'Halloran, 1998). Developing students' mathematical literacy requires teaching students how to read mathematical language, symbols, and visual images, as well as how to use them in mathematical problem-solving. Since students' prior experiences with academic language in contexts outside of school may differ, students need opportunities to learn academic language for them to have equitable access to academic knowledge (Schleppegrell, 2004). At the same time, students possess knowledge from experiences outside of school that shape their mathematical understanding of language, symbols, and visual images. Considering students' prior knowledge from out-of-school experiences is fundamental (National Research Council, 2000). When teachers draw upon students' prior knowledge from these experiences, they can solidify students' understanding and empower them by validating their knowledge.

The teaching and learning of geometry in school provides a particular case for studying how disciplinary literacy can draw from students' out-of-school experiences. Geometric thinking is special because its reliance on visual images opens opportunities for students to draw inferences based on their perceptions of a diagram (Duval, 1995). At the same time, students' perceptions of a diagram are insufficient for geometry problem-solving. Learning how to interact with diagrams by applying other reasoning skills in addition to perception is fundamental for students to develop mathematical understanding through geometry problem-solving. Geometry students need to know how to interpret the symbolic notation in a diagram such as markings for angles, how to identify relevant parts within a diagram's configuration, and how to purposefully add auxiliary lines that would aid in proving geometric properties (Duval, 1995; Herbst, 2004). These actions exemplify new ways of interacting with diagrams for many students.

The U.S. National Council of Teachers of Mathematics identified what they called "big ideas" in relation to specific mathematical domains such as algebra and geometry. Each big idea has various implications for mathematics teaching and learning, called "essential understandings." One big idea in high school geometry (grades 9 through 12) is that working with diagrams is a fundamental aspect of geometric thinking (Sinclair, Pimm, & Skelin, 2012).[1] Four essential understandings follow this big idea. First, diagrams serve the dual purposes of communicating mathematical ideas and supporting mathematical thinking. Second, diagrams have a "history" in terms of the sequence of steps that were used to construct them and a purpose that emphasizes the relationships among geometric objects based on this history.[2] Third, a diagram requires interpretation. Specifically, "learning how to read a diagram can be like learning a new language" (Sinclair, Pimm, & Skelin, 2012, p. 17). This last point highlights the importance of teaching students to make sense of diagrams to develop their geometric thinking. Diagrams include symbolic notation that illustrates geometric properties such as congruence. However, reading a diagram also involves both emphasizing and suppressing attention to some of its parts, as well as visualizing a diagram as dynamic, even when it appears to be static. Students' interactions with diagrams in geometry can lead them to make conjectures to establish the variances or invariances of geometric objects. The process of "building reasoned conjectures" (Herbst, 2004) refers to the use of deductive reasoning to establish mathematical propositions. For students to build reasoned conjectures in geometry, they need to read and modify a diagram.

Goals of the study

In this study, I apply linguistic analysis to a teacher's implementation of a geometry lesson. In the lesson, the teacher used the context of visual arts to teach a geometric concept in the high school geometry curriculum. Students' everyday experiences and their experiences with visual arts were entry points in the lesson for them to develop mathematical understanding.

From the perspective of the *realistic mathematics education* (RME) theory, students need opportunities to mathematize by discovering mathematical ideas that are known in society but new to them (Freudenthal, 1991). The proponents of RME argue that students should solve realistic problems with mathematics. These are problems that students perceive as realistic and that motivate students' mathematical work (Freudenthal, 1991; Gravemeijer & Doorman, 1999; van den Heuvel-Panhuizen, 2003). I apply linguistic analysis to address two questions concerning a teacher's use of a problem embedded in a visual arts context: *How does a teacher engage his students in mathematizing? What literacy practices regarding the use of geometric diagrams does the teacher promote?*

With the first question, my goal is not to evaluate a teacher's lesson enactment but to unpack the complexity of teaching. Systemic Functional Linguistics (SFL) (Halliday & Matthiessen, 2004) allows an examination of the intricacies of teacher–student interactions. With the second question, I examine the literacy practices that the teacher promoted during geometry problem-solving. I use SFL to identify the teaching moves that supported students' literacy practices in working with a diagram during geometry problem-solving. In a problem-based lesson, students learn mathematical ideas by solving mathematical problems with other students (Boaler, 2008; Lampert, 2001). This approach is difficult to implement in classrooms because it requires teachers to examine students' problem-solving strategies during the lesson and use these strategies to promote student learning. In geometry instruction, problem-based instruction can be particularly challenging because it challenges the typical interactions in geometry classrooms (Herbst, 2006). Examining how teachers can support students during geometry problem-solving is fundamental for making problem-based instruction viable in geometry classrooms. Ultimately, my goal is to illustrate how linguistic analysis can unpack the teaching strategies that other mathematics teachers can apply when implementing problem-based instruction in their own classrooms.

Context of the study

I selected classroom episodes from a lesson taught by a high school geometry teacher, Gian (a pseudonym), with ten years of experience teaching geometry. He was a participant in a two-year professional development intervention. The intervention aimed at increasing teachers' attention to students' prior knowledge through their participation in a modified version of lesson study. Lesson study is a professional development cycle that originated in Japan to improve instruction (Fernandez, 2002). During the cycle, a group of teachers plans a lesson to observe student thinking in relation to specific learning goals. Each teacher teaches the lesson to their own students. Using insights from their lesson observations, teachers revise and reteach the lesson to a new group of students.

The teachers who participated in the professional development intervention planned a lesson to teach the geometric concept of dilation. Dilation is a geometric transformation that makes an object larger or smaller by a specific ratio under two conditions (see Figure 4.1): (1) the lines through corresponding points in the image and the preimage pass through the center of dilation ($\overleftrightarrow{AA'}$, $\overleftrightarrow{BB'}$, and $\overleftrightarrow{CC'}$) and (2) the segments connecting corresponding points that do not pass through the center of dilation are parallel ($\overline{AB}\|\overline{A'B'}$, $\overline{BC}\|\overline{B'C'}$, and $\overline{CA}\|\overline{C'A'}$). In Figure 4.1, triangle $A'B'C'$ is the dilation image of the triangle ABC. Point O is the center of dilation and all of the lines connecting corresponding vertices pass through that point. In the U.S., the recent adoption of the *Common Core State Standards for Mathematics* (National Governors Association Center for Best Practices, Council of Chief State School Officers, 2010) includes dilation as a new topic in the geometry curriculum. Although there are some examples of teaching a one-point perspective in relation to mathematics in a primary school in Italy (Bartolini Bussi, 1996), this topic is typically taught in art classes in the U.S. Historically, perspective drawings have intrigued mathematicians and are related to projective geometry, an important branch of mathematics (Pedoe, 1976). However, this topic is not traditionally taught in school geometry. Reading a perspective diagram requires different skills to those that are applied when reading typical diagrams in geometry textbooks (Dimmel & Herbst, 2015).

The teachers started the cycle by discussing animations prepared by the research team with examples of two problem-based lessons that they could teach (González & DeJarnette, 2018). The teachers decided to modify a lesson shown in one of the animations that used the context of visual arts, namely, the "one-point perspective" lesson (DeJarnette & González, 2017). In the lesson, students had to use the diagram in Figure 2 to answer two questions: (1) Are the real-life heights of the two houses the same or different? How can you tell? (2) Are the trees the same height in real life? How can you tell? To answer these questions, students had to draw perspective lines, which are lines that pass through corresponding points and the vanishing point. If the lines that pass through corresponding points intersect at the same point, the vanishing point, then the diagram is in a one-point perspective. In the diagram in Figure 4.2, the houses are in perspective, but the trees are not. If we were to draw a line through the top of the trees, that line will

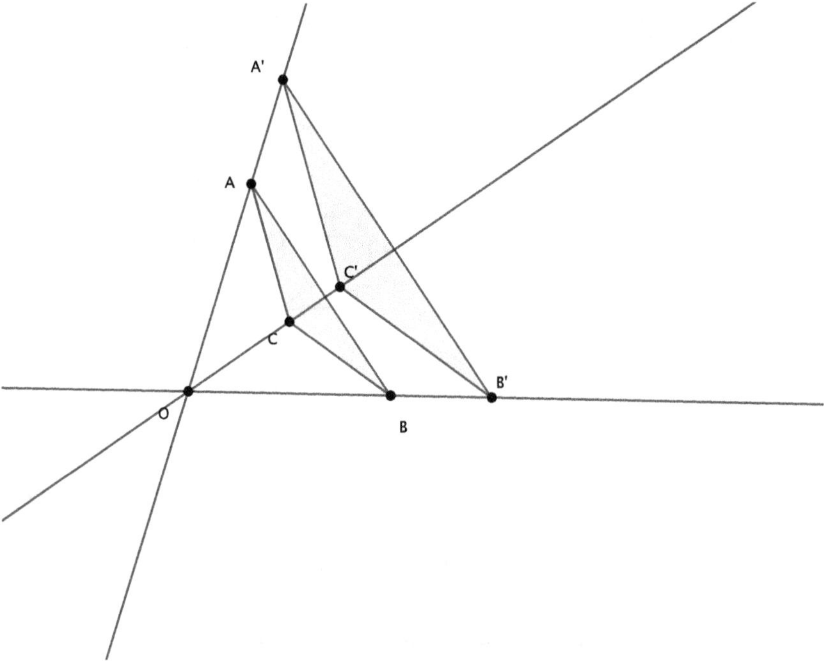

Figure 4.1 Dilated figure with *O* as the center of dilation.

not pass through the given vanishing point. This means that the trees are not the same height in real life if one considers the given vanishing point. For the diagram to be in one-point perspective, the line through the top of the trees and the line through the top of the houses should intersect at the given vanishing point. In addition, all of the lines connecting the vertices of similar figures in the diagram should go through the giving vanishing point as well. Mathematically, a one-point perspective drawing is an example of dilation, with the vanishing point being the center of dilation. The "one-point perspective problem" requires students to establish a relationship between the figures and the vanishing point, which opens opportunities for students to notice the center of dilation in relation to dilated figures. As part of the professional development intervention, the research team video-recorded the lessons taught by the teachers in their own classrooms. In a study group session, the teachers discussed examples of students' solutions across all of the classrooms in an activity called "video clubs" (Sherin & Han, 2004).[3] Based on the animations, the video club discussions, and their own observations during the lesson enactment, the teachers modified the dilation

Linear perspective is a method designers use to show three dimensions in a picture. The simplest way to use linear perspective is to select one point in the distance, called a "vanishing point". The objects in the picture below follow lines called "perspective lines" back to the vanishing point.

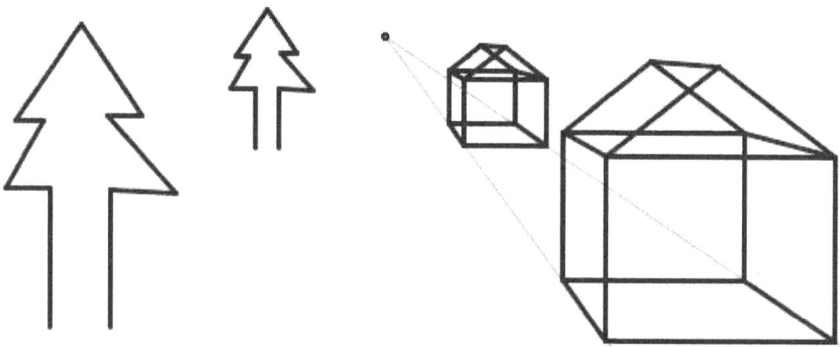

Figure 4.2 Diagram and instructions provided in the one-point perspective lesson.

lesson and taught the new version to a new group of students in the second year (Skultety, González, & Vargas, 2017). Gian's lesson enactment in the second year of the professional development intervention incorporated the changes that the teachers discussed.

I selected Gian's enactment of the dilation lesson in the second year for three main reasons. First, he addressed the potential difficulties that students may have when interpreting the geometric diagram based on the teachers' study group discussion regarding the lesson's enactment during the previous year. Second, during my observation of the lesson, I noticed that Gian used the problem's context to promote students' understanding of the learning goals of the lesson. Finally, in the lesson summary, Gian elicited the various solutions that students displayed during the lesson by following the teaching strategies discussed in the professional development intervention (González, 2018). A problem-based lesson typically has three parts, the *launch*, when the teacher introduces the problem, the *exploration*, when students solve the problem in groups, and the *summary*, when the teacher discusses various solutions and establishes the main concept of the lesson (Lappan, Fey, Fitzgerald, Friel, & Phillips, 1998/2002/2005). I focus on public discussions during the launch and summary because in these discussions, the teacher had to manage the input of the entire class and clarify the lesson's goal for all students.[4]

Research questions and methods

Two research questions guide the linguistic analysis. The first question is: *How does a teacher launch a problem intended to target the concept of dilation?* In linguistic terms, the question can be stated as: *How can analysis of lexical and nuclear relations reveal the connections between the problem's context and mathematical content of the lesson?* The second question is: *How does a teacher support students in establishing reasoned conjectures from their interactions with a diagram?* In linguistic terms, the question can be stated as: *How can conjunction analysis reveal the teacher's linguistic strategy to draw from students' statements about their interactions with a diagram?* Together, the two questions examine how a teacher constructs mathematical meanings in class discussions by using linguistic strategies that connect students' everyday and mathematical understandings.

With the first question, I unpack how the teacher set up the problem for students to start their exploration. Learning more about the content discussed through the study of taxonomic, expectancy, and nuclear relations in the discussion allows observations as to whether and how the teacher established relationships between the realistic context and the mathematical content. Specifically, I focus on identifying lexical relations, both taxonomic and expectancy, and trace these through lexical strings developed in the teacher's discourse (Eggins, 2004; see also Halliday & Hasan, 1976; Martin & Rose, 2007). Taxonomic lexical relations involve terms related through *repetition, synonyms, contrast, class*, and *part* (Martin & Rose, 2007). For example, the terms "triangle" and "side" are in a whole/part relation, since a triangle has sides. Expectancy relations are connections between nominal and verbal elements that are plausible in relation to the context of the text. For example, the terms "diagram" and "construct" are plausible to be related in text since many geometric diagrams involve constructing them with a compass and straightedge. An important consideration regarding lexical and expectancy relations is that these can involve more than one word (Martin, 1992, p. 293). For example, "one-point perspective" and "vanishing point" can appear in a lexical string to achieve lexical cohesion. I also investigate nuclear relations to identify how the teacher introduced the diagram (Martin & Rose, 2007). I identify the *participants, processes,* and *circumstances* in the clauses that pertain to the diagram. To answer the second question, I use conjunction analysis to identify the logical relations that the teacher made explicit in the discussion (Halliday & Hasan, 1976; Martin & Rose, 2007). I identify whether the four types of logical relations

– *addition, comparison, consequence,* and *time* – supported the teacher's actions in summarizing the solutions to the problem. By using these analytical approaches, my goal is to identify the linguistic resources that the teacher used for students to establish connections between the context of one-point perspective drawings and the mathematical goal of learning the properties of dilation. I focus on the teacher's reading of the diagram because this is an important aspect for teaching geometry students how to use the diagram to build reasoned conjectures.

In my analysis of the classroom discussions, I share the assumption from SFL that speakers draw upon language resources to fulfill three metafunctions (Halliday & Matthiessen, 2004). Specifically, speakers convey meanings by using the resources from the *ideational* metafunction, engage speakers in conversations using the resources from the *interpersonal* metafunction, and organize a text using the resources from the *textual* metafunction.[5] The first research question is aligned with the ideational metafunction by examining the content of the talk. The second question inquires about the ways in which the teacher used resources from the textual and ideational metafunctions – in this case, from the system of conjunction – to state the conjectures concerning the geometric diagram. Speakers fulfill these metafunctions of language simultaneously, and consequently they may draw on the same linguistic resources. This is the case of the conjunctions that are resources for the textual and the ideational metafunctions. Nevertheless, in my analysis, I concentrated on one of the metafunctions in relation to specific linguistic resources. Table 4.1 shows the lesson segments analyzed and the linguistic analysis used for that segment, and identifies what each analysis strategy helps us understand about the instructional work the teacher is doing.

Table 4.1 Linguistic analysis for the lesson segments

Lesson segment	Analysis strategy	What the analysis reveals about the teacher's actions
Launch	Taxonomic and expectancy relations (lexical strings)	How to connect students' everyday and mathematical understandings
	Nuclear relations	How to support students' reading of the diagram
Summary	Conjunction analysis	How to turn students' ideas into reasoned conjectures

Findings

Launching the one-point perspective lesson

The launch of the one-point perspective lesson was approximately six minutes. Using the overhead projector, the teacher showed a slide with a collection of photos in one-point perspective including landscapes. He opened the discussion by asking students if they have heard the term "one-point perspective." Students discuss their experiences in their English class when talking about "personal experience," and in their art and technology class when creating one-point perspective drawings. With this discussion, the teacher attempted to establish connections with students' prior knowledge about the term one-point perspective before introducing other meanings. After eliciting students' experiences, the teacher called students' attention to the photos shown and asked, "What do you notice about all these pictures in one-point perspective?" The students mentioned "distance," and the teacher established connections between the one-point perspective drawings and distance:

> Teacher: Yeah. So, they all have like it just keeps going to one point, right. Kind of comes together in one point. And it has to do with distance. So, what do you notice about things in a distance versus things up close?

The students replied that objects at a distance are smaller. The teacher asked further questions, clarifying that objects at a distance in a one-point perspective are not smaller than objects that are closer to the observer. (When revising the lesson, the teachers agreed to address the notion that, in a one-point perspective drawing, the objects that are far from the observer's perspective appear to be smaller; Skultety, González, &Vargas, 2017.) At the end of the launch, the teacher read the instructions in the worksheet and asked students to collaborate during group work.

Analysis of the taxonomic, expectancy, and nuclear relations

The analysis of taxonomic, expectancy, and nuclear relations helps comprehension of the relationships between people and things in a text. A lexical string shows these relationships develop beyond a particular clause, pointing to ways in which a text builds cohesion, relating terms that follow the same theme. I identified two lexical strings in the launch pertaining to the one-point perspective problem. One lexical string includes terms related to one-point perspective drawings such as *one-point perspective, two-point perspective, single-point perspective, vanishing point*, and *perspective lines*. Figures 4.3 and 4.4 show this lexical string. (Although it is only one lexical string, I show them in two figures to make them readable. I repeat the term "it kind of keeps going to like one point" in the two figures to illustrate where Figures 4.3 and 4.4 overlap; the teacher did not repeat this term.) The lexical items from the discussion are in italics; between the items I specify the type of relationship holding between the items, connected through *repetition, synonyms, contrast, class*, and *part* (Martin & Rose, 2007). For example, in Figure 4.3, the first two items stated by the teacher are "one-point perspective" and "one-point perspective," which are noted in italics. These two items are related by repetition.

At the beginning of the launch, the teacher did not define specialized terms and asked students to share their ideas on the meaning of "one-point perspective." However, he defined the terms at the end of the launch, when reading the instructions. Most of these terms were connected through repetition or synonyms (a type of "similarity" according to Eggins, 2004, p. 43). Specifically, he used repetition twice referring to "one-point perspective" and synonyms five times. By using synonyms, the teacher connected the terms "one point perspective" and "single-point perspective," "these pictures in one-point perspective" and "they all have like it keeps going to one point," "it kind of keeps going to like one point" and "one point perspective," "one-point perspective" and "all going to one point," and "all going to one point" and "linear perspective." The teacher contrasted the one- and two-point perspectives using the terms "single-point perspective," "two-point perspective," and "one-point perspective." The teacher established that one-point perspective is one method for drawing by using a classification relationship of class/sub-class. Reading from the worksheet, the teacher said, "And it says, 'Linear perspective is a method designers use to show three dimensions in a picture.'" This means that while there are various methods for designers to represent three dimensions, linear perspective belongs to the set of methods and thus is part of a class of methods. He identified parts of a one-point perspective diagram such as the vanishing point and the perspective lines. Specifically, at the end of the lexical string he used the terms "vanishing point" and "perspective lines," which are part of "linear perspective" drawing and related among themselves as co-parts (see Figure 4.4). With these references to the parts of the diagram, he promoted students' shifts in attention from perceiving the diagram as a whole to focusing on essential parts. The instructions in the worksheet that the teacher read established that one-point perspective is a method for drawing two-dimensional figures so that they represent three dimensions. These instructions explained the visual arts context to all of the students. Through his language, the teacher shifted the discussion from one-point perspective as a characteristic of a diagram to one-point perspective as the basis for illustrating three dimensions in two dimensions.

The term "distance" is in the lexical string that characterizes one-point perspective diagrams (see Figure 4.3). The teacher mentioned this term five times in the launch. The first two times were when revoicing a student's answer. The teacher asked, "When you look at these pictures they are all one-point perspective, what do you think that kind of it means?" When a student replied, mentioning the term "distance," the teacher repeated the student's answer by saying, "**Distance**. They have something to do with **distance**, right?" After the student elaborated, the teacher said, "Yeah, they all have like it keeps going to like one point, right. It kind of keeps going to like one point. And it has to do with **distance**. So, what do you notice about things at a **distance** versus things up close?" These other two mentions of distance involve a lexical relation of expectancy. A one-point perspective diagram has a particular way of representing the distance from the viewer to the objects in the diagram. It is predictable that a person viewing a one-point perspective diagram would evoke a sense of the distance between the viewing point and the objects in the diagram, perceiving these objects as far or close. The term "distance" also appeared in another lexical string (see Figure 4.5), connecting the one-point perspective and the students' experiences. When the same term appears in more than one lexical string, the term helps to establish connections between the meanings conveyed in each string. Eggins (2004, p. 44) states that having the same term in various lexical strings supports the "texture" of the text. That is, the use of a term in relation to two or more strings adds to the sense that the text has unity. The teacher mentioned "distance" for the fifth time when he repeated students' perception of things in the diagram, "Smaller in a **distance** than they are close." Here the term distance is used to characterize things that are far away.

A second lexical string, also at the beginning of the launch, includes references to students' experiences with a one-point perspective (Figure 4.5). These experiences can be categorized according to school experiences and everyday experiences. School experiences pertain to specific courses (i.e., English, Technology, and Art).[6] Some of the activities in these courses included discussing a personal view in a text, illustrating how to stand and view something in a diagram, making an image, and building scale models. I classified these activities as "part" because they are activities within a

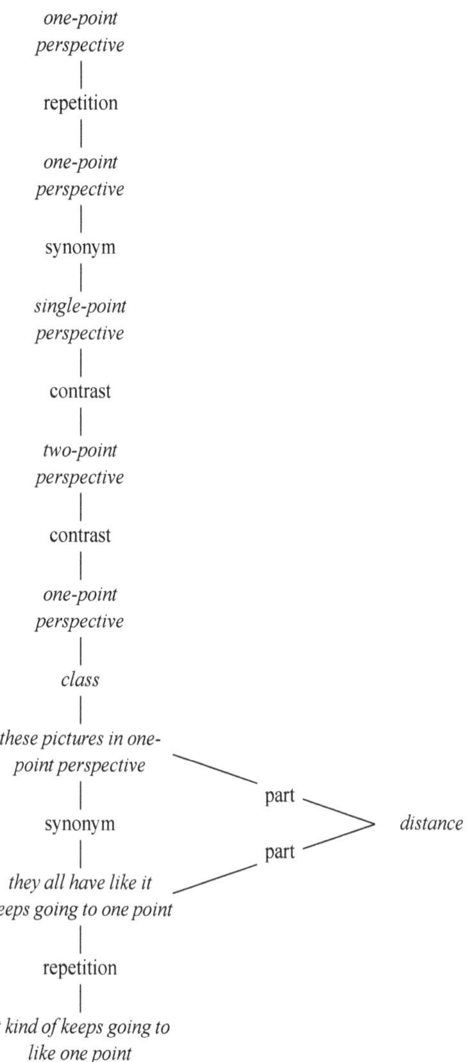

Figure 4.3 Lexical string regarding the one-point perspective introduced by the teacher in the launch (Part 1).

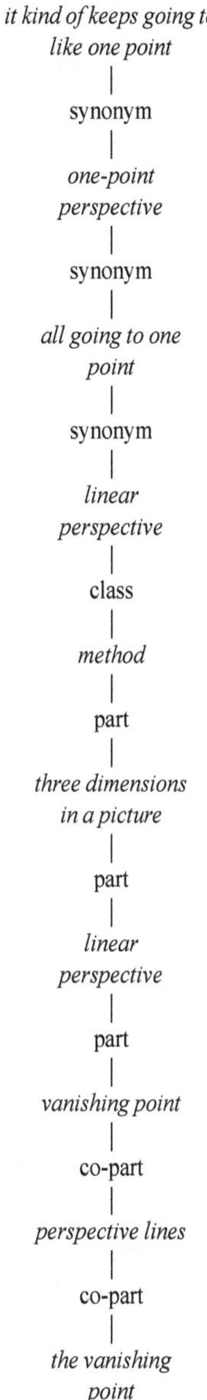

Figure 4.4 Lexical string regarding the one-point perspective introduced by the teacher in the launch (Part 2).

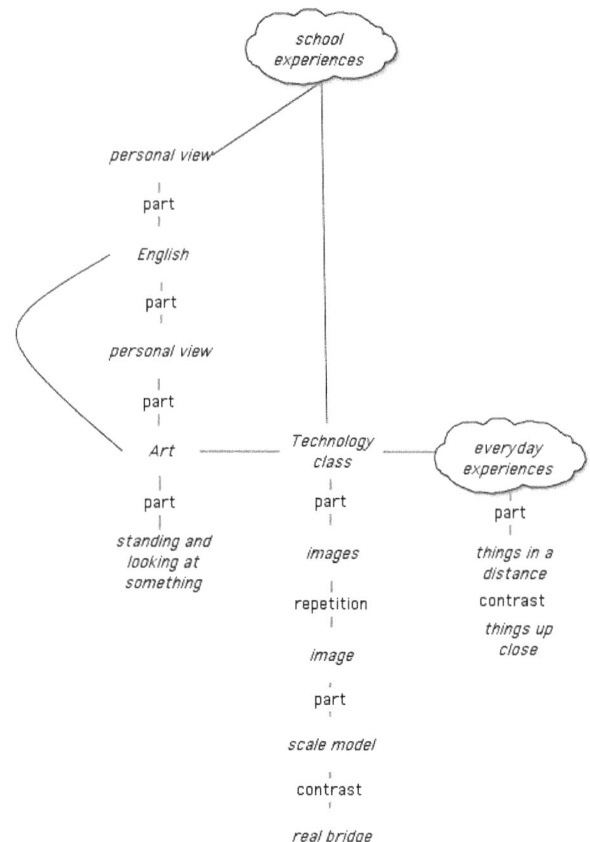

Figure 4.5 Lexical string regarding students' everyday and school experiences with the one-point perspective in the launch.

school course. The activity of building a scale model is related to the mathematical concept of similarity, but this connection was not explicit in the discussion. It is possible that students were making connections with prior knowledge from school mathematics. Another personal experience is that of "noticing" objects in real life. The teacher elicited this experience when he said, "So, what do you notice about things in a distance versus things up close?" While students' knowledge of one-point perspective may differ according to their school experiences, all students could potentially relate to the everyday experience of perceiving the size of objects that are far and close. The term "distance" is in this lexical string. A student first mentioned "distance" when the teacher asked, "When you look at these pictures, they are all one-point perspective; what do you think that kind of it means?"

The teacher elaborated by discussing "things in a distance."[7] The teacher, following what the student had stated, used the term "distance" to qualify the position of the observer in a one-point perspective diagram, which models the experience of seeing objects at a distance in real life. The term "distance" connected the two lexical strings regarding students' experiences and one-point perspective diagrams.[8]

An analysis of nuclear relations shows that the teacher promoted a shift from a static to a dynamic view of the diagram. Nuclear relations establish relationships between parts of a clause with the purpose of understanding how the participants (i.e., people or things) are involved in a process. From this analysis, we can later identify activity sequences in a text by going beyond a clause. For example, the teacher asked the following.

> <u>Teacher:</u> Alright. So, what do you notice about all these pictures in one-point perspective? What's – What does it – When you look at these pictures, they are all in one-point perspective, what do you think that kind of it means?

The teacher discussed one-point perspective as a characteristic of the pictures by using "one-point perspective" as a qualifier (Table 4.2). This property suggests a static view of the diagram, where parts of the diagram are not moving.

However, in further discussions concerning the diagrams during the launch, the teacher shifted to a dynamic view of the diagrams. He said:

> <u>Teacher:</u> Yeah. So, they all have like it just keeps going to one point, right. Kind of comes together in one point. And it has to do with distance. So, what do you notice about things in a distance versus things up close?

In this excerpt, "they all have" is a false start, signaled by the use of "like" to reformulate.[9] The teacher said "it just keeps going to one point." Although the diagrams were not actually moving, such as when diagrams are constructed with dynamic geometry software, the teacher discussed visualizing

Table 4.2 Nuclear relations that show a static view of the pictures

these pictures	are	[in] one-point perspective
they [all]		
Participant	**Process** (Being)	**Qualifier**

Table 4.3 Nuclear relations that show a dynamic view of the pictures

it [the picture]	just keeps going	to one point
Participant	**Process** (Doing)	**Circumstance** (Where)

each diagram as moving towards one point. This point is the vanishing point in a one-point perspective diagram (Table 4.3).

After introducing a dynamic view of the one-point perspective pictures, the teacher opened the discussion to students' perceptions of objects close and far in a one-point perspective diagram. This is important because the teacher asked the students to conceive of the diagram in relation to their position as a viewer by perceiving objects at different distances. Overall, the analysis of taxonomic relations demonstrates that the teacher used students' experiences and their observations of the photos in one-point perspective to build a mathematical definition of "one-point perspective." The analysis of nuclear relationships indicates his emphasis on visualizing the diagram as dynamic, which is crucial for understanding the mathematical concept of dilation. Specifically, the teacher shifted the discussion from qualifying the pictures as one-point perspective pictures to visualizing the pictures as moving to one point. By calling attention to the configuration of the diagram in relation to the point, the teacher started to seed important ideas when introducing the mathematical concept of dilation, which depends upon the identification of a point (i.e., the center of dilation). In terms of the process of creating a text through dialogue (i.e., a "logogenetic" perspective; Eggins, 2004, p. 51), the teacher's introduction of a dynamic view of the diagram supported students' development of reasoned conjectures that apply this view of the diagram. In the same way that once a term has been introduced in a text, there are new opportunities for connecting to that term in the future, introducing a new way to visualize the diagram invited students to build on that new way of visualizing the diagram as moving to one point.

Summarizing the one-point perspective lesson

The exploration phase of the lesson where students worked in groups to solve the problem was approximately 35 minutes. During this time, the teacher walked around the classroom, recording students' solution strategies. He used his notes to select and sequence the discussion of students' solutions during the summary, as suggested in a book that was discussed in the professional development intervention (Smith & Stein, 2011). The summary was 13 minutes. The teacher discussed three strategies to solve the problem during the summary. The first strategy required adding selective perspective lines and making inferences about the lines. Specifically, the students drew perspective lines through the bottom of the trees and the top of the trees to check if they also passed through the vanishing point (Figure 4.6). With the second strategy, the students added multiple perspective lines to see if they all passed through the vanishing point (Figure 4.7). The final strategy involved measuring corresponding parts to see whether the figures were proportional. At the end of the summary, the teacher discussed frustrations in problem-solving as a sign of learning by making an analogy with fatigue when playing basketball. The teacher used the analogy to commend the students for their perseverance. While this string was excluded from this analysis since it covers broader issues pertaining to

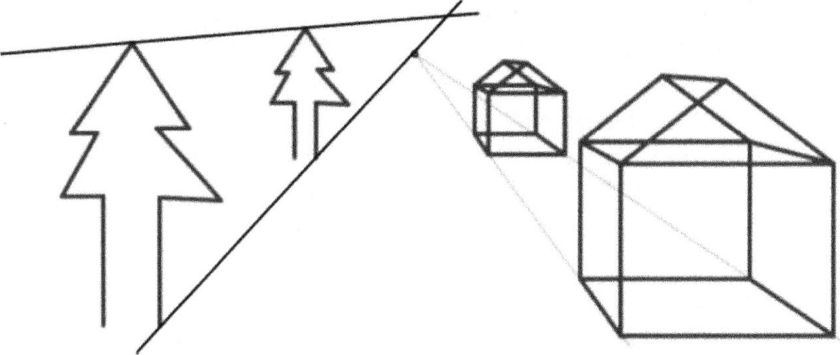

Figure 4.6 Reproduction of the first strategy for solving the one-point perspective problem.

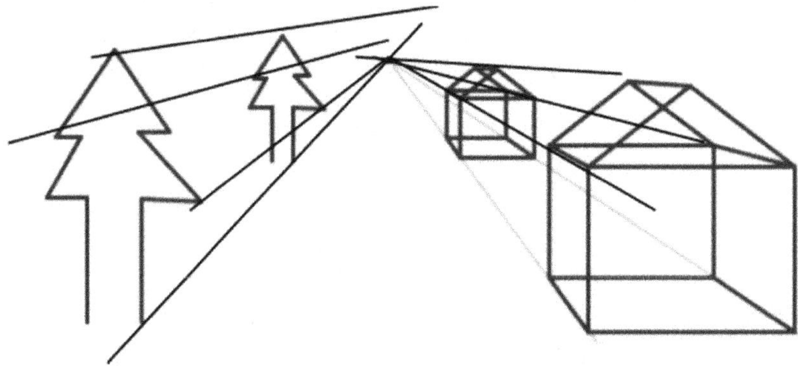

Figure 4.7 Reproduction of the second strategy for solving the one-point perspective problem.

students' problem-solving experiences, it shows the teacher's intention to make these experiences explicit and to highlight the value of perseverance, a trait stressed in the current Standards.

Conjunction analysis

During the summary, the teacher discussed three strategies that students applied during the solution of the problem and turned these strategies into reasoned conjectures. I performed an analysis of the conjunctions that the teacher used from the time that he started the summary until he concluded the discussion of the third strategy. In a total of 32 turns of speech, the teacher used 117 conjunctions. That is, he used approximately 4 conjunctions per turn of speech. Table 4.4 shows the number of conjunctions for each logical relation and the list of conjunctions that he used. In this context, the teacher used "okay" as a conjunction for framing the addition of new information (see González & Herbst, 2013; Martin & Rose, 2003). Most of the conjunctions denoted consequence and illustrated how the logical connections were fundamental in the discussion of solutions. Conjunctions to denote consequence are particularly important in written mathematical work (O'Halloran, 2005). In class discussions, the conjunctions for denoting consequence organize the structure of an oral proof (González & Herbst, 2013).

In the summary of the one-point perspective lesson, the conjunctions to denote consequence allowed the teacher to state the conjectures that could be deduced from students' work on the problem. This is significant because the teacher's talk illustrated how to make *reasoned conjectures* based on students' reading of the diagram. That is, the teacher helped students to translate their interactions with the diagram into *if–then statements,* which follow the structure of typical mathematical propositions. Teachers' use of conditional if–then statements supports mathematizing by generalizing the relationship between conditions and results (Shreyar, Zolkower, & Pérez,

Table 4.4 Conjunctions that the teacher used in the summary

Logical relation	*Number of conjunctions*	*Conjunctions*
addition	29 (25%)	*and, okay, or*
comparison	3 (2%)	*like*
consequence	75 (64%)	*because, but, "cause, if, so, then*
time	10 (9%)	*when*

2010). In terms of mathematical literacy, the teacher modeled for students how to use mathematical discourse to establish reasoned conjectures.

For example, when discussing the first strategy, Gian started by asking students in one group the actions to the diagram that they had performed. One of the students said that he had "matched up" similar elements from the diagram such as the lower limbs of two trees or the upper limbs of two trees. The teacher asked for clarification about the elements that they were "matching up" and asked "**When** you guys were matching things up, what should have been matching up? What were you matching up?" Here, the use of "when" as a logical conjunction of "time" illustrates the condition that needed to be met when adding a line to the diagram; also construing "condition" in this context. The condition was that the corresponding points of the diagram and the vanishing point needed to be collinear, which students referred to as "matching." The students stated that they had used three points: two corresponding parts of the diagram and the vanishing point. The teacher summarized the conjecture as follows:

> Teacher: [While drawing.] **So,** we might match – the three things he matched up are the bottom of the first tree, bottom of the second tree, **and** the point, right? **And, if** you line those up, you can get all three of those in one straight line, correct?

The first conjunction in the excerpt, "so," framed the summary of the strategy: matching three points. The teacher used the conjunction of addition, "and," to add the vanishing point to the list of points that should be connected. The teacher used the consequence conjunction "if" to establish the condition that is met in this case when he said, "if you line those up." With this conjunction, the teacher stated that the three points must be collinear.

In contrast, the line passing through the top of the trees did not line up with the vanishing point. The teacher made this contrast explicit by using the conjunction "but." By showing a contrasting case, the teacher established the reasoned conjecture regarding the conditions needed for the objects to have the same height in real life.

> Teacher: **If** you line them all up, you can get the bottom of the trees to match up. **But** what he – what he's saying is on the second side, **when** he did it – Did this one go – did you line up the tops of the trees? **And** did your line go above **or** below that dot?

The strategy of drawing a line through corresponding points of the trees did not yield the same result as with the houses. Specifically, the line going through the top of the trees did not pass through the vanishing point, "the dot." Alternatively, the line passed either above or below the vanishing point. He summarized the conjecture by stating the conditions that must be met by using the conjunction "if": "**If** you drew the line, **if** it hit the point, it would all be the same size." The teacher also discussed the alternative: "**And if** they don't match up, we know they're not the same size." The examples illustrate how the teacher used the conjunction "if" to state the expectation about what to "see" in the diagram and the consequence that results from meeting (or not) this expectation.

The teacher's summary of the second strategy included 11 conjunctions. The teacher used "so" several times to link different ideas in his talk as he discussed the strategy reported by David, a student.[10] The conjunction "so" denotes consequence, as the teacher establishes reasoned conjectures based on the students' work with the diagram.

> Teacher: **So**, he took corresponding points on both of them. He took different parts of the house. For every point that you see, every vertex you see here. Do you know what a vertex is? It's where two segments meet. **So,** for every vertex on here, he had drawn a line. **So,** he had matched up every possible vertex. **So,** he checked lots, a lot of points. Which is good, **'cause then**, **if** they all match up, **then** you know they're exactly the same. **But, if** they don't match up, something is not the same, right? **So**, that was David's approach.

The second strategy was similar to the first strategy because the students were connecting corresponding points in the diagram. However, in the second strategy, David connected various pairs of corresponding points (Figure 4.7). The teacher made the conjecture explicit: "'**cause then**, **if** they all match up, **then** you know they're exactly the same." This conjecture follows from their work on the diagram. The conjunctions "cause" and "then" allowed the teacher to identify the conjecture that resulted from the students' work with the diagram: "**if** they all match up, **then** you know they're exactly the same." The use of *if–then* statements is explicitly taught in the traditional geometry curriculum (for example, see Jurgensen, Brown, & Jurgensen, 1994, p. 33–34). With "if," the teacher established the condition that all the corresponding points in the diagram needed to be connected to the vanishing point. With "then," the teacher established the result: the sizes of the objects in the one-point perspective drawing are the same in real life.

With the conjunction "but," the teacher contrasted the conditions in the first and second conjectures: "**But, if** they don't match up, something is not the same." This second conjecture leads students to establish that the lines connecting corresponding parts that do not pass through the vanishing point are not the same size in real life.

The third strategy involved measuring corresponding parts and making calculations with these measurements. For example, the students measured the height of the two houses or the height of the two trees. The teacher used consequence conjunctions to make explicit their conjecture.

> Teacher: **So,** they took corresponding measurements **and** they compared them, **and if** the measurements, **when** they set them into proportions they got exactly the same thing, which means that the ratios are equal. **If** the ratios are equal, the shapes are similar, right? **So,** tell me what you did on the trees, **then.** What happened there?

The teacher used "if" and "when" to describe the conditions. The teacher's use of "when," a conjunction to denote time, allowed him to retell the story of their mathematical procedure. First, the students measured parts of the diagram and then they set these measurements into proportions. The teacher framed the conjecture by using "if" to denote the condition that must be met: "If the ratios are equal." The consequence of meeting this condition is that the figures are similar. The teacher commended the students for this strategy but also stated that it can be difficult to identify which tree is larger in real life by relying only on measurements. The teacher used "but" to apparently lessen a veiled critique of the method, which did not allow the students to answer the main question of comparing the size of the trees.

> Teacher: **So, when** they did the xy, these values came out not to be the same. **So,** they're not proportional. Which means the ratios are not the same, which means the shapes are not going to be the same, right. More difficult to determine which one is higher or lower in that case. **But,** that, that's a really good approach. That's a different approach, which looks pretty good.

The teacher had written on the board the proportion $\frac{x}{x} = \frac{y}{y}$. Although he used the same variable twice, the terms of the proportion compared the height of the first house with the height of the second house and the side of the first house with the side of the second house. The teacher used algebraic notation to denote a generalization of the measurements that the students had made and the product of the two terms in the proportion: *xy*. If the two cross products are not the same, then the figures are not proportional. As a result, the figures are not similar. The conjunction "when" helped to establish the condition, and the conjunction "so" allowed the teacher to state the conclusion of the conjecture.

In the discussion of the three strategies, the teacher used the students' work with the diagram to make generalizations. The three strategies illustrate the cases where the students interacted with the diagrams following a *generative* mode of interaction (Herbst, 2004) by adding auxiliary lines or purposefully measuring some of its parts. In the summary, the teacher elicited the strategies and extended the students' understanding of the underlying mathematics concepts in the lesson by discussing how to state their conclusions as conjectures. The first two strategies resulted in conjectures where the students relied on the perception of the diagram; students reached conclusions in relation to whether the lines were concurrent or not. The third strategy required calculations to see whether the figures in the diagram were proportional. The teacher's use of conjunctions supported the process of making students' reasoned conjectures explicit. The use of *if–then* statements provided a template for students to identify the conditions that needed to be met and the consequences of meeting these conditions.

Discussion

Reading a diagram is essential in geometry problem-solving. In the one-point perspective lesson, students needed to work with the diagram to solve the problem of determining whether the houses and the trees were the same height in real life. The students' problem-solving strategies included specific operations with the diagram such as adding the perspective lines, selectively measuring corresponding segments, and focusing their attention on specific parts. During the launch, the teacher elicited the students' prior experiences with the one-point perspective. Drawing on these experiences, the teacher provided cues to read the diagram in a dynamic way. If a teacher tells too much about a solution strategy during the launch, then students may not apply their own solution strategies, which thus limits students' opportunities to learn (González & Eli, 2017). With the launch, the teacher provided scaffolds without limiting students' opportunities for discovery. The teacher's linguistic choices helped students to transition from a static to a dynamic view of the diagram. The first two strategies discussed in the summary relied on a dynamic view of the diagram by drawing perspective lines. The teacher could use these solutions to introduce the concept of dilation in further discussions.

The third solution presented in the summary relied on a static view of the diagram. The students who worked on these solutions did not add the perspective lines. Instead, these students identified and measured the length of corresponding segments, such as the height of the houses. Additionally, the students performed numerical calculations, similar to other calculations that they had performed in the days prior to the lesson when discussing ratios and rates. The third solution had limitations for introducing dilation. Specifically, students did not have the need to attend to the vanishing point to establish that two figures were similar. Additionally, the third strategy did not help to answer the question of which tree is larger, as the teacher noted. By using the conjunction "but" when saying "**But**, that, that's a really good approach," the teacher signaled his preference for a dynamic view of the diagram that would lead them to answer the question. Nevertheless, it was valuable for the teacher to discuss this solution during the summary since it showed the students' work on the problem, initiated future connections with the concept of similarity, and provided a contrast with the solutions that relied on adding the perspective lines.

In the summary, the teacher translated the students' perceptions of the diagram and actions to the diagram into reasoned conjectures. The analysis shows how conjunctions helped him establish a structure for the conjectures. Specifically, the teacher established the conditions that needed to be met by using "if" and the results of these conditions by using "then." Although the teacher did not use "then" in all of the instances where he established a conjecture, most clauses followed the typical *if–then* structure of mathematical propositions. By making the conjectures explicit, the teacher prompted students to make generalizations based on their work on the problem. These generalizations are reasoned conjectures, because the teacher was able to establish the consequences of reading the diagram in specific ways. A teacher's actions are important to provide an environment that supports justifying and proving in geometry classrooms (Martin, Soucy, Wallace, & Dindyal, 2005). In this case, the teacher promoted the students' justifications of their conjectures with explanations concerning their work with the diagram.

Mathematics requires students to read visual images in special ways. This is particularly important in geometry. Lemke (2003) argued that in mathematics classrooms, students should learn how to translate visual representations into other representations, if possible. The teacher promoted this translation by stating the students' reasoned conjectures about the diagram.

Lemke (2003) also recommended connecting school mathematics to mathematical practices. In the case of the one-point perspective lesson, students had the opportunity to approach the problem of representing three dimensions in two dimensions, a problem that has been a source of inspiration in the history of mathematics. The practice of reading and working with a one-point perspective diagram supported students' development of mathematical understanding. Figure 4.8 shows a representation of how the lesson had different layers of mathematical literacy.

In the one-point perspective lesson, students' experiences of examining objects that are close and far in real life provided an entry point to a mathematical problem: how to represent three dimensions in two dimensions. In the lesson, the problem provided an entry point to study school geometry. Specifically, the one-point perspective lesson used the context of visual arts for students to learn a mathematical concept in the curriculum: dilation. The lesson's goal was for students to identify the properties of dilation by using a one-point perspective diagram. At its core, the lesson provided opportunities

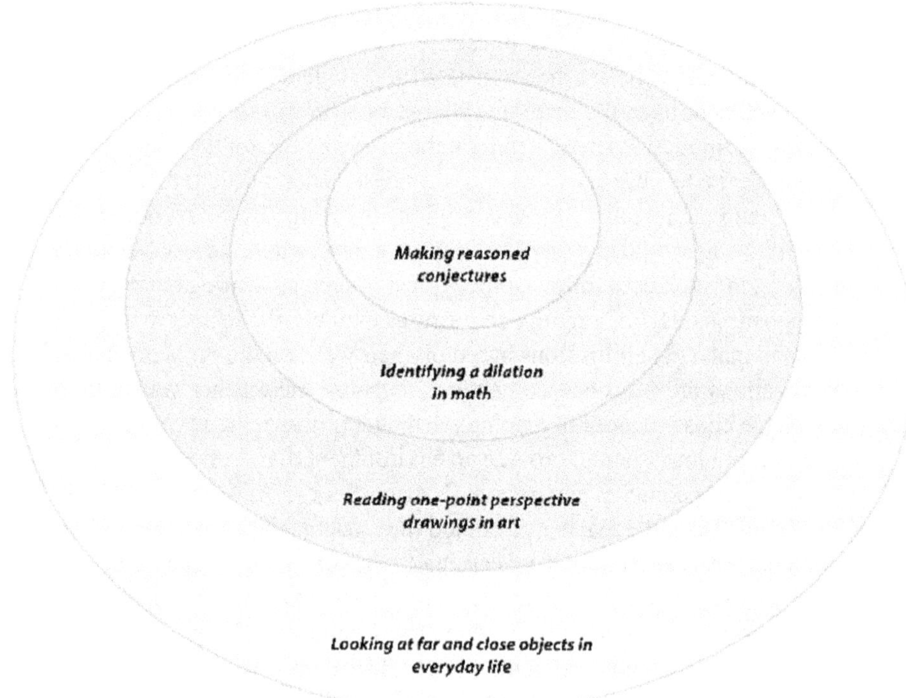

Figure 4.8 Layers of mathematical literacy in the one-point perspective lesson.

for students to use a geometric diagram to make reasoned conjectures. The teacher modeled the literacy practice of formulating conjectures in mathematics by using students' solution strategies and generalizing statements with the aid of conjunctions that established logical consequences.

Mathematizing from realistic contexts is fundamental for students to develop mathematical understanding and an appreciation for mathematics. In this lesson, the students were able to draw on their experience and extend these experiences to a mathematical situation. The context of visual arts is atypical in geometry instruction. However, it provided the students with an entry point to the concept of dilation, with a novel way to perceive diagrams as dynamic. Moreover, the visual arts context provided an opportunity for students to build reasoned conjectures by working with a diagram. The teacher's deliberate efforts to support students in learning how to read the diagram during the launch, and when formulating reasoned conjectures during the summary, supported students' mathematical literacy.

Conclusion

As a mathematics education researcher, I use Systemic Functional Linguistics to unpack the complexities of mathematics classroom talk. By making explicit the work of teachers, teacher educators can consider ways to support teachers in promoting literacy practices for reading a diagram in their classrooms. When planning the one-point perspective lesson, the teachers intended to elicit and use students' prior knowledge to support students' mathematical understanding. The linguistic analysis of the launch made explicit the strategies that one teacher used to elicit students' ideas by positioning them as experts and connecting to their prior experiences. During the launch, the teacher also instilled in students a dynamic view of the diagram, which was critical to solving the problem, by adding auxiliary lines. During the summary, the teacher used conjunctions to establish reasoned conjectures based on students' solution strategies, which thus supported the students in mathematizing. While the professional development did not target these literacy practices directly, the teacher promoted ways to read the diagram and establish conjectures that promoted students' mathematical understanding. The multisemiotic discourse of mathematics requires teachers to promote connections among visuals, symbols, and written and oral texts. Learning more about the ways in which teachers promote mathematical understanding through literacy practices can help other teacher educators to make these practices explicit. Future professional development initiatives can build on teachers' use of linguistic strategies that support the development of students' mathematical reasoning in classrooms.

About the author

Gloriana González is Associate Professor of Mathematics Education in the Department of Curriculum and Instruction at the University of Illinois at Urbana-Champaign. Her research interests are problem-based instruction, classroom discourse, and teacher professional development. She has a special interest in the teaching and learning of geometry. She led a grant funded by the National Science Foundation, CAREER: Noticing and using students' prior knowledge in problem-based instruction. Methodologically, she uses Systemic Functional Linguistics to analyze classroom talk and discussions among teachers. She received the 2015 Emerging Scholar Award from the North American Systemic Functional Linguistics Association.

Acknowledgements

This work was supported by a National Science Foundation grant to Gloriana González for the project entitled "CAREER: Noticing and Using Students' Prior Knowledge in Problem-Based Instruction," Grant No. DRL-1253081. Opinions, findings, conclusions, or recommendations are those of the authors and do not necessarily reflect the views of the National Science Foundation. I appreciate useful feedback from George K. Francis, Claudia E. Lundsgaard, Michelle Samet, Lisa Skultety, and Gabriela E. Vargas on earlier versions of this chapter. I appreciate the valuable comments of Mary Schleppegrell.

Notes

1 The document includes four big ideas, but for this discussion on literacy, the first big idea is most relevant.
2 For example, to construct an angle bisector, one must start with an angle. A diagram does not show the order of the construction. However, the diagram has a history in terms of the sequence of steps performed in the construction of the angle bisector of a given angle.

3 This was a modification of the lesson study model. Instead of conducting live observations of one teacher teaching the lesson, all of the teachers taught the lessons and discussed examples of students' thinking (González & Skultety, 2018).

4 Following requirements by the Institutional Review Board (IRB), we only include students' comments in the transcriptions if we had permission from them and their parents.

5 I conducted an analysis of the *negotiation exchanges* (Berry, 1981; Ventola, 1987) in the launch. I found that the teacher drew on students' contributions in eight out of ten exchanges. For brevity, I did not include this analysis in the chapter. Nevertheless, the analysis suggests that the students were the main source of information during the launch, different from a typical initiation–reply–feedback exchange (Lemke, 1990).

6 The school has a technical education program aiming at preparing students for various careers.

7 The lexical strings only include terms used by the teacher. Although a student was the first to mention the term "distance" in the launch, the teacher appropriated the term.

8 In school mathematics, there are specific ways to define "distance," such as the distance between a point and a line or the distance formula. However, during the discussion, the teacher and students did not connect this term to school mathematics.

9 Thanks to Mary Schleppegrell for assisting with the analysis of this clause.

10 Following IRB requirements, I use pseudonyms for the teacher and the students.

References

Bartolini Bussi, M. G. (1996). Mathematical discussion and perspective drawing in primary school. *Educational Studies in Mathematics*, **31**, 11–41. https://doi.org/10.1007/bf00143925

Berry, M. (1981). Systemic linguistics and discourse analysis: a multi-layered approach to exchange structure. In M. Coulthard & M. Montgomery (eds.), *Studies in Discourse Analysis.* London: Routledge and Kegan Paul. https://doi.org/10.4324/9781315857336-14

Boaler, J. (2008). *What's Math Got to Do with It?* New York: Penguin Books.

DeJarnette, A. F., & González, G. (2017). Geometry students' arguments about a 1-point perspective drawing. *REDIMAT, 6*(1), 7–31. https://doi.org/10.17583/redimat.2017.2015

Dietiker, L., Baldinger, E., Cabana, C., Gulick, D., Shreve, B., & Lomac, L. (2006). *College Preparatory Mathematics*. Sacramento, CA: Author.

Dimmel, J. K., & Herbst, P. G. (2015). The semiotic structure of geometry diagrams: How textbook diagrams convey meaning. *Journal for Research in Mathematics Education, 46*(2), 147–195. https://doi.org/10.5951/jresematheduc.46.2.0147

Duval, R. (1995). Geometrical pictures: Kind of representation and specific processings. In R. Sutherland and J. Mason (eds.), *Exploiting Mental Imagery with Computers in Mathematics Education* (pp. 142–157). Berlin: Springer. https://doi.org/10.1007/978-3-642-57771-0_10

Fernandez, C. (2002). Learning from Japanese approaches to PD: The case of lesson study. *Journal of Teacher Education, 53*(5), 393–405.

Freudenthal, H. (1971). Geometry between the devil and the deep sea. *Educational Studies in Mathematics, 3*, 413–435. https://doi.org/10.1007/bf00302305

Freudenthal, H. (1991). *Revisiting Mathematics Education: China Lectures.* Dordrecht, The Netherlands: Kluwer.

González, G. (2018). Moving toward approximations of practice in teacher professional development: Learning to summarize a problem-based lesson. R. Zazkis, & P. Herbst (ed.), *Mathematical Dialogue: Scripting Approaches in Mathematics Education* (p. 115–146). Springer. https://doi.org/10.1007/978-3-319-62692-5_6

González, G., & DeJarnette, A. F. (2018). Designing animated stories of instruction for teacher education: The process of making an animation to promote teacher noticing of students' prior knowledge. *Journal of Technology and Teacher Education, 26*(1), 79–102.

González, G., & Eli, J. A. (2017). Prospective and in-service teachers' perspectives about launching a problem. *Journal of Mathematics Teacher Education, 20*(2), 159–201. https://doi.org/10.1007/s10857-015-9303-1

González, G., & Herbst, P. (2009). Students' conceptions of congruency through the use of dynamic geometry software. *International Journal of Computers for Mathematical Learning, 14*, 153–182. https://doi.org/10.1007/s10758-009-9152-z

González, G., & Herbst, P. (2013). An oral proof in a geometry class: How linguistic tools can help map the content of a proof. *Cognition and Instruction, 31*(3), 271–313. https://doi.org/10.1080/07370008.2013.799166

González, G., & Skultety, L. (2018). Teacher learning in a combined professional development intervention. *Teaching and Teacher Education, 71*, 341–354. https://doi.org/10.1016/j.tate.2018.02.003

Gravemeijer, K., & Doorman, M. (1999). Context problems in realistic mathematics education: A calculus course as an example. *Educational Studies in Mathematics*, **39**(1/3), 111–129. https://doi.org/10.1023/a:1003749919816

Halliday, M. A. K., & Hasan, R. (1976). *Cohesion in English.* London: Longman.

Halliday, M. A., K., & Matthiessen, C. (2004). *An Introduction to Functional Grammar* (3rd ed.). London: Hodder Arnold.

Herbst, P. (2004). Interaction with diagrams and the making of reasoned conjectures in geometry. *Zentralblatt für Didaktik der Mathematik*, **36**(5), 129–139. https://doi.org/10.1007/bf02655665

Herbst, P. (2006). Teaching geometry with problems: Negotiating instructional situations and mathematical tasks. *Journal for Research in Mathematics Education*, **37**(4), 313–347.

Jurgensen, R. G., Brown, R. G., & Jurgensen, J. W. (1994). *Geometry.* Boston, MA: Houghton Mifflin.

Lampert, M. (2001). *Teaching Problems and the Problems of Teaching.* New Haven, CT: Yale.

Lappan, G., Fey, J. T., Fitzgerald, W. M., Friel, S. N., & Phillips, E. D. (1998/2002/2005). *Connected Mathematics Project.* Upper Saddle River, NJ: Prentice.

Lemke, J. (1990). *Talking Science: Language, Learning, and Values.* Westport, CT: Ablex.

Lemke, J. (2003). Mathematics in the middle: Measure, picture, gesture, sign, and word. In M. Anderson, A. Sáenz-Ludlow, S. Zellweger, & V. V. Cifarelli (eds.), *Educational Perspectives on Mathematics as Semiosis: From Thinking to Interpreting to Knowing* (pp. 215–234). Brooklyn, NY, and Ottawa, Ontario: Legas.

Martin, J. R. (1992). *English Text: System and Structure.* Amsterdam: Benjamins.

Martin, J. R. & Rose, D. (2003). *Working with Discourse: Meaning Beyond the Clause* (1st ed.). London: Continuum.

Martin, J. R. & Rose, D. (2007). *Working with Discourse: Meaning Beyond the Clause* (2nd ed.). London: Continuum.

Martin, T., Soucy, S., Wallace, M., & Dindyal, J. (2005). The interplay of teacher and student actions in the teaching and learning of geometric proof. *Educational Studies in Mathematics*, **60**, 95–124. https://doi.org/10.1007/s10649-005-6698-0

National Governors Association Center for Best Practices, Council of Chief State School Officers. (2010). *Common Core State Standards for Mathematics.* Washington, D.C.: Author.

National Research Council. (2000). *How People Learn: Brain, Mind, Experience, and School,* J. Bransford, J., Pellegrino, D. Berliner, M. Cooney, A. Eisenkraft, H. Ginsburg, et al. (eds.). Washington, D.C.: National Academy Press.

O'Halloran, K. (1998). Classroom discourse in mathematics: A multisemiotic analysis. *Linguistics and Education*, **10**(3), 359–388. https://doi.org/10.1016/s0898-5898(99)00013-3

O'Halloran, K. (2005). *Mathematical Discourse: Language, Symbolism and Visual Images*. London: Continuum.

Pedoe, D. (1976). *Geometry and the Visual Arts*. Courier Corporation.

Schleppegrell, M. J. (2004). *The Language of Schooling: A Functional Linguistics Perspective*. Routledge.

Sherin, M. G., & Han, S. Y. (2004). Teacher learning in the context of a video club. *Teaching and Teacher Education*, **20**(2), 163–183. https://doi.org/10.1016/j.tate.2003.08.001

Shreyar, S., Zolkower, B., & Pérez, S. (2010). Thinking aloud together: A teacher's semiotic mediation of a whole-class conversation about percents. *Educational Studies in Mathematics*, **73**, 21–53. https://doi.org/10.1007/s10649-009-9203-3

Sinclair, N., Pimm, D., Skelin, M., & Zbiek, R. (2012). *Developing Essential Understanding of Geometry for Teaching Mathematics in Grades 9–12.* Reston, VA: NCTM.

Skultety, L., González, G., & Vargas, G. (2017). Using technology to support teachers' lesson adaptations during Lesson Study. *Journal of Technology and Teacher Education*, **25**(2), 5–33.

Smith, M., & Stein, M. K. (2011). *Five Practices for Orchestrating Productive Mathematics Discussions*. Reston, VA: National Council of Teachers of Mathematics.

van den Heuvel-Panhuizen, M. (2003). The didactical use of models in realistic mathematics education: An example from a longitudinal trajectory on percentage. *Educational Studies in Mathematics*, **54**, 9–35. https://doi.org/10.1023/b:educ.0000005212.03219.dc

Veel, R. (1999). Language, knowledge and authority in school mathematics. In F. Christie (ed.), *Pedagogy and the Shaping of Consciousness: Linguistic and Social Processes* (pp. 185–216). London: Continuum.

Ventola, E. (1987). *The Structure of Social Interaction: A Systemic Approach to the Semiotics of Service Encounters*. London: Frances Pinter.

Part II

Studies in student and faculty development with respect to academic writing at the university level

5 Exploring new perspectives and degrees of delicacy in *Appraisal* studies: An analysis of *Engagement* resources in academic discourse in Spanish

Julio César Valerdi Zárate
Universidad Nacional Autónoma de México

Introduction

During the last decade, academic writing analysis has become an important area of interest for linguists working within the systemic functional paradigm in Latin America. This is particularly true regarding the development of studies around the interpersonal dimension of academic writing in Spanish, for which Martin & White's *Appraisal* model (Martin & White, 2005; White, 2001) has proved especially productive. As a result of such development, we have come to understand more about the evaluative features which model academic discourses in Spanish.

Current developments in this field explore the implications of the generic properties of authors' attitudinal and ideological positioning in university contexts (Ignatieva, Herrero, Rodríguez-Vergara & Zamudio, 2015; López, 2008; Navarro, 2014; Rodríguez-Vergara, 2010, 2014;) as well as prototypical attitudinal trigger selections in their texts (Zamudio, 2016). There is also a better understanding of strategies authors use to position themselves with respect to other voices (Castro, 2013), and the relationship between appraising realizations and academic evaluation by teachers and writing instructors (Castro & Sánchez, 2013). Also, pedagogical material analysis has seen interesting advances through studies such as those by Moss (2011) and Moss & Mizuno (2011), which have revealed meaningful implications of intertextual features in textbooks.

Works like those cited above represent important progress in the study of evaluative language in academic contexts, in terms of both the construction of interpersonal relations and the positioning of an ideal reader (Martin & White, 2005; Perales & Sandoval, 2016). However, despite their contributions in the Latin American educational context, *Appraisal* studies share the core methodological feature of basing their conclusions on relative frequencies of evaluative realizations in the global structure of the texts being analyzed, which may limit the scope of the descriptions developed. *Appraisal* studies generally start by identifying the most and least frequent evaluative choices in texts and then explain the rhetorical workings of such choices through the discussion of individual instances at the clause level. In the switch of focus from general evaluative tendencies to individual instances, meaningful rhetorical dynamics taking place above the clause level, but below the general structure of the text and its stages, may remain unnoticed.

The purpose of this chapter is to propose an argumentative approach to the analysis of *Appraisal* systems in academic writing. This approach is applied by analyzing *Engagement* resources within argument structure deployed in introductions of MA theses from the field of Applied Linguistics in Spanish. This research is based upon the consideration of argument structure, as proposed by Toulmin (1958), as an intermediate level of realization – between the clause and the general structure of texts – through which specific rhetorical functions and relations of speakers' linguistic evaluations can be identified with higher degrees of delicacy. Since the descriptive move from general tendencies to individual instances of evaluative language is found in studies about academic English, too (Lee, 2008; 2014; Valerdi, 2016; Wu, 2006, 2007), the results of this work can inform applied linguists analyzing languages different from Spanish in various contexts beyond Latin America.

Appraisal and argumentation in discourse

In this chapter, concepts related to *rhetoric* are used in the sense of informal argumentation as conceived by Perelman & Olbrechts-Tyteca (1958) and Toulmin (1958). From this perspective, the focus of rhetoric is to analyze the mechanisms through which speakers justify the propositions they assert. Such focus allows for the acknowledgement of both formal and informal argumentation as persuasive practices where "it is possible to adhere oneself not only to a thesis, but also to ways of thinking, seeing, and feeling" (Amossy, 2009, p.70) in the context of various types of discourse, including academic instances of language use.

The joint consideration of ideas, opinions and emotions in contemporary rhetoric confirms a pertinent connection between the frameworks of Martin & White's *Appraisal* model and Toulmin's Argumentation Model (1958, 2003). Both relate to three classical dimensions of argumentation that remain valid in today's discourse analysis: *pathos, ethos* and *logos* (Hyland, 2005). The first is related to the appeal and manipulation of the audience's emotions. The second involves the speaker's projection toward an audience and vice versa. The latter relates to the coherent, purposeful organization of propositions in discourse.

Through the systems of *Attitude, Engagement,* and *Graduation,* the *Appraisal* model analyzes linguistic realizations of *pathos* and *ethos,* while Toulmin's model approaches the dimension of *logos* through the study of the strategic unfolding of arguments, their organization and composition. Together, both models provide useful tools for the analysis of the rhetorical workings of evaluative language in academic discourse. In the following section, I summarize the constructs of both models that are pertinent for this study.

The model of *Appraisal* and the *Engagement* system

The model of *Appraisal* (Martin & White, 2005) represents an extension of the systemic study of the interpersonal dimension of language use. It offers a comprehensive systemic view of resources employed by speakers for purposes of subjective projection in discourse. The model considers the appraising systems of *Attitude, Engagement,* and *Graduation.* The first involves the linguistic expression of emotions, and opinions derived from them. The second has to do with the speaker's positioning in relation to other voices and his/her audience. The system of *Graduation* relates to the resources employed for the intensification and attenuation of realizations of *Attitude* and *Engagement.*

Resources comprised by these systems have a rhetorical influence in as much as they get involved in the projection of emotions and values through a community's texts, as well as in the speakers' authorial construction of personalities for themselves and their audiences. Such configuration of personae provides discourse with potential for aligning or disaligning the speakers' stance with those of real or potential interlocutors. The ultimate objective of using appraising language is to mobilize attitudes and beliefs in order to modify those held by one's interlocutor(s). This chapter focuses on the *Engagement* system.

Founded upon the Bakhtinian notions of dialogism and intertextuality (Bakhtin, 1981, 1982), this system includes linguistic resources speakers use to consider the presence and influence of other speakers' voices and discourses in their own discursive performance. By employing *Engagement* resources, utterances are "represented as taking up, responding to, acknowledging, endorsing, rejecting, discounting, challenging or anticipating some prior or potential utterance" (Derewianka, 2007, p. 162). Thus, through realizations of *Engagement*, speakers position themselves before their audience's and third parties' voice, aligning or disaligning their stances, and creating or eroding dialogical solidarity.

The absence of *Engagement* resources results in *monoglossic* discourse which denies or ignores the dialogic nature of linguistic exchanges. In contrast, the use of *Engagement* realizations conveys *heteroglossic* propositions, involving two subsystems of options for dialogic negotiation: *Contraction* and *Expansion*. *Contraction* comprises resources that contradict, reject or subordinate voices different from the speaker's. These, on the one hand, are analyzed in terms of the subsystem of *disclaim,* comprising resources of *denial* and *countering*. Disclaiming resources in Spanish include adverbs like *no, nunca, ni, tampoco,* etc., and pronouns like *nadie* and *ninguno* for *denial* (1). As for *countering,* we find counter-expectancy and contrast operators like *pero, mas, incluso, hasta,* etc. (2)

(1)   [...] el significado procedimental **<u>no</u>** es tan poco flexible [...]
       [...] procedural meaning is not that inflexible [...]

(2)   [...] el silencio se ha definido como oposición a la palabra.
       <u>Sin embargo</u>, también puede ser definido en relación con la palabra.
       [...] silence has been defined as an opposition to words. However, it can also be defined in relation to words.

Resources of *disclaim* involve a high dialogic cost since they present propositions as contradictions to others' ideas and stances, which reduces opportunities for discursive solidarity between speaker and audience. These resources can be oriented toward the speaker's interlocutors, or toward a third indirect dialogic party. When oriented toward a third party, resources of *disclaim* align the speaker's and audience's view. When oriented toward the audience, its voice and the speaker's voice disalign, reducing opportunities for discursive solidarity.

In addition to these disclaiming options, I propose a third category which has not yet been considered by any of the consulted works on *Appraisal* in Spanish or English: *rectification*. This paradigm occurs in propositions where resources of *denial* and *countering* interact, explicitly correcting a proposition the speaker believes to be held by the audience. In Spanish, this correction is prototypically introduced through the connector *sino* (usually realized as *but rather* in English) as shown in (3):

(3)   Los proclíticos ergativos en yucateco no están relacionados morfológica ni sintácticamente con el verbo, **sino** con una posición sintáctica diferente
        Ergative proclitics in Yucatec are not related to the verb morphologically nor syntactically, but rather to a different syntactic position

In (3), contractive choices work together to realize two moves: first, they reject two propositions supposedly held by the audience (two syntactic relations in Yucatec Mayan); and then, they replace these propositions with one which is presented as the right one. Although Martin & White take the interaction of *denial* and *countering* into consideration, they analyze them as separate dialogic operations construing concession rather than rectification: *"Even though he had taken all his medication, his leg didn't look any better"* (2005, p. 120). In Spanish, the rectifying function of negation and opposition interactions is so particular that speakers use the specialized operator *sino*. This kind of rhetorical move has been described recently by García Negroni (2009) and Tosi (2015) as a metadiscursive negation with the potential to "disqualify others' discourse by cancelling the discursive framework it invokes [...] always establishing a discursive space different from the one which is challenged" (Tosi, 2015, p.127. The translation is mine).

Dialogic *contraction* can also be realized via expressions of *proclamation*, which include the subsystems of *pronunciation* (4), *concurrence* (5), and *endorsement* (6). *Pronunciation* carries an emphatic weight that positions the speaker's voice as challenging or taking distance from a dialogic alternative. In Spanish, this is done through discourse markers (*de hecho*), adverbial modifiers (*precisamente*), and emphatic first person (*yo sostengo que ...*). *Concurrence* encodes a certain degree of agreement between the speaker and alternative voices through two subsystems. On the one hand, it can *affirm* a proposition as something generally accepted, potentially alienating speakers who disagree via expressions like *obviamente, por supuesto, naturalmente*, etc. On the other hand, it can provisionally give credit to other voices only to reject them or deny them later (*si bien X, no* ...; *aunque X, no* ...; *aunque no X, sí*...). Finally, *endorsement* presents a proposition as highly valid or warrantable via factual verbs such as *demostrar*, *comprobar*, etc., removing or disqualifying alternative views in discourse.

(4)   [...] el proceso de investigación-acción **verdaderamente** pro-
        fundizó la comprensión [...]
        *[...] this action research process truly deepened our compre-
        hension [...]*

(5)   [...] **si bien** (*el alumno*) no las ha utilizado nunca, **sí** puede
        reconstruir el sentido (*de las palabras*).
        *[...] even though he (the learner) has never used them, he can
        figure out their meaning (of words).*

(6)   Ello queda **confirmado** por los ejemplos registrados en la
        literatura.
        This was confirmed by the examples found in literature.

The system of dialogic *expansion* comprises resources used to express one's propositions as alternatives to other voices, equally valid and reliable. Thus, *expansion* consists of widening the dialogic space to increase opportunities for discursive solidarity and alignment. *Expansion* is realized through the systems of *entertainment* and *attribution*. The first one includes operators that invite the audience to consider the existence of positions different from the speaker's. At the same time, those resources represent an attenuation of the speaker's commitment regarding his propositions. *Entertainment* (7) is prototypically realized by modals of epistemicity (*poder*, *deber*, etc.), deonticity (*tener*, *poder*), and evidenctiality (*parecer*). Rhetorical questions, adverbial adjuncts (*probablemente*), and interpersonal metaphors (*es posible*) realize *entertainment,* too.

(7)   **Puede decirse** que el cuerno es el eje de la fiesta brava.
        It can be said that the horn is the axis of bullfighting.

Attribution cites propositions from other speakers as valid dialogic alternatives, which increases opportunities for discursive solidarity. This can be realized encoding two paradigmatic positions regarding the cited proposition. The first one is the speaker's *acknowledgement* and agreement with the cited voice (8a). This usually has the rhetorical effect of adding support for the speaker's own position. *Acknowledgement* is realized via reportative processes (*decir*, *pensar*, *explicar*, etc.), adverbial adjuncts (*de acuerdo con*), and nominalizing experiential metaphors. The second attributive paradigm is *distance*, used to cite other voices and take distance from the content of their propositions, encoding a certain degree of disagreement without disqualifying them (8b). In Spanish, *distance* is expressed by similar choices as those of *acknowledgement*, although these are realized as impersonal clauses (*se piensa que*, *se ha dicho que*, etc.) supported by contractive expressions that make the divergence clear. Figure 5.1 summarizes the *Engagement* system.

(8)   a. […] a partir de lo cual **Edwards (1985) denomina** un caso específico […]
[…] on the basis of which Edwards (1985) establishes a specific case […]

b. […] las categorías de nombre y verbo, que **se presumen** universales […]
[…] the categories noun and verb, which are believed to be universal […]

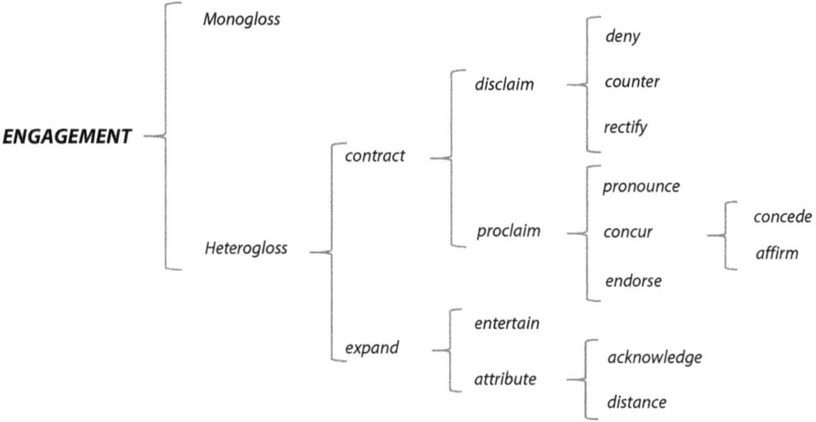

Figure 5.1 System of *Engagement.* **Adapted from Martin & White (2005)**

Toulmin's Argumentation Model

The second theoretical referent of this chapter is Toulmin's Argumentation Model (1958). Toulmin based his observations on the construct of *justification* and developed a model for arguments as "the products of argumentative acts" (Bermejo, 2010, p. 21), which aims at describing the capacity of arguments to provide justification for the statements speakers affirm. Within this framework, an argument is defined as a group of propositions which support a thesis based on certain kinds of evidence, and are joined by the argumentative relation of justification (Freeman, 1991, 2005; Renkema, 1999). All propositions in an argument have a rhetorical function as parts of argumentative components that justify the speaker's thesis.

Toulmin's argument structure consists of three basic components (Figure 5.2). The first is the *claim* (*C*), or the main point stated by the speaker. This component is supported by one or more propositions that function as its *data* (*D*), or evidence which justifies presenting the corresponding *conclusion.* This justificatory move is realized by a *warrant* (*W*), a generalizing statement without which a proposition remains as a bare assertion without reaching argument status (Létourneau, 2010).

Almost invariably, *W* remain implicit in the argument when the speakers consider the justificatory relation between *D* and *C* to be self-evident. Freeman (2005) proposes the identification of four types of implicit *W* through the recognition of the kind of reasoning linking *D* and *C*: *empirical* (based on experiential knowledge and observations the speaker presumes shared by the audience), *institutional* (based on references to recognized institutional authorities), *a priori* (based on "natural" logical relations such as *if x is blue, then it is not red*), and *evaluative* (based on purely subjective observations).

Toulmin's model "reflects a particular dialectic structure for arguments" (Hitchcock, 2003, cited in Santibañez, 2010, p. 192), since the presentation of *D* to justify *C* responds to potential questionings by virtual or real dialogic partners the speaker intends to persuade. Because of such rhetorical motivation, it is possible for speakers to introduce three optional components:

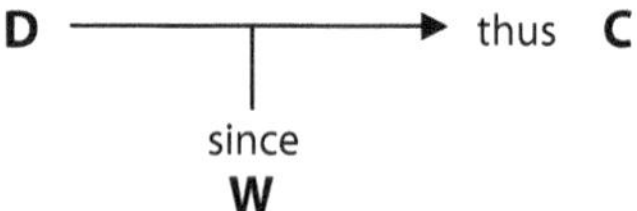

Figure 5.2 The three basic necessary components of an argument. Adapted from Toulmin (2003)

backings (**B**), *rebuttals* (**R**), and *modal qualifiers* (**Q**). Toulmin refers to *backings* as "other *warrants*" that support the legitimacy of **W** (1958, p. 103). They take the form of categorical statements and citations of other voices – usually some sort of authority. *Rebuttals* introduce conditions of exception for the argument's validity, somehow recognizing weak points in the argumentation. Finally, a **Q** moderates or intensifies the force of the main point of the argument. It is realized via modal operators, *counter* connectors, and conditional clauses. By adding these optional components to their arguments, speakers avoid possible counter arguments before they are even advanced by other speakers. Figure 5.3 illustrates an argument analyzed in this research.

The argument in Figure 5.3 incorporates both necessary and optional argumentative components. As it illustrates, Toulmin's componential representation of argument structure is particularly useful for the purposes of this chapter, since it allows for a detailed account of the various rhetorical functions of propositions making up arguments inside paragraphs and other organizational units of texts. This more detailed account increases the potential delicacy of argumentative analysis in contrast with argument structure proposals considered in previous systemic functional works, such as Miller & Pessoa (2016). These authors explore academic argumentation through

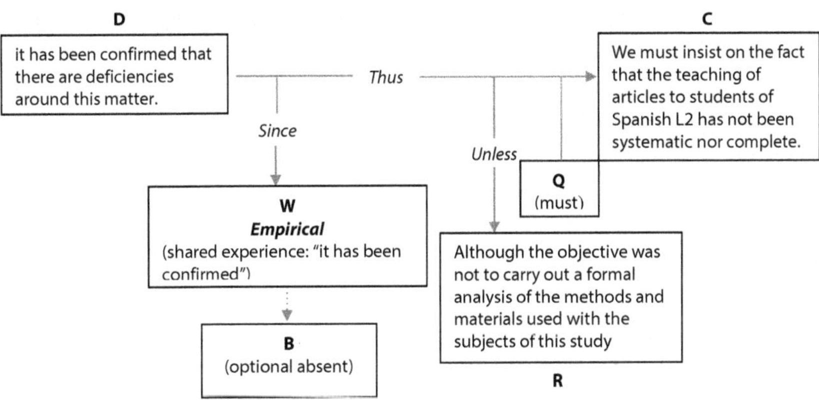

Figure 5.3 Argument supported by an implicit empirical *W* (based on shared experience). There is a *R* recognizing a limitation to the argument (the validity of the observation in relation to the kind of study reported). No *B* is presented

the constructs of macro-Themes and hyper-Themes. These constructs focus, on the one hand, on the supportive connection between introductory sentences in paragraphs and the contents of those paragraphs. On the other hand, they focus on the thematic links established between paragraphs in texts in relation to their introductory sentences. This approach, however, does not consider argumentative functions of sentences beyond observations about the thematic support that paragraphs give to their introductory sentences.

Similarly, Lee (2014) analyzes argument structure in academic essays based on *functional stages* from genre pedagogy. Such functional stages stand for argumentative functions of whole paragraphs rather than propositions inside paragraphs. Depending on the purposes of a study, this might be a limitation since, as toulminian analysis reveals, propositions inside paragraphs play rhetorical roles making up subarguments that ultimately work together to characterize the rhetorical force and nature of such paragraphs. These roles remain unnoticed in Lee's approach in a similar fashion as would happen if Swales' (1990) rhetorical moves perspective were to be adopted. Thus, the greatest advantage of implementing Toulmin's Model in systemic analysis is the possibility to track arguments developing inside the structure of larger arguments realized by functional stages; to analyze the argument inside the argument, so to say.

Interestingly, Lee (2014) draws upon Toulmin's components *claim*, *data*, and *warrant* to explain the rhetorical workings of some functional stages of the texts she analyzes. However, she does not describe rhetorical dynamics of other types of components (*backings*, *rebuttals*, and *qualifiers*). Still, her reference to Toulmin's argumentative components stands as a precedent signal of the model's pertinence in systemic functional studies. In the following sections, I elaborate on the methods used to benefit from the argumentative delicacy of Toulmin's Model for the *Appraisal* analysis purposes of this chapter.

Methodology

In this research, the introductory sections of 20 MA theses from the field of Applied Linguistics written in Mexican Spanish by graduate students at a public university in Mexico City were analyzed. MA theses are important as one of the main forms of knowledge production and communication at university level (Marín, 2015). This work contributes to research and pedagogy of the rhetorical implications of evaluative language in academic writing.

The selection of the introduction subgenre is pertinent for its prominent argumentative features (Perales, Sima & Valdez, 2012), which make it an ideal discursive environment for the rhetorical exploration of *Appraisal* resources. Finally, analyzing academic writing in Spanish serves the purpose of broadening the still developing study of *Appraisal* systems in academic genres in this language, resulting in useful information for academic writing instruction in Spanish and English for Spanish speakers.

Every text was subjected to two analyses. The first one had the purpose of identifying the evaluative features of *Engagement* in the corpus. All the realizations of *Engagement* were recorded and then quantified in relation to the total number of clauses composing each text, including sentences without *Engagement* resources. This made it possible to calculate the relative frequencies of *Engagement* types in the whole texts and, in turn, the whole corpus. For realizations of *denial, countering* and *pronunciation*, the contractive orientation toward the readers or a third party was recorded. General tendencies in the corpus were identified through calculation of relative frequencies of realizations of *Engagement* via the function # *Engagement type/total # clauses*.

The second analysis identified argumentative patterns in the corpus. First, an argumentative passage per introduction was selected by taking the first cluster of propositions that displayed at least one realization of heteroglossic discourse and were topically related to the same *claim/conclusion*. Textual operators such as *en primera instancia (first)*, *en relación con ... (in relation to)*, *en cuanto a ... (regarding)*, *por lo tanto (thus)*, *aunque (although)*, etc. were instrumental in distinguishing the beginning, continuation, and end of arguments. The selected passages were analyzed according to Toulmin's model; the argumentative functions of their propositions (*D, C, B, R* y *Q*) were identified and their argumentative components were organized in argumentative schemes and subschemes.

In this corpus, all *warrants* linking *C* and *D* remained implicit. Thus, the identification of their nature in Freeman's terms (2005) was carried out with the main purpose of confirming a justificatory presentation of *C* in the analyzed arguments. For this reason, examples of argumentative analysis in Appendices A–C only include the label of the justificatory nature – empirical, evaluative, institutional, or *a priori* – of *W* in each case.

Resulting argumentative schemes were classified in patterns. These were defined based on the presence/absence of *D* in their structure, as well as the relations held among their main subargument (labelled α) and the secondary subarguments (labelled β, γ, etc.). Again, textual operators signaled the beginning and the end of subarguments as well as their status as main or secondary subarguments (see Appendix A).

The final step was the evaluative–argumentative crossing of the models of *Appraisal* and argumentation. This step aimed at identifying the rhetorical functions of *Engagement* resources in the corpus in relation to the argumentative component in which they appear (*C, D, B, R* and *Q*). Schemes following each argumentative pattern identified in the previous analysis were quantified in terms of the number of clauses that compose them and their elements. Then, using the information that resulted from the *Engagement* analysis, the components of the argumentative schemes were characterized according to the types of heteroglossic resources they display. This procedure shed light on the rhetorical workings of *Engagement* with higher degrees of delicacy than those obtained through the usual general characterization of evaluative prosody. The results of the whole process are presented in the following section.

Results

Evaluative prosody

The properties revealed by the evaluative analysis are similar to prototypical academic writing in Spanish as described in previous work (Zamudio, 2016; Castro, 2013; Castro & Sánchez, 2013). The first main feature of the corpus is the minimal presence of heteroglossic discourse, which represents 15% of the total propositions in the corpus. This finding coincides with those by Castro (2013), who identified a "scarce presence of resources acknowledging the existence of alternative proposals different from the authors'" in academic essays (p. 104).

In heteroglossic terms, the corpus reflects a marked preference for the use of contractive resources when alternative voices are introduced in the texts. While expansive resources add up to 35% of the heteroglossic propositions, *contraction* is realized in a proportion of 65%. Again, Castro (2013) and Castro & Sánchez (2013) report the same tendency to reduce opportunities of dialogue between the authors' stance and that of potential interlocutors. Interestingly, the contractive tendency of the corpus continues by favoring *disclaim* over *proclaim* with proportions of 83% and 17% of the contractive propositions. Additionally, resources of *denial* and *countering* are oriented towards the audiences in proportions of 85% and 87%. When resources of *proclamation* take place, *pronunciation* dominates over *concurrence* and

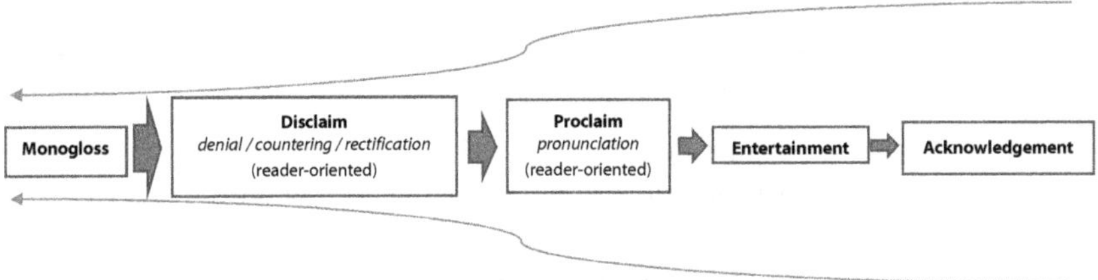

Figure 5.4 Heteroglossic flow representing the dynamics of dialogic space in the corpus

endorsement with 75% of the realizations. Moreover, resources of *pronunciation* are oriented towards the texts' readers in an 88% proportion, which extends the marked tendency to put alignment and discursive solidarity at stake.

The expansive features of the corpus favor *entertainment* over *attribution*, with 62% of the expansive propositions considering alternative voices via modality and 38% referring to other speakers explicitly. Finally, when speakers attribute propositions to others, they do so by signaling some sort of agreement with the cited voice via *acknowledgement* choices. This represents the only variation in the global tendency to reject, contradict or disagree with alternative views. Considering the results of the *Engagement* analysis, the evaluative prosody of the corpus can be said to conform to the heteroglossic flow illustrated by Figure 5.4. Thick arrows flowing from left to right indicate the most and least frequently realized options of *Engagement*, showing expansive choices have a reduced presence in the corpus. Thin external arrows flowing from right to left represent the behavior of the dialogic space negotiated in the corpus, indicating it tends to be contracted. In the *ENGAGEMENT* and argumentation and Discussion sections, I explain the significance of this characterization of evaluative tendencies in terms of its connection with argumentative patterns found in the corpus.

Argumentative patterns

The argumentative analysis of the corpus revealed five different patterns (see Table 5.1). Argumentative patterns I (Appendix B) and III (Appendix A) incorporate *D* in their main subarguments, while pattern II (Appendix C) compensates for the absence of *D* in the main subargument with the support of secondary subarguments. Patterns IV and V are particular in their features and realization frequencies. Arguments in pattern IV, on the one hand, instantiate partially unjustified argumentation with no *D* in their main subargument and through the inclusion of bare assertions. On the other,

Table 5.1 Argumentative patterns of schemes identified in the corpus

Pattern	Scheme*	Description	Occurrence
I	$\beta + \beta + \alpha$	A main sub argument which incorporates at least one **D** in its sub scheme and has additional support of one or more secondary sub arguments working as external **D**.	8 (40%)
II	$(\beta + \beta)\,\alpha$	A main sub argument which does not incorporate **D** in its sub scheme, but is supported by one or more secondary sub arguments – marked in brackets – working as its **D**.	3 (15%)
III	$\beta + \alpha + c$	A main sub argument which incorporates at least one **D** in its sub scheme and has additional support of one or more secondary sub arguments working as external **D**. The scheme incorporates one or more bare assertions with no **D** or **W.**	7 (35%)
IV	$(\beta+ \beta+c)\,\alpha$	A main sub argument which does not incorporate **D** in its sub scheme, but is supported by one or more secondary sub arguments – marked in brackets – working as its **D**. The scheme incorporates one or more bare assertions with no **D** or **W.**	1 (5%)
V	$c+c+c$	The scheme is only composed by bare assertions which are intended to defend a thesis with no **D** or **W.**	1 (5%)
Total:			20

* Only in argumentative schemes, α = main sub argument, β = secondary sub argument, and c (lowercase) = bare (unjustified) assertion.

subschemes in pattern V instantiate totally unjustified *assertions*. Both argumentative dynamics occurred only once in the whole corpus. For this reasons, patterns IV and V are briefly described in Table 5.1, but they are not further discussed so that focus remains on the role of *Engagement* in fully argumentative (justified) discourse.

Engagement and argumentation

The advantages of the argumentative approach to *Appraisal* analysis applied in this research can be seen from the general evaluative–argumentative scenario displayed by Figure 5.5. As we can see, the analysis made it possible to go beyond the general description of relative frequencies of evaluative realizations in the corpus; it allowed the identification of the rhetorical functions where contractive and expansive *Engagement* resources operate in the corpus by linking them to specific components of argument structure. The results indicate that speakers mainly engage in dialogic negotiation in non-central argumentative components (***B***, ***R***, and ***Q***), while central rhetorical functions (***C*** and ***D***) instantiate highly monoglossic propositions. This means that, from a general perspective, optional components, whose influence consists of supporting the core elements of arguments, are the grounds where discourse is made negotiable by the speakers. On the other hand, the most determining rhetorical functions are introduced in discourse as propositions where speakers hold the most valid or reliable stances. It is important to bear in mind that, according to the heteroglossic flow in Figure 5.4, discursive spaces where *Engagement* takes place are predominantly contractive. Thus, the general rhetorical strategy in the corpus consists of dominating dialogic space, with more abundant and varied heteroglossic interaction in the optional supports of *conclusions*.

Through evaluative–argumentative analysis, descriptions of the rhetorical workings of *Engagement* can be even more detailed. The evaluative analysis of argument structure in the corpus resulted in three heteroglossic dynamics of *Engagement* interrelated with the argumentative patterns

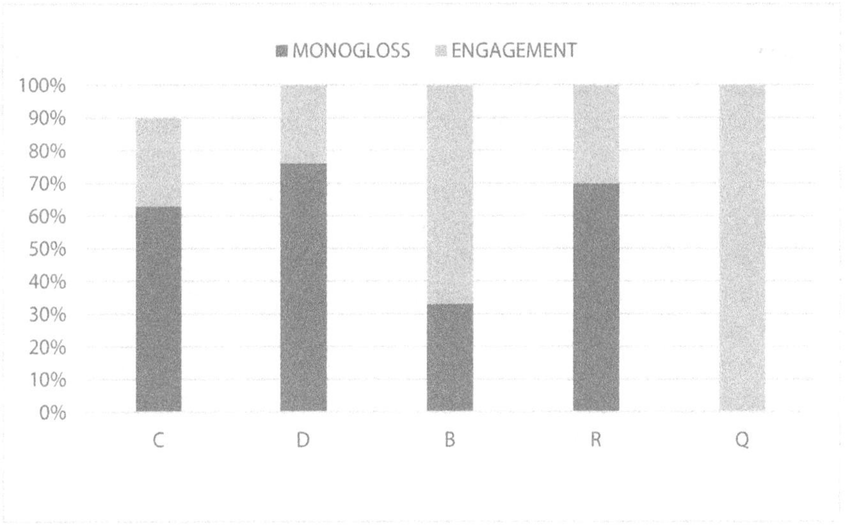

Figure 5.5 *Engagement* in argumentative components

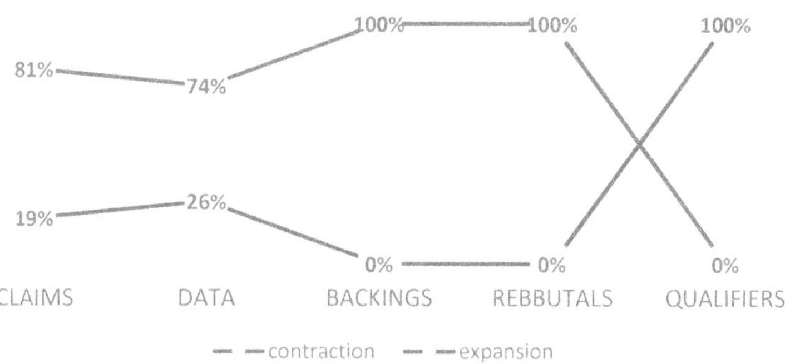

Figure 5.6 Heteroglossic dynamic in argumentative pattern I

reported in the previous section of this chapter. The most frequent dynamic corresponds to pattern I (Figure 5.6), where dialogic contraction leads the negotiation of heteroglossic discourse. This is especially true for the rhetorical functions *B* and *R*, where 100% of the heteroglossic propositions are contractive. In *C* and *D*, dialogic space is meaningfully contracted in proportions of 81% and 74%, respectively. Not surprisingly, only *Q* display major proportions of expansion, with 100% of the heteroglossic propositions. We can see how an augmentative approach to *Engagement* analysis allows the identification of the most and the least frequent heteroglossic choices in discourse, as well as the specific rhetorical functions they have according to the argumentative component where they are used.

The second most representative heteroglossic dynamic is found in pattern III (Figure 5.7). Here, dialogic space is negotiated in less unequal terms in *C* and *D*, where the distance between *contraction* and *expansion* is reduced. This changes in *B*, where contractive and expansive choices are deployed by speakers in relatively similar distributions with a slight tendency toward expansion. Heteroglossia in *R* is totally contractive, while *Q* display completely expansive *Engagement*.

Pattern II is the third one in frequency (Figure 5.8). Here, the strategic negotiation of dialogic space varies more significantly. On the one hand, proportions of expansive and contractive resources get closer to each other both in *C* and *D*. On the other hand, *B* is realized in completely monoglossic terms while there is a null presence of *Q*.

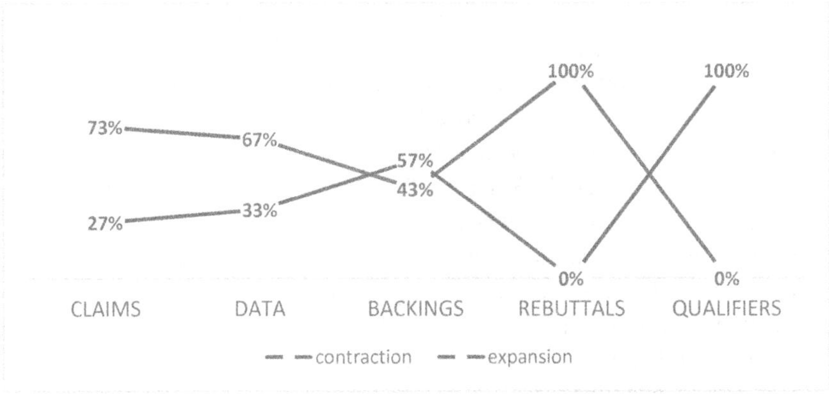

Figure 5.7 Heteroglossic dynamic in argumentative pattern III

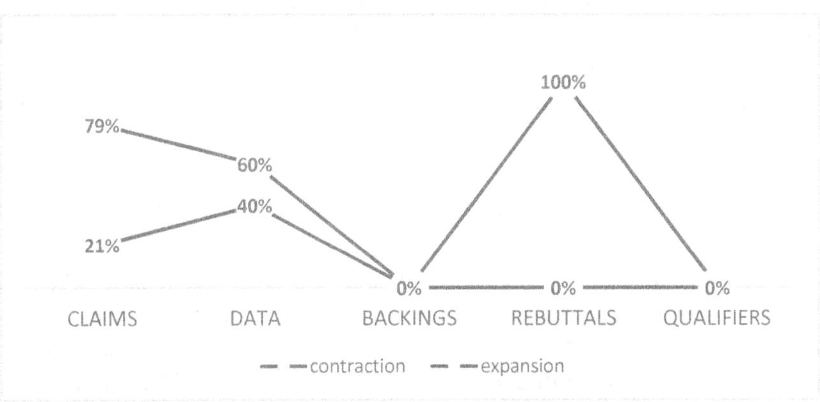

Figure 5.8 Heteroglossic dynamic in argumentative pattern II

Discussion of the results

The relation between the findings of each of the analyses involved in this research reveals the advantages of an argumentative approach to *Engagement* analysis. The first observation about the corpus is that its heteroglossic features conform to prototypical expectations about academic writing in Spanish. As part of their studies, Oteíza (2009, cited in Navarro, 2014) and Castro & Sánchez (2013) described the general tendency to realize monoglossic discourse and to contract dialogic space when integrating other voices. This is also the case in the current analysis and is even accentuated along the heteroglossic flow illustrated by Figure 5.4.

While confirming these tendencies in Spanish is relevant for academic instruction in the language, such information has interesting implications for the field of English for Academic Purposes in Spanish speaking countries. In a contrastive study, Valerdi (2016) analyzed English texts written by Mexican undergraduate students and found heteroglossic tendencies become meaningfully more contractive as writers gained experience – the opposite of texts by native English speakers analyzed in the same work. This suggests a preference in writers to project the kind of authorial stance they develop in their L1 and signals the importance of considering cultural contrasts in processes of academic literacy in foreign languages. Such importance is also proposed by Lee & Deakin (2016), who found similar tendencies in texts written by Chinese learners. Interestingly, Wu (2007) reported that Singaporean instructors valued English texts with highly heteroglossic features (70%) more positively, adding to the contrasts that justify the need for a meaningful awareness of interpersonal differences among languages and cultures.

Besides the identification of general evaluative tendencies, the evaluative–argumentative analysis allows a more specific tracing of the rhetorical workings of *Engagement* resources. *Appraisal* studies based on general evaluative prosody would describe the monoglossic and contractive nature of academic discourse by presenting examples of individual realizations of *Engagement* at the clause level. However, such a move could imply the risk of focusing too much on the most representative types of heteroglossia, neglecting the fact that the least frequent realizations may play an important strategic role in the linguistic exchange not in terms of their frequency, but in relation to the specific argumentative stage in which they participate. From the argumentative approach adopted in this work, the specific rhetorical workings of both frequent and infrequent realizations have been traced in relation to the argumentation patterns and argument components in which they appear.

The latter can be seen in the authorial projection in optional components of arguments in pattern I, where heteroglossic dynamics are predominantly contractive in *C*, *D*, *B*, and *R*. *Backings* and *rebuttals* display totally contractive features (9), which suggests the speakers' rhetorical strategy is reducing the negotiability of elements intended to bring additional support to the *data* and *warrants* presented. Since *qualifiers*, which are 100% expansive, modify *claims* directly, they add a slight load of expansion to the co-text around *C*, *W*, and *D*. This generates a dialogic impression of progressive expansion, which may result in solidarity and alignment between interactants despite the monoglossic features spreading throughout the general structure of the texts and the authorial contractive dominance in optional components used for persuasion enhancement (*B* and *R*). Although the presence of expansive resources, such as those of *entertainment,* is incipient from a global perspective and, in principle, they can be realized anywhere in the argument structure, their centrality in the rhetorical effects of argumentation is evidenced by their incorporation as *qualifiers* in this strategy (10).

    (9)   a. [...] **Sin embargo**, según un informe oficial, la suma real [...]
        [...] however, according to an official report, the real sum [...]

        b. **Aunque no** las podríamos calificar de fastuosas [...]
        Although we couldn't label them as lavish [...]

        c. [...] **sí** podemos hablar de un derroche impresionante de recursos.
        [...] we CAN speak of an impressive waste of resources.

    (10) **Quizás** el público recuerde spots televisivos que [...]
         Perhaps the public remembers spots which [...]

In pattern III, the most distinctive contrast resides in *backings*, where expansive *Engagement* leads the way. Heteroglossic choices in this pattern present *B* as reliable supports through expansive choices of *attribution* (11). However, despite this display of apparent authorial dialogic flexibility, *rebuttals* – which acknowledge the weak points of arguments – remain contractive, displacing any potential alternative reading of what the weak points of the arguments represent (12). Again, these rhetorical uses of *Engagement* could not be identified based on general tendencies alone.

    (11) Estudios **indican** que la entonación [...]
         Studies report that intonation [...]

    (12) **Si bien** últimamente existe gran interés hacia el uso del lenguaje en contextos educativos [...] hace falta realizar más exploraciones sobre la escritura académica de autores mexicanos.
         Even though there is recent interest in language use in educational contexts [...] more explorations on academic writing by Mexican authors is needed.

The third most representative pattern, II, is heteroglossically peculiar. Resources of *Engagement* cannot realize *backing* nor *qualifying* since these functions are not incorporated. Thus, dialogic space is particularly restricted, as the absence of these components nullifies opportunities of negotiation in functions which would imply integrating diverse voices. Nonetheless, some balance is brought in by using more expansive resources in *data* than the rest of the patterns. Here, the incorporation of *attribution > acknowledgement* and *entertainment* gives arguments both an expansive impression and justificatory authority (13)

(13)   a. **Diferentes autores han destacado** el hecho de que [...]
Different authors have highlighted the fact that [...]

b. Asimismo, se **debe** considerar la forma en que se procesa la L2.
Also, we should consider how the L2 is processed

From these observations, we can see an argumentative approach to *Engagement* analysis makes it possible to trace specific rhetorical functions in which expansive and contractive heteroglossia operate. This kind of exploration of evaluative language represents the possibility of going beyond the interpretation of general tendencies in the global structure of texts in favor of a more delicate understanding of the rhetorical effects of *Engagement* resources. Moreover, descriptions attained through this evaluative–argumentative approach can still be more precise if the results of the evaluative analysis are taken into consideration in a more delicate way.

Let us take the case of *disclaim* as an example. Considering the dialogic cost of *disclaim* resources, it is relevant to notice they have a remarkable presence in central components of arguments (*C*, *D*, and *W*) in pattern I. These resources also dominate propositions in *B* and *R* in this pattern, something which does not happen in patterns II and III, which eventually lack evidence and display bare assertions. Since *denial, countering*, and *rectification* resources are predominantly oriented toward the readers of the analyzed texts (Figure 5.4), we can conclude that discursive solidarity and alignment are put at stake more significantly in argumentative grounds where justification compensates for the interpersonal negative effects of dialogic confrontation. In argumentative patterns with less justificatory solidity, speakers make more cautious heteroglossic choices, as shown by the increasing presence of expansive realizations in patterns II and III. These and previously described results corroborate the descriptive possibilities and advantages of an evaluative–argumentative analysis compared to more conventional *Appraisal* analyses.

Conclusions

This chapter has shown that an argumentative approach to *Engagement* analysis in academic discourse makes it possible to describe the rhetorical workings of evaluative language in more detail than conventional focus on global tendencies in general text structure. This has been demonstrated through three main achievements of this research. First, three different argumentative patterns with meaningful rhetorical contrasts among them were found in the corpus. From the perspective of an exclusively evaluative analysis, such patterns would have remained unnoticed. This demonstrates that rhetorical dynamics involving propositions which convey evaluative *Engagement* would have remained unnoticed, too.

Second, both expansive and contractive paradigms of *Engagement* were effectively linked to particular forms of argumentation based on the argumentative patterns and specific rhetorical functions in which they are deployed. In other words, the rhetorical functions that *Engagement* resources accomplish in the discourse of the analyzed corpus were revealed. This achievement proves toulminian argumentative structure to be a pertinent intermediate level of *Engagement* instantiation and analysis between clause level and full text.

Finally, the enhanced delicacy of heteroglossic description through this evaluative–argumentative approach was demonstrated by the specific identification of rhetorical dynamics involving the paradigm of *disclaim*. Such a tracing of rhetorical dynamics can be applied to every *Engagement* paradigm in discourse by referring to the results of the evaluative and argumentative analyses. Exemplifications through individual realizations become more pertinent in the context of such delicate descriptions than in those developed in conventional *Appraisal* studies.

The most remarkable contribution of this chapter is the proposal of an analytical approach applicable to academic corpora in languages different from Spanish. Although one of the primary purposes of this work is to extend *Appraisal* analysis in academic Spanish, the results of the analysis and the research review suggest that contexts of academic instruction in languages like English can benefit from the evaluative–argumentative approach developed in this work. Since current systemic explorations of argument structure focus on rhetorical moves instantiated at the level of paragraphs, the evaluative–argumentative proposal of this chapter could support application and analysis in future research around *Appraisal* systems in different linguistic contexts.

About the author

Julio César Valerdi Zárate holds a PhD on Linguistics from the National Autonomous University of Mexico (UNAM). His teaching experience has focused on English and Spanish for general and academic purposes as well as teacher training. He has taught several language and Applied Linguistics courses and workshops at the Autonomous University of Puebla, UNAM and Iberoamerican University (Ibero Puebla). As a full-time professor, Valerdi was head of the departments of English, Spanish, German, and Asian Languages at the Intercultural Language Center of Ibero Puebla. He is currently full-time Associate Professor at the Applied Linguistics Department of UNAM. His fields of interest are Second Language Acquisition, Discourse Analysis, Linguistic Argumentation, and Interculturality.

References

Amossy, R. (2009). Argumentación y análisis del discurso: Perspectivas teóricas y recortes disciplinarios. In L. Puig (ed.), *El Discurso y sus Espejos* (pp. 67–98). México: Universidad Nacional Autónoma de México.

Bakhtin, M. (1982). *Estética de la Creación Verbal.* México: Siglo XXI.

Bakhtin, M. (1981). *The Dialogic Imagination.* Austin: University of Texas Press.

Bermejo, L. (2010). El programa de *Los usos de la argumentación* de Stephen Toulmin. In R. Marafioti & C. Santibañez (eds.), *Teoría de la Argumentación a 50 Años de Perelman y Toulmin* (17–38). Buenos Aires: Biblos. https://doi.org/10.32735/s0718-2201201900049752

Castro, M. (2013). Posicionamiento discursivo en el ensayo de opinión escrito por estudiantes universitarios. *Lenguas en contexto*, **10**, 98–107.

Castro, M. & Sánchez, M. (2013). La expresión de opinión en textos académicos escritos por estudiantes universitarios. *Revista Mexicana de Investigación Educativa*, **18**(57), 483–506.

Derewianka, B. (2007). Using appraisal theory to track interpersonal development in adolescent academic writing. In R. Whittaker, M. O'Donell & A. McCabe (eds.), *Advances in Language and Education* (pp. 142–165). London: Continuum. https://doi.org/10.5040/9781474212045.ch-007

Freeman, J. (1991). *Dialectics and the Macrostructure of Arguments: A Theory of Argument Structure.* New York: Foris. https://doi.org/10.1515/9783110875843

Freeman, J. (2005). Systematizing Toulmin's warrants: An epistemic approach. *Argumentation*, **19**, 331–346. https://doi.org/10.1007/s10503-005-4420-0

García Negroni, M. (2009). Negación y descalificación: a propósito de la negación metalingüística. *Ciências & Letras*, **45**, 61–82.

Hyland, K. (2005). *Metadiscourse: Exploring Interaction in Writing.* London: Continuum.

Ignatieva, N., Herrero, L., Rodríguez, D. & Zamudio, V. (2015). Analizando procesos verbales en géneros académicos de las humanidades en español. *Signos Lingüísticos*, **17**, 53–79.

Létourneau, A. (2010). Una discusión sobre la lectura y el uso del modelo de argumentación de Stephen Toulmin en Jürgen Habermas. In R. Marafioti & C. Santibañez (eds.), *Teoría de la Argumentación a 50 Años de Perelman y Toulmin* (pp. 131–145). Buenos Aires: Biblos. https://doi.org/10.32735/s0718-2201201900049752

Lee, S. (2008). Attitude in undergraduate persuasive essays. *Prospect: An Australian Journal of TESOL*, **23**, 43–58.

Lee, S. (2014). Argument structure as an interactive resource by undergraduate students. *Linguistics and Human Sciences*, **9**(3), 277–306.

Lee, J. & Deakin, L. (2016). Interactions in L1 and L2 undergraduate student writing: International metadiscourse in successful and less-successful argumentative essays. *Journal of Second Language Writing*, **33**, 21–34. https://doi.org/10.1016/j.jslw.2016.06.004

López, C. (2008). La valoración y la emoción en español en discursos especializados. In A. Moreno (ed.), *Actas del VIII Congreso de Lingüística General (25–28 de junio de 2008)* (pp. 1142–1155). Madrid: Universidad Autónoma de Madrid. https://doi.org/10.1515/9783110963571.271

Marín, M. (2015). *Escribir Textos Científicos y Académicos.* México: Fondo de Cultura Económica.

Martin, J. R. (2000). Beyond exchange: *APPRAISAL* systems in English. In S. Hunston & G. Thompson (eds.), *Evaluation in Text: Authorial Stance and the Construction of Discourse* (pp. 142–175). Oxford: Oxford University Press. https://doi.org/10.1177/14614456020040041104

Martin, J. R. (2004). Sense and sensibility: Texturing evaluation. In J. Foley (ed.), *Language, Education and Discourse: Functional Approaches* (pp. 270–304). London: Continuum.

Martin, J. R. & White, P. (2005). *The Language of Evaluation: Appraisal Systems in English.* Basingtoke: Palgrave Macmillan.

Miller, R. & Pessoa, S. (2016). Where's your thesis statement and what happened to your topic sentences? Identifying organizational challenges in undergraduate student argumentative writing. *TESOL Journal*, **7**(4), 847–873. https://doi.org/10.1002/tesj.248

Moss, G. (2011). La negación: un diálogo exigente. In N. Barleta & D. Chamorro (eds.), *El Texto Escolar y el Aprendizaje: Enredos y Desenredos*

(pp. 181–194). Barranquilla: Universidad del Norte. https://doi.
org/10.4067/s0718-09342015000200006

Moss, G. & Mizuno, J. (2011). Las voces del texto. In N. Barleta & D.
Chamorro (eds.), *El Texto Escolar y el Aprendizaje: Enredos y Desenredos*
(pp. 123–148). Barranquilla: Universidad del Norte. https://doi.
org/10.4067/s0718-09342015000200006

Navarro, F. (2014). GRADACIÓN y COMPROMISO en escritura académica
estudiantil de humanidades. Análisis contrastivo desde la Teoría de la
Valoración. *Estudios de Lingüística Aplicada*, **32**(60), 9–33.

Perales, M., Sima, E., & Valdez, S. (2012). Movimientos retóricos en las
conclusiones de tesis de licenciatura en Antropología Social: un estudio
sistémico-funcional. *Escritos, Revista del Centro de Ciencias del Lenguaje*,
45, 33–60.

Perales, M. & Sandoval, R. (2016). La lectura retórica desde la enseñanza
discursivo-cognitiva: Una alternativa discursiva para la alfabetización
académica. In G. Bañales, M. Castelló, & N. Vega (eds.), *Enseñar a Leer y
Escribir en la Educación Superior: Manual de Buenas Prácticas Basadas
en la Investigación* (pp. 55–76). Ciudad Victoria: Universidad Autónoma de
Tamaulipas. https://doi.org/10.35537/10915/44649

Perelman, C. & Olbrechts-Tyteca, L. (1958). *Traité de l'Argumentation. La
Nouvelle Rhétorique.* Bruxelles: Université de Bruxelles. https://doi.
org/10.1017/s0012217300033114

Puig, L. & García, D. (2011). Introducción. En L. Puig y D. García (eds.),
Retórica y Argumentación: Perspectivas de Estudio (pp. 7–24). México:
Universidad Nacional Autónoma de México. https://doi.org/10.22201/
fi.25940732e.1998.01n1.004

Renkema, J. (1999). *Introducción a los Estudios Sobre el Discurso.* Barcelona:
Gedisa

Rodríguez-Vergara, D. (2014). El papel de la metáfora experiencial en la
escritura académica. In N. Ignatieva & C. Colombi (eds.), *CLAE: El
Lenguaje Académico en México y los Estados Unidos: Un Análisis
Sistémico Funcional* (pp. 101–126). México: Universidad Nacional
Autónoma de México. https://doi.org/10.1353/hpn.2016.0122

Rodríguez-Vergara, D. (2010). *Metáfora Gramatical en el Lenguaje Académico
en Español: Una Exploración Sistémico Funcional a la Escritura
Estudiantil.* Tesis de maestría, Universidad Nacional Autónoma de México.
https://doi.org/10.22402/j.rdipycs.unam.4.0.2017.159.21-44

Santibañez, C. (2010). Los usos de la argumentación: ¿retórica, dialéctica
o pragmática? In R. Marafioti & C. Santibañez (eds.), *Teoría de la
Argumentación a 50 Años de Perelman y Toulmin* (pp. 181–204). Buenos
Aires: Biblos. https://doi.org/10.4067/s0718-23762015000100014

Swales, J. (1990). *Genre Analysis: English in Academic and Research Settings.*
Cambridge: Cambridge University Press.

Tosi, C. (2015). Mitos y certezas en el discurso de la divulgación científica para chicos. Un análisis sobre la posición ante la doxa y la reinterpretación del topoi. In M. García Negroni (ed.), *Sujeto(s), Alteridad y Polifonía. Acerca de la Subjetividad en el Lenguaje y en el Discurso* (pp. 121–145). Buenos Aires: Ampersand. https://doi.org/10.15448/1984-7726.2016.1.21981

Toulmin, S. (1958). *The Use of Argument*. New York: Cambridge University Press.

Toulmin, S. (2003). *The Use of Argument* (Updated Edition). New York: Cambridge University Press.

Valerdi, J. C. (2016). La heteroglosia en la redacción académica en inglés: Una exploración de la propiedad lingüística en el ensayo académico universitario. In N. Ignatieva & D. Rodríguez-Vergara (eds.), *Lingüística Sistémica Funcional en México: Aplicaciones e Implicaciones* (pp. 147–176). México: Universidad Nacional Autónoma de México. https://doi. org/10.19130/iifl.adel.5.1.2017.1423

White, P. R. R. (2001). *An Introductory Tour Through Appraisal Theory.* Retrieved from http://grammatics.com/appraisal.

Wu, S. (2006). Creating a contrastive rhetorical stance: Investigating the strategy of problematization in students' argumentation. *Regional Language Centre Journal*, **37**(3), 329–353. https://doi. org/10.1177/0033688206071316

Wu, S. (2007). The use of engagement resources in high- and low-rated undergraduate geography essays. *Journal of English for Academic Purposes*, **6**, 254–271. https://doi.org/10.1016/j.jeap.2007.09.006

Zamudio, V. (2016). La expresión de opiniones y puntos de vista en textos académicos estudiantiles sobre literatura. *Lenguaje,* **44**, 35–39. https://doi. org/10.25100/lenguaje.v44i1.4629

Appendix A

Argumentative scheme in the introduction of thesis 13 (AIT13) in its original language. *Claims* in each subargument are located in cells from line C. *Data, warrants, backings,* and *rebuttals* are organized in lines D, W, B and R, respectively. This is a main subargument (α) supported by two *data* and a secondary subargument (β). The scheme includes a bare assertion (c). Both subarguments are supported by empirical *warrants*. The bare assertion is not justified; the space of its *warrant* is marked as "null." There are no *rebuttals* nor *qualifiers* in this argument. The scheme corresponds to argumentative pattern III.

	α			β				c
C	El área de la lingüística aplicada en que se inscribe este trabajo corresponde a la enseñanza de una segunda lengua en el nivel bachillerato y busca abordar la comprensión auditiva en inglés y la formación docente en ambientes digitales a la luz de los planteamientos metodológicos de la investigación-acción.			El desarrollo de la comprensión auditiva en los alumnos, en particular, ha ofrecido dificultades para la planta docente				que en la práctica resultan inadecuadas para solucionar los problemas específicos de percepción, comprensión y respuesta a textos orales.

D		Durante el ciclo 2009–2010 en los 5 planteles del Colegio de Ciencias y Humanidades -subsistema de bachillerato de la Universidad Nacional Autónoma de México- el enfoque de comprensión de lectura que predominó durante más de 20 años dio paso a la enseñanza de la lengua extranjera en sus "cuatro habilidades."	Surgió entonces la problemática de instrumentar un modelo de enseñanza-aprendizaje que no solo fomentara la autonomía del estudiante en el marco del modelo educativo del Colegio, sino que además integrara todas las habilidades lingüísticas para lograr "el desarrollo de la competencia comunicativa del alumno a un nivel básico … para … interactuar en una lengua extranjera acorde con sus necesidades académicas y personales,"		debido a la aparente similitud en cuanto a estrategias didácticas con aquellas usadas en la comprensión de textos escritos,	Además, existe la necesidad institucional de mejorar la vinculación entre el proceso de enseñanza/ aprendizaje, los medios electrónicos disponibles y los centros de auto-acceso recién instalados en cada plantel.		
W	EMPÍRICAL			EMPÍRICAL				NULL
B			según señala el objetivo general de la materia, (Aguilar et. al, 2011: 35).				Vandergrift (2007), a partir de su revisión de otros autores, señala que la comprensión auditiva en L2 es el área menos estudiada y la habilidad que mayores dificultades presenta para su enseñanza y evaluación.	

Appendix B

Argumentative scheme AIT1, from pattern I, in its original language. The main subargument (α) incorporates *data* and has additional support of a secondary subargument (β) which works as its *data*. Subarguments are supported by evaluative *warrants* as justificatory links between *data* and *claims*. No *backings* are included.

	α					β			
C	En el año de 2010, México celebró 200 años de haber iniciado su independencia como país, y 100 de haber iniciado la revolución que tuvo como primer objetivo terminar con un sistema de gobierno dictatorial. Esta conmemoración fue vigorosamente promovida por distintas instituciones tanto gubernamentales como privadas.					Por su parte, las distintas dependencias gubernamentales federales se erigieron como los principales artífices de la celebración y [...] sí podemos hablar de un derroche impresionante de recursos.			

D	Por ejemplo, ese año el torneo de fútbol de la primera división mexicana llevó por nombre "torneo bicentenario"	hubo además competencias de tenis, de regata y de otros deportes que llevaban la palabra "bicentenario(a)" dentro de sus nombres;	lo mismo sucedió en el plano artístico e incluso en el rubro comercial	(un caso destacado, o al menos curioso, es el de la relojería suiza Audermars Piguet, que produjo el reloj conmemorativo Royal Oak Offshore Pride of Mexico).	También instituciones como el Banco de México o Correos mexicanos produjeron monedas y timbres conmemorativos.		Según un informe1 de Banjército, fiduciario del "Fideicomiso del Bicentenario," los gastos realizados con motivo de estas celebraciones, registrados tan sólo del 21 de febrero de 2009 al 31 de agosto de 2010, alcanzaron la impresionante suma de mil 813 millones 196 mil 134 pesos.	Sin embargo, la suma total presupuestada tocó el techo de los 2 mil 971 millones 600 mil pesos	
W	EVALUATIVE					EVALUATIVE			
B									
R									si bien no podríamos calificar de fastuosas a la mayoría de las actividades realizadas por dichas dependencias,

Appendix C

Fragment of argumentative scheme AIT2, from pattern II, in its original language. The main argument (α) does not incorporate *data* in its subscheme, but it has three secondary subarguments (β1, β2 and γ) working as its "external" *data*. The role of the main subargument is marked by textual marker *por lo anterior* (*For all the previously mentioned*). Subargument β1 is justified by an *a priori* relation (of the kind "if something is x, then it is not y"). This fragment does not incorporate *backings*, *rebuttals* nor *qualifiers*.

	β1		*β2*		*γ*		*α*
C	En este sentido, el presente estudio contribuye a explorar el conocimiento que se tiene acerca de las redes semánticas entre los sistemas léxicos de la lengua materna y la lengua extranjera.		Este aspecto es importante también para la didáctica de segundas lenguas,		ya que es en el salón de clases donde se pueden hacer actividades para señalar la diferencia o similitud de los equivalentes significado en las dos lenguas.		Por lo anterior, consideramos que las características de adquisición de la L2 son determinantes para entender de forma integral las dificultades que enfrentan los estudiantes en los diferentes contextos del bilingüismo
D		Asimismo, se debe considerar la forma en que se procesa la nueva información de la L2 con el sistema lingüístico de la L1.		ya que es en el salón de clases donde se pueden hacer actividades para señalar la diferencia o similitud de los equivalentes significado en las dos lenguas.		ya que tiene implicaciones en cuanto a la adquisición del vocabulario, y específicamente al fenómeno de la transferencia,	
W	A PRIORI		EVALUATIVE		EMPÍRICAL		EMPÍRICAL

6 A functional study of Transitivity and Attitude in student writing in Spanish across disciplines: Making connections

Natalia Ignatieva, Daniel Rodríguez-Vergara and Victoria Zamudio Jasso
Applied Linguistics Department, National School of Languages, Linguistics and Translation, National Autonomous University of Mexico

Introduction

This chapter presents a systemic analysis of process types in academic texts in literature, history and geography from the Appraisal perspective. This work is part of the ongoing research study *Verbal typology and evaluation in academic writing of the humanities: a systemic functional study,* developed at the National Autonomous University of Mexico (UNAM), which, in turn, is included in the international *SAL* (*Systemics Across Languages*) project in its Latin American version (Scotta Cabral & Barbara, 2018a; 2018b). We had already participated in the *SAL* project with a lexicogrammatical analysis of verbal processes in student texts (Ignatieva, 2011; Ignatieva & Zamudio, 2012; Ignatieva & Rodríguez-Vergara, 2015). The present project extends this research to all types of processes, as our goal now is to explore how process types in Spanish are related to the expression of appraisal in academic texts. We used student texts from the CLAE corpus (*Corpus del Lenguaje Académico en Español*, or Corpus of Academic Language in Spanish), the product of one of our previous studies (Ignatieva & Colombi, 2014). The texts, collected at the Faculty of Arts, belong to three disciplines (literature, history and geography) but to only one type of text which is usually labelled as "essay" in the university setting.

In their analysis of different types of discourse, Martin & White (2005) mention that there exists a certain relation between ideational and interpersonal meanings and, as a consequence, between the systems of Transitivity and Appraisal. For that reason, our main goal is to examine this relation between process types and the expression of evaluation in the clauses containing them. In accordance with this, our study has to do with two levels of analysis (lexicogrammatical and discourse semantic) and two systems (Transitivity and Appraisal). Although there are studies which connect some process types with different kinds of evaluation (e.g., Chen, 2005; 2007; Hyland, 1999; Lavid, 2008) they do not treat this relation from the angle adopted in this work. Besides, since most of these studies explore English, taking a different language as a basis can enrich this exploration and add new aspects to it.

Our purpose is to explore how writers exploit process types to represent the outer and inner worlds and how interpersonal meanings unfold in student writing in the context of three disciplines: history, geography and literature. We are especially interested in what options students choose for encoding semantic categories of Attitude. The final result will be to observe the interaction of the two metafunctions (ideational and interpersonal) and the two systems (Transitivity and Attitude) and establish their relation to disciplines. Thus, a more delicate analysis of this interaction can give us a better understanding of their functioning in academic language. In addition, the results may have pedagogical implications for teaching academic writing within these disciplines.

Theoretical assumptions

SFL on metafunctions

Our study draws on Systemic Functional Linguistics (SFL) created by M. A. K. Halliday (1976, 1978, 1985, 1994) and developed by other exponents of this theory (Martin, 1985; 1992; Martin; Rose, 2003; Matthiessen, 1995; Thompson, 1996; etc.). The theory presents a holistic model of language and its social context which conceives language as a meaning construing resource.

The SFL model describes and explains language from multiple and complementary perspectives to provide a global vision of linguistic phenomena. One of the fundamental perspectives is functional. Halliday considers language as a system of meanings conditioned by its functions. He labels them *metafunctions*, i.e., the most abstract and general functions that are common to all human languages (Halliday & Matthiessen, 2014). These are three: the *ideational metafunction,* which reflects world reality and our experiences in the world, the *interpersonal metafunction,* which has to do with the interactions of participants and their opinions, feelings, etc., and the *textual metafunction,* which organizes the text. These metafunctions, which act and coexist in the language simultaneously, permit us to express three respective types of meaning: ideational, interpersonal and textual.

Ideational meanings and, in particular, experiential ones, are those that a writer or speaker manipulates to encode his experiences about the exterior and interior world; they are materialized in the clause via the linguistic system of Transitivity. Interpersonal meanings have to do with social relations, i.e., how people interact, how they express and exchange their opinions. Their basic systems are Mood, which defines the type of exchange (giving and demanding information or giving and demanding services); Modality, which expresses indeterminacy between the positive and negative poles; and Appraisal (Martin & White, 2005), which will be defined later. Textual meanings deal with information flow and they organize and distribute ideational and interpersonal meanings into a coherent text; they are realized through a system of Theme.

Thus, the metafunctional approach to analysis is important, as this approach can facilitate our recognizing the ways in which "interpersonal meanings relate to ideational choices in the discourse" (Hood, 2010). Therefore, our main interest concerns the interaction between the ideational and interpersonal meanings realized through the Transitivity and Appraisal systems, respectively.

Transitivity system

In construing the SFL architecture, Halliday takes a traditional concept of transitivity and gives it a new life. While in traditional grammar transitivity refers to a grammatical category of the verb, in SFL it represents a lexicogrammatical category of the clause (Matthiessen, 1999, p. 2). That means Halliday applied not only grammatical, but also semantic criteria to the phenomenon and extended it to the whole clause. Thus, systemic functional transitivity concerns different combinations of participants organized around a process in the clause. It refers to "a way of representing patterns of experience [...] of imposing order on the endless variation and flow of events" (Halliday, 1994, p. 106). In other words, it is the organization of the sentence which construes the world of experience into

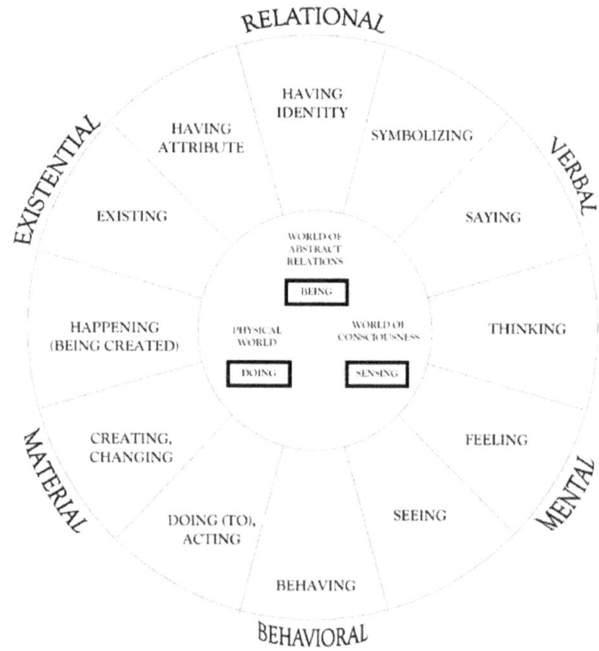

Figure 6.1 Transitivity "wheel" (taken from Matthiessen, 2018, p. 42)

a set of process types. Halliday first divided processes into three types, "material," "mental" and "relational" (Halliday 1968), and then he added three more types, "verbal," "behavioral" and "existential" (Halliday 1994), but he considered the original three as the main types while the types in the second group were thought of as "borderline" cases. Thus, the whole set of process types can be represented as a wheel (see Figure 6.1), which first appeared on the cover of the second edition of *Introduction to Functional Grammar* (Halliday, 1994).

Matthiessen (1995), however, extended the main types to four (material, mental, relational and verbal) and in this way he included verbal processes in the primary group, arguing that verbal processes have their own characteristic traits that set them apart from the other process types.

Appraisal system

The Appraisal system can be considered as an extension in the analysis of interpersonal meanings realized by Halliday (1994). Created within the research group known as the Sydney School (Martin, 1992; Martin & Rose,

2008), this model explores and describes evaluative aspects of language in a much more detailed way through a set of established categories (Martin & White, 2005). It permits us to describe the speaker's intersubjectivity in terms of systems. On the other hand, the Appraisal framework can also be seen as one of the systems of textuality, which gives cohesion to the text from the point of view of values, attitudes and the author's stance – and in this way contributes to textual coherence on the discursive semantic level.

The Appraisal system is divided into three subsystems: Attitude, Engagement and Graduation; here we shall analyze only one, Attitude. As a construct, Attitude models linguistic resources which are grouped under the term *evaluation* in some other theories (e.g. Thompson & Hunston, 2000). The subsystem of Attitude includes linguistic options to express emotions (*affect*), to appraise things and abstract entities using aesthetic criteria (*appreciation*) and to evaluate persons on the basis of ethical criteria (*judgment*). In accordance with that, the Attitude subsystem is also divided into three respective regions: Affect, Appreciation and Judgment (Martin & White, 2005, p. 35). Attitudes can be invoked or inscribed, i. e., clearly expressed with linguistic means. We are concerned here only with inscribed attitude.

Another important criterion to take into consideration is an attitude's polarity or orientation (Matthiessen, Teruya & Lam, 2010, p. 161), i.e., if an evaluation is positive or negative. We illustrate this with some examples from our corpora:

Affect/positive
1. *En la actualidad a Marc Bloch, le daría* **gusto** *encontrarse con que … (H4)*

   (At present, Marc Bloch would be **glad** to find out that …)
2. *Me atrevo sin* **temor** *a comparar esto … (G1)*

   (I dare without **fear** to compare this …)
3. *Don Quijote* **ama** *profundamente a su emperatriz (L5)*

   (Don Quixote deeply **loves** his empress)

Affect/negative
4. *Esto me* **disgusta** *totalmente (H3)*

   (I totally **dislike** this)
5. *El hoy lo dejamos de lado, [...] lo* **despreciamos** *(G5)*

   (We leave behind the present, […] we **despise** it)
6. *Don Quijote deja expresar una aguda* **angustia** *(L4)*

   (Don Quijote expresses a sharp **anguish**)

Appreciation/positive

7. *Este último punto es **importante*** (H6)
   (This last point is **important**)
8. *Un elemento **fundamental** para la ampliación de esas opciones* (G3)
   (A **fundamental** element for the expansion of those options)
9. *El discurso romántico es vasto de imágenes **preciosas*** (L3)
   (The romantic discourse is full of **beautiful** images)

Appreciation/negative

10. *La situación se torna **tensa*** (H9)
    (The situation becomes **tense**)
11. *El ejemplo más claro lo tenemos en la **escasa** oferta* (G4)
    (The clearest example we have is the **meager** offer)
12. *Las cosas del entorno aparecen **confusas*** (L2)
    (The surrounding things appear to be **confusing**)

Judgment/positive

13. *… considerados como **héroes** de la historia* (H6)
    (… considered as **heroes** of history)
14. ***Presumimos** de ser seres racionales* (G1)
    (We **boast** of being rational beings)
15. *No podemos olvidarnos de su **valentía y tenacidad*** (L2)
    (We cannot forget his **courage and persistence**)

Judgment/negative

16. *… denuncia los **atropellos** cometidos por los gobiernos* (H6)
    (… denounces the **outrages** committed by governments)
17. *… habla de la **incompetencia** de las autoridades para resolver situaciones inesperadas* (G2)
    (… talks about the **incompetence** of authorities to solve unexpected situations)
18. *El convite es aceptado por el **rudo** militar republicano* (L3)
    (The treat is accepted by the **tough** republican soldier)

To sum up, the model of Appraisal provides "a basis for a theoretically informed analysis of the interpersonal meanings" construed in the student texts (Hood, 2010). It is worth noting that most work on appraisal has been done analyzing English, while little research has been conducted in Spanish (Moss & Mizuno, 2015; Navarro, 2014; Perales-Escudero, 2018;

Rodríguez-Vergara & Contijoch, 2016; Zamudio Jasso, 2016). We believe, however, that the appraisal model in its basic terms has universal potential, i.e., it can be applied to Spanish or any other language. Therefore, there is a need for more applications of this model in order to prove its total or partial applicability and see if there is any specificity for particular languages.

Methodology of analysis

For this study, we analyzed 15 texts written by undergraduate students from the Faculty of Philosophy and Arts at UNAM. We used student texts from the CLAE corpus (*Corpus del Lenguaje Académico en Español*, or Corpus of Academic Language in Spanish), which was the product of one of our previous studies (Ignatieva & Colombi, 2014), made freely available on the internet[1]. We randomly chose five essays by students majoring in history, five in geography, and five in literature. All 15 texts were written as part of the students' regular workload in different courses and submitted voluntarily for analysis. As such, the history and geography texts were written by freshman students while the literature texts were written by senior students. Even if these texts come from different disciplines and therefore cover different topics, both faculty and students refer to them as "essays."

These essays, however, have different purposes and might actually be considered different genres (according to Martin & Rose's taxonomy, 2008). The literature essays, for instance, have to do with character and/or theme analysis of different literary works and have an evaluative purpose that brings them closer to the argumentative family of genres. The history texts deal with questions of defining history as a science and outlining its goals. Students have to compare different points of view in order to arrive at conclusions about the role of history in a modern society, so the texts can also be classified as arguments. Finally, the geography essays are concerned with the application of geographical theory to the study of public health issues such as emerging diseases, traditional medicine and medical care. Since their main purpose is to describe the relationship between the management of human resources and the development of geographic information systems, these texts contain the properties of the genre family known as reports.

Since our research group consists of three members, each one of us analyzed texts from a different discipline. One of our purposes was to observe if there were considerable differences or similarities as far as the Transitivity and Attitude resources employed by students are concerned. In addition,

Table 6.1 Number of clauses (verbal groups)

	Text 1	*Text 2*	*Text 3*	*Text 4*	*Text 5*	*TOTAL*
History	173	148	174	126	76	697
Literature	142	329	87	506	296	1,360
Geography	105	109	70	161	178	623

although our main focus was the variation among disciplines, we were also interested in observing if there were differences related to the experience of the students (freshman vs. senior).

The first step was to identify and quantify the verbal groups, and thus the number of clauses in each text. Whereas the number of clauses in history and geography essays is similar, literature essays are significantly longer (see Table 6.1). Despite this difference, as we will show later, we were able to compare the results from the three subcorpora by taking into account the proportion of units to be compared.

The following step was to determine the process type realized by every verbal group. Because Attitude expressions (the other aspect to be studied in connection with Transitivity) can occur in any linguistic fragment, all verbal groups were coded regardless of their finiteness and embeddedness. As a consequence, there were cases where several processes were coded in a single ranking clause:

> 19. *El presente escrito no tiene*[RELATIONAL] *por finalidad* [[*extenderse*[VERBAL] *o profundizar*[VERBAL] *en la idea* [[*que tengo*[RELATIONAL]]] *sobre la competitividad*]] (G1)
>
> (The present text does not have the objective of [[elaborating or delving into the idea [[I have]] about competitiveness]])[2]

The next step was to identify and quantify the evaluative expressions, which allowed us to determine the proportion of clauses that contained appraisal in each text. After that, each expression was coded as 1) affect, appreciation or judgment, and as 2) positive or negative evaluation. We built tables (see Table 6.2) where we inserted single clauses taken from the essays and where we identified the process type realized by each verbal group, whether it contained appraisal or not, the type of appraisal (where contained) and the orientation (positive/negative).

With the help of these tables, we identified the connections between the instantiations of Transitivity and Appraisal in the following way. A whole

Table 6.2 Fragment of a table used in the analysis (G2)

Clause (processes are underlined and attitude expressions in bold)	Process type	Attitude type (if present)	Orientation
En los últimos años la situación sanitaria mundial <u>ha estado dominada</u> por la prevalencia de las enfermedades transmisibles (In the last years the world's healthcare situation has been dominated by the prevalence of communicable diseases)	Material	Not present	–
*las cuales <u>representan</u> una **pesada** carga de morbilidad y mortalidad para muchos países, especialmente los subdesarrollados.* (which represent a heavy load of morbidity and mortality for many countries, especially the underdeveloped ones.)	Relational	Appreciation	Negative
*En ese panorama las llamadas enfermedades emergentes y reemergentes <u>ocupan</u> el lugar más **importante**.* (In that panorama the so-called emerging and re-emerging diseases hold the most important place.)	Relational	Appreciation	Negative
Hasta hace aproximadamente 30 años el impacto de las enfermedades trasmisibles <u>parecía</u> controlado como consecuencia de los progresos en la prevención específica y de la sanidad Until approximately 30 years ago the impact of communicable diseases seemed controlled as a consequence of the progress in specific prevention and healthcare	Relational	Not present	–
*al <u>disponer</u> de drogas **eficaces*** by having effective drugs available	Relational	Appreciation	Positive

clause was considered as an instantiation of a process type. Thus, if a clause contained, say, a mental process and an expression of affect, we counted it as an instance of co-occurrence between Transitivity and Appraisal and between "mental process" and "affect evaluation." With this information, we calculated the statistics concerning 1) ratio of clauses with a process type containing no appraisal; 2) ratio of clauses with a process type containing appraisal; and 3) ratio of clauses with a process type and a specific appraisal type. In this way, we suggest that there are either experiential meanings that trigger the expression of appraisal, or expressions of appraisal that trigger experiential meanings.

Results

Transitivity

When we compare the frequency of process types in the three corpora (see Figure 6.2), we observe similar trends: material and relational processes are the most frequent types; mental and verbal are in the middle of the chart; and existential and behavioral are the less frequent types. However, there are some particularities that deserve attention. First, the highest overall percentage is 38.20% belonging to relational processes in geography essays, which contain the lowest percentages of mental and verbal processes. The high frequency of relational processes in geography essays might be due to the fact that these texts are reporting and classifying in nature (Cope & Kalantzis, 1993). These texts give an account of the natural and social phenomena related to issues of health, medicine and disease. They usually start with a general classification of the particular phenomenon in question, followed by an account in terms of qualities, uses or habits. Here we present a fragment with extensive use of relational processes.

> 20. *Globalmente el año mas caluroso fue*[RELATIONAL] *el de 1998 y los noventas fueron*[RELATIONAL] *la década mas caliente de la cual se ha tenido*[RELATIONAL] *registro; muchos países principalmente de latitudes medias y altas han tenido*[RELATIONAL] *un aumento en la cantidad de precipitación anual; en algunas regiones de Asia y África las sequías se han intensificado*[MATERIAL] *en la última década; fenómenos como el Niño han sido*[RELATIONAL] *mas frecuentes, intensos y persistentes desde la década de los setentas.* (G4)

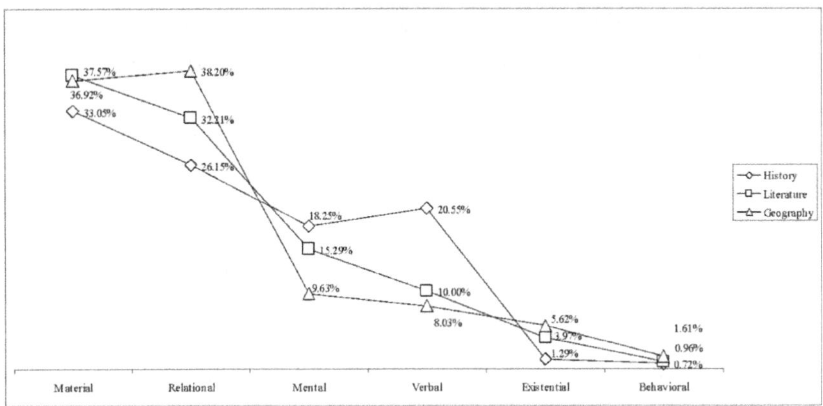

Figure 6.2 Process type frequency

(Globally, the hottest year was 1998, and the 1990s was the hottest decade ever registered; many countries (mainly those of mid to high latitude) have had an increase in the quantity of annual precipitation; in some regions of Asia and Africa, droughts have intensified in the last decade; phenomena such as El Niño have been more frequent, intense and persistent since the decade of the 1960s.)

On the other hand, history essays contain the highest percentages of mental and verbal processes. The percentage of mental processes in history essays is double that of geography essays (18.2% and 9.6% respectively), whereas the percentage of verbal processes in history is double that in literature (20.5% to 10%), and more than double that of geography (8%). One final particularity is that history essays have the lowest percentages of material and relational processes. In sum, there seems to be a correlation between material/relational experience and the geography discipline, and another one between mental/verbal experience and the history discipline. An extract from a history text with verbal and mental processes is presented in (20).

21. *... esta subjetividad inherente al historiador cómo lo menciona*[VERBAL] *Gaos en sus "Notas sobre la historiografía"; una subjetividad que también recalca*[VERBAL] *Hobsbawm en su texto al hacer mención*[VERBAL] *de que, cuando un historiador escribe no puede dejar de lado sus vivencias, y menos en un tema tan delicado cómo el de las matanzas alemanas que trata*[VERBAL] *él; y del mismo modo, nos*

*sentiremos*MENTAL *tentados a interpretar*MENTAL *nuestros descubrimientos de la manera más favorable a nuestra causa.* (H1).
(… this subjectivity inherent to a historian as Gaos mentions it in his "Notes about the historiography"; a subjectivity that Hobsbawm emphasizes in his text, having mentioned that when a historian writes he cannot leave behind his experiences, and less so in such a delicate theme as the one of German killings which he treats; and in the same way, we shall feel tempted to interpret our discoveries in the most favorable manner for our cause.)

As we have already mentioned, history texts deal with different perspectives on the subject of history as discipline and its role in modern society; consequently, as students describe what historical authors think and say on the topic, they also have to argue in order to take sides and express their own opinions based on their interpretations of different points of view. Thus, the use of verbal (*mencionar, recalcar, tratar*) and mental (*sentir, interpretar*) processes is justified and logical. We may deduce that among the most important functional meanings in history texts of our corpus are arguing, interpreting and criticizing, which might be a discipline characteristic.

In literature, on the other hand, material and relational processes appear in 37.5% and 32.2% of the clauses respectively. These two processes combined represent nearly 70% of the total number of processes in the texts. As mentioned, student literature texts are mostly based on the analysis of characters and/or themes in a literary work. On the one hand, these texts establish relationships between different elements of a literary work and provide an interpretation for them, as in the following example:

22. *[el autor]* *tomó*RELATIONAL *[la ciudad] como escenario idóneo para retratar*MATERIAL *los males sociales que había que erradicar*MATERIAL. *La provincia representa*RELATIONAL *el atraso e incluso la inocencia de los integrantes de la familia protagonista, ya que todo lo citadino es*RELATIONAL *para ellos motivo de asombro.* (L9)
([the author] took [the city] as an ideal scenario to portray the social ills that had to be eradicated. The province represents the backwardness and even the innocence of the members of the main family, since everything in the city is a source of astonishment for them.)

Therefore, literature texts, as those in geography, have a strong presence of material and relational processes. However, they also have a higher number of mental and verbal processes, which may be explained by the students' choice of focusing their analysis on the characters in the literary work, their actions, thoughts and sayings. The processes in literature texts indicate that the students' construction of meanings is related mostly to functions such as narration, description and interpretation.

In the section below 'Transitivity and Appraisal' we will show the results of the analysis of the processes whose host clauses contain attitudinal meaning.

Appraisal

Regarding the analysis of Appraisal, the main question we wanted to explore was the presence of inscribed Attitude in the texts. From the total number of clauses in the texts, we took only those in which an explicit element of evaluation was present. To be able to establish a comparison between the texts in spite of the difference in length, we considered solely the percentage of evaluative clauses in each discipline. As we can see in Figure 6.3, history and geography texts show very similar results; in both cases the number of clauses with evaluation is close to 50%. However, in the literature essays (the middle columns) the amount of attitude expressed is significantly lower, with only 25% of evaluative clauses. Considering that the literature essays were, as mentioned, written by students in their senior year, the lower percentage may indicate the choice of different, more invoked, evaluative resources.

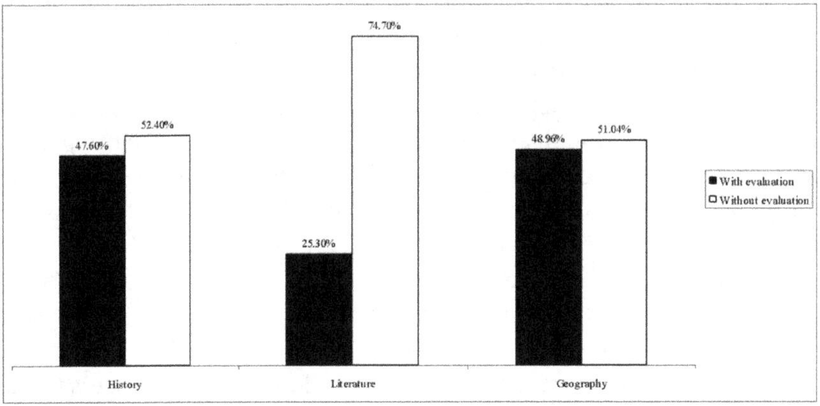

Figure 6.3 Percentage of evaluative and non-evaluative clauses

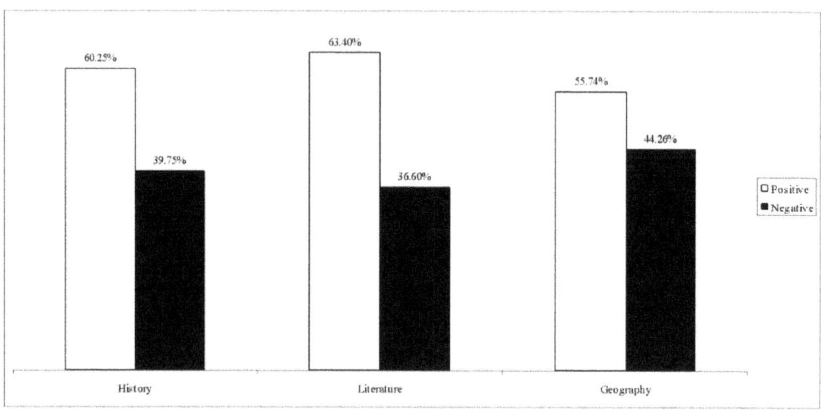

Figure 6.4 Polarity in students' attitudinal expressions

For the next step in the analysis, we examined the attitudinal polarity of those clauses where inscribed Attitude is expressed; that is, we identified whether the values expressed in the texts were positive or negative. Figure 6.4 shows how evaluation is predominantly positive in all disciplines. In literature and history, a positive attitudinal polarity is present in more than 60% of all evaluative clauses while in geography texts it appears in 55% of the instances, showing thus a slightly higher amount of negative expression of attitude.

The third aspect to explore regarding the expression of evaluation was the type of attitudinal meanings present in the essays. All instances of attitude were therefore classified in terms of Affect, Judgment and Appreciation. In Figure 6.5 we can see that, as is the case in most academic discourse, Appreciation is the preferred form of evaluation overall. In all three disciplines, it represents more than half of all attitudinal expressions.

However, even if the expression of evaluation in terms of Appreciation is the most common kind in all these essays, it is interesting to note a greater number of instances of evaluation by Judgment in the case of literature and geography essays (almost 35% and 31% respectively) compared to history (19%) and a greater expression of Affect in the latter (17% in history, 13% in geography and only 7% in literature)[3].

We have presented the results from two types of analysis, Transitivity and Appraisal; in the following section we show how attitudinal expressions interact with patterns of Transitivity as expressed by the use of process types.

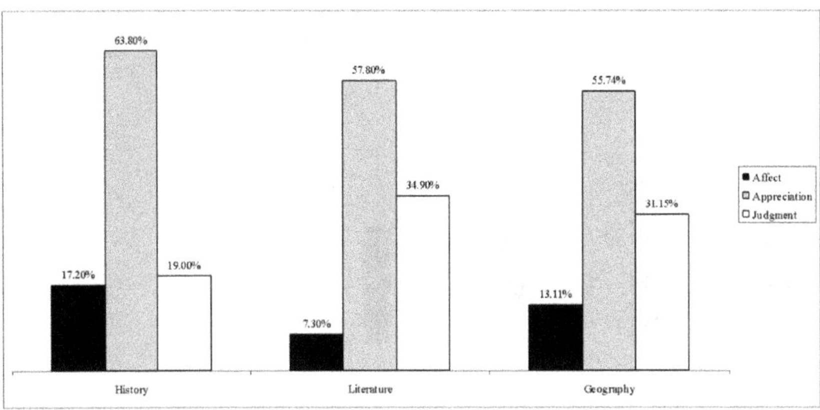

Figure 6.5 Type of Attitude in student texts

Transitivity and Appraisal

If we count only the processes whose host clauses contain attitudinal meaning (see Figure 6.6), the panorama looks very similar to the one in Figure 6.2 (overall transitivity) with the exception that now mental processes are more frequent than verbal ones in history essays. This suggests that the relationship between mental transitivity and attitude may be stronger than the one between verbal transitivity and attitude.

The idea of a stronger link between mental transitivity and attitude is supported by the data in Figure 6.7, where we observe that, of the total 127

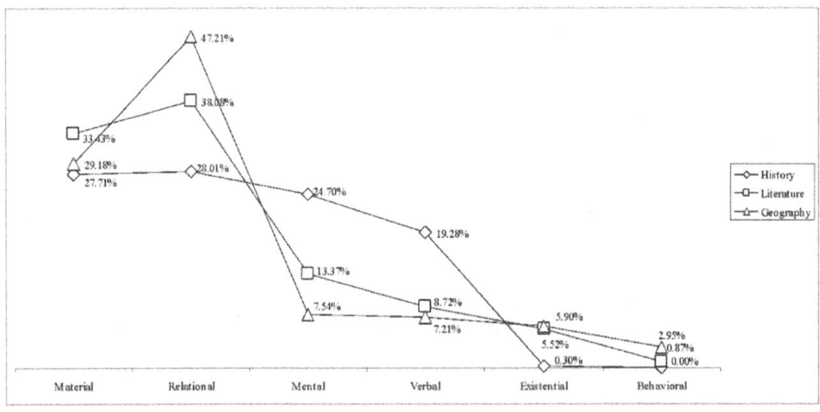

Figure 6.6 Frequency of processes that appear in clauses with attitude

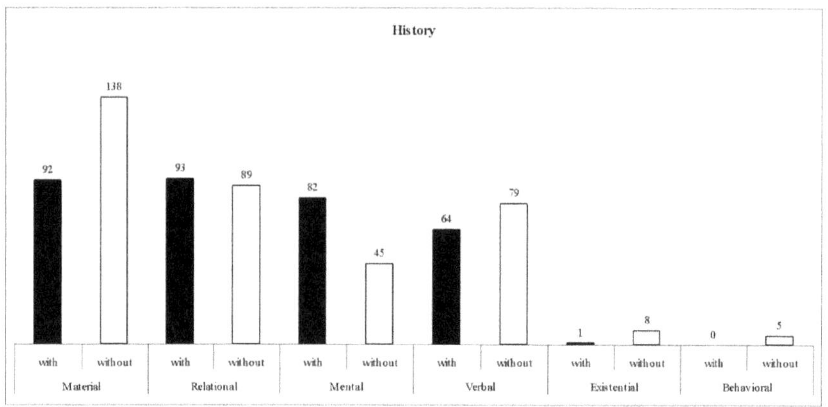

Figure 6.7 Process type tokens with and without attitude in history texts

mental processes in history essays, 82 (65%) appear in clauses with attitude, and 45 (35%) in clauses without attitude. In contrast, of the total 143 verbal processes in history essays, 64 (45%) appear in clauses with attitude, and 79 (55%) in clauses without attitude.

In history essays, both relational and mental processes have more instances that co-occur with attitude than instances that do not. In turn, considering now the data in Figure 6.8, in geography essays, there are three process types (relational, existential, and behavioral) whose instances that co-occur with attitude in clauses are more frequent than the ones that do not. The co-occurrence of relational process and attitude thus appears both

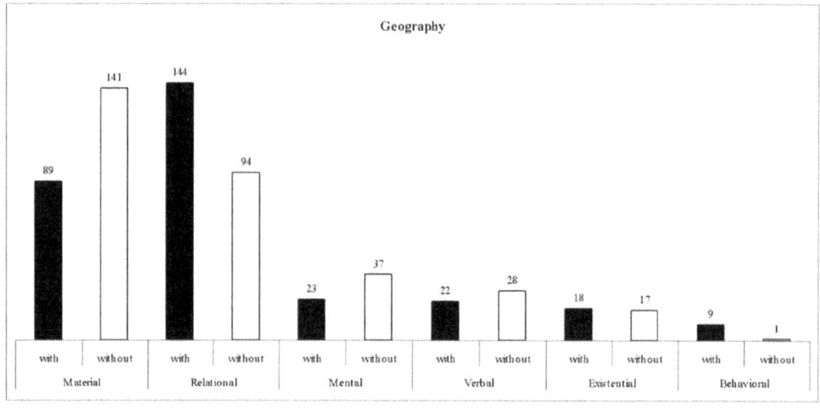

Figure 6.8 Process type tokens with and without attitude in geography texts

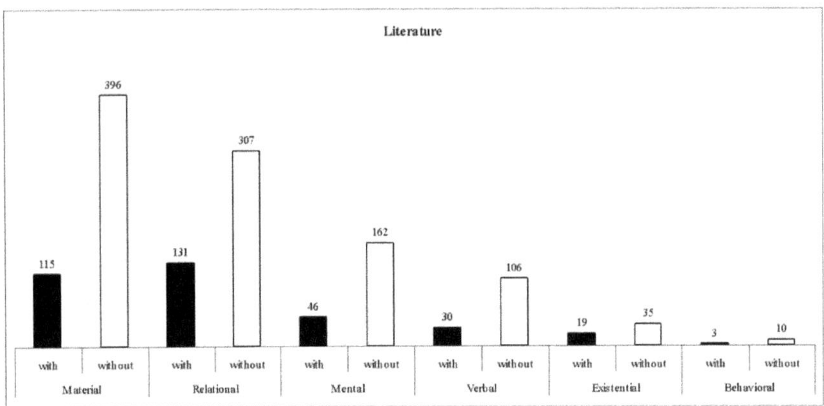

Figure 6.9 Process type tokens with and without attitude in literature texts

in geography and history essays, which indicates that relational processes show a stronger correlation with attitude than any other process type. However, we can also see that the picture is different in literature essays (Figure 6.9), where the instances that do not co-occur with attitude are always more frequent than the ones that do in all process types.

We will end this section with the exploration of the correlation between process type and attitude type. Due to their low frequency, existential and behavioral processes show unusual patterns, but if we consider the four other processes, we observe that, with one exception, Appreciation appears first in all of them, Judgment second, and Affect third (Figures 6.10–6.12).

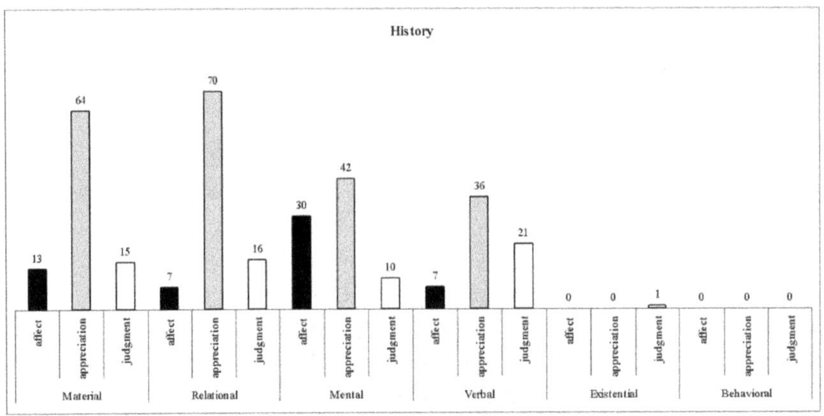

Figure 6.10 Process type tokens with specific attitude types in history texts

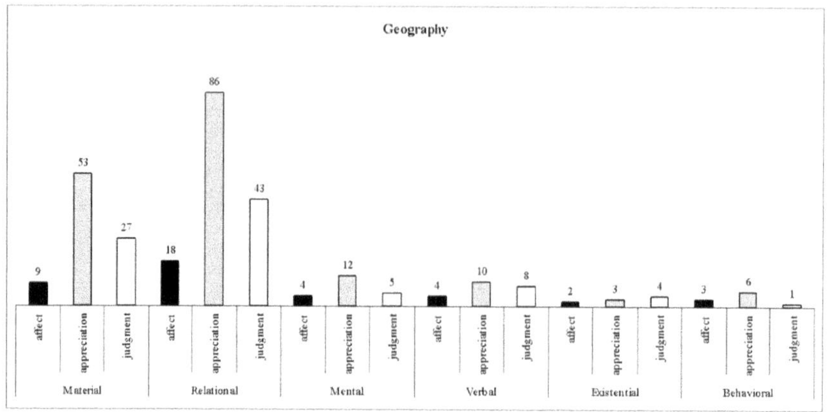

Figure 6.11 Process type tokens with specific attitude types in geography texts

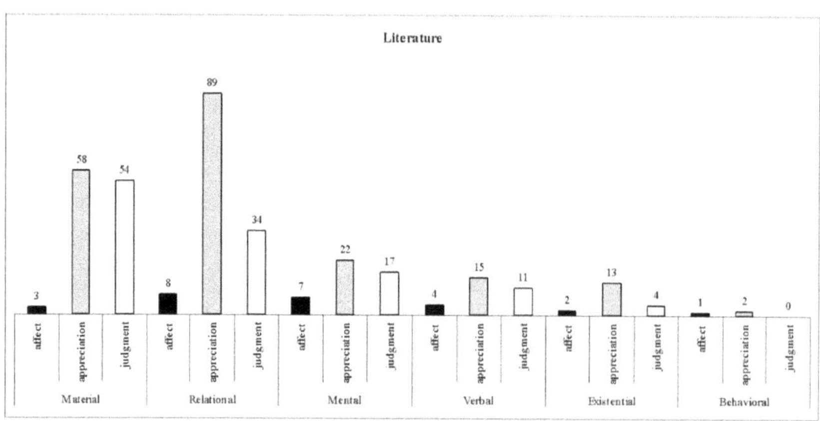

Figure 6.12 Process type tokens with specific attitude types in literature texts

The exception is found in history essays (Figure 6.10), where, as far as mental processes are concerned, Affect appears in second position, and Judgment in third.

Although behavioral processes have a low number of tokens, of the ten instances that appeared in geography essays, nine contained expressions of attitude in their host clauses: six with Appreciation, three with Affect and one with Judgment (Figure 6.11). As we already mentioned, the correlation between Transitivity and Attitude seems to depend on the field of discourse of the texts and their purpose. Even if they are referred to as "essays" by teachers and students, they present different rhetorical modes, and they belong to different domains of experience, sometimes even within each discipline. In the case of the geography essays, for example, the topics covered are emerging diseases, traditional medicine and health care, therefore, the use of (mainly negative) expressions of attitude within behavioral clauses may be one of the aspects triggered by their field of discourse.

Discussion

The main objective of the study presented here was to explore the relationship between ideational and interpersonal meanings by analyzing texts from three different disciplines within the humanities. First, ideational meanings were explored through the Transitivity system, specifically, through the analysis of the use of different process types. Material and relational processes were, as expected, the main types of processes used in all three disciplines; however, there are differences worth noting. In geography essays, for instance, there is a very clear preference for two types of processes: material and relational. These two represent more than 75% of all processes and it is the only field in which relational processes are slightly higher than material ones. Even though these two types of processes are also the most common in the other two fields, a difference can be seen in the percentage of use (69% in literature essays and 59% in history essays) which is lower in both. The highest percentage of relational processes in geography essays could be interpreted as a preoccupation of the authors to identify participants and attribute to them certain qualities (a potential context where evaluation can be used). It might also be due to the fact that, as already mentioned, geography essays are closer to the report genre, in terms of Martin & Rose's taxonomy (2008):

23. *El progreso en el ámbito de la educación es*[RELATIONAL] ***esencial***[APPRECIATION] *para el desarrollo humano por sí mismo, pero también lo es*[RELATIONAL] *por las relaciones [[que guarda*[RELATIONAL] *con la salud, la equidad y la adquisición de poder]]. Una vez más, el resultado es*[RELATIONAL] *el de un progreso* ***a medias***[APPRECIATION]. (G3)
    (Progress in terms of education is itself essential for human development, but also for the relationships [[that it has with healthcare, equity and power acquisition]]. One more time, the result is a halfway progress.)

The results of our analysis of geography texts show a frequent use of "being" and "having" clauses which supports the idea that the main purpose of these texts is informing and describing, bringing them closer to reports (Cope & Kalantzis, 1993). History and literature essays, on the other hand, are closer to the argumentative genres. They present and discuss points of view on a diversity of topics. The different purpose of these essays partly explains the differences found in the percentage of use of other process types as well. For instance, in geography texts, the other types of processes appear in less than 10% of the clauses. At the same time, mental and verbal processes are relatively more common in literature and, especially, history. Since Halliday (1994) considers verbal processes, along with existential and behavioral, as a "secondary" type in that they occupy an intermediate position between relational and mental ones, one would expect mental processes to be more frequent than verbal ones across corpora, as is the case in Matthiessen (2006). This is true in the case of literature and geography, where mental and verbal processes appear in similar amount, with mental processes in a slightly higher degree, but not in the case of history. History essays show the highest percentage of mental and verbal processes involved but in these texts verbal processes appear more frequently than mental ones. In fact, the amount of verbal processes in history texts (20.5%) is practically double the amount in the literature (10%) and geography (8%) texts. The increased use of verbal processes in history texts might be explained by the nature of the discipline itself, which is partly built by referencing past authors and texts. Other studies have also found that verbal processes are more frequent than mental ones (e.g. Banks, 2008, in scientific writing in English, and Martínez, 2016, in newspaper articles in Spanish), supporting the argument that verbal transitivity is one of the major experiential domains (Ignatieva, 2016).

On the other hand, interpersonal meanings were explored through Appraisal analysis focusing on the attitudinal meanings present in student texts. The results, in general terms, follow closely the kind of evaluation usually present in academic texts; that is, an increased use of positive attitude expressed through Appreciation (Hood, 2010). However, some differences in the frequency of use of inscribed instances of attitude and of the three types of attitude were found. Comparing the three disciplines included in this study, literature seems to be characterized by fewer instances of inscribed attitude. The low percentage of evaluative clauses in literature texts might be explained in part by a difference in the familiarity with academic discourse between the students who wrote the history and geography essays, in their freshman year of college, and the literature students who were all seniors. Familiarity and experience might be relevant as previous research on academic discourse (see Hood, 2004 for example) has shown that professional academic writing (published texts) has a greater amount of invoked attitude; that is, evaluation presented in a more implicit, subtle way. Given that in this study we only considered the expression of inscribed attitude, it is possible that freshman writers use evaluation in a more explicit way while seniors are more familiar with an implicit way of expressing attitude in their texts. However, previous studies of student literature texts (Zamudio Jasso, 2016; Macías, 2018) also show that essays written by freshman literature students have lower use of Attitude than was found in history and geography texts, which might indicate that evaluation within the field of literature is not as frequent and explicit as in other disciplines, regardless of the writers' familiarity with the discourse. Further exploration is needed to establish if this is due to a more covert realization of evaluation or to a different nature and function of the literature essay as a genre. In this regard, it might be useful to analyze published texts in the discipline to see how evaluative meanings are realized and thus be able to establish connections between student and published texts.

In comparison to literature, geography essays are more explicitly evaluative, as almost half the clauses (48.9%) in these texts have some kind of attitudinal meaning involved. These texts also have a higher degree of negative polarity in the values expressed. This might be explained by an apparent preference for attributing qualities to participants in a higher frequency than in the other two disciplines. As mentioned, the geography essays analyzed for this study center on issues of disease, medicine and health, which might explain the fact that geography students seem more inclined to attribute negative values than students from the other disciplines. However, it may also indicate the adoption of a more explicitly critical stance towards the participants, as we can see in these texts an increased presence of Judgment. Judgment is usually centered around the evaluation of people and their behavior and its higher presence in both geography and literature might be a reflection of a preference for focusing their critical stance in the attribution of qualities (mostly positive in literature, slightly more negative in geography) to people, whether real (in geography) or fictional (as might be the case in literature where the judgment of fictional characters is more common). History students have a clear preference for expressing values linked to the Appreciation of things, as more than 60% of the attitudinal meanings in their texts are realized in these terms. It may be deduced that they tend to evaluate things, happenings and events and, considerably less, historic figures. History texts also show a similar frequency in the use of evaluation in terms of Affect and Judgment (17% and 19% respectively) while texts in geography and literature show a clear preference for judgment over affect: in these two cases, instances of Judgment are almost three times more frequent than Affect. This might indicate that emotional responses towards real facts and characters related to history (and to a lesser degree geography) are more common in student texts than emotions towards fictional actions and characters as discussed in literature.

Finally, as mentioned, the results found both in the transitivity and the attitudinal analyses allow us to explore the interplay between these two systems. For instance, if we consider briefly the subtypes of Attitude within the Appraisal system, we can see that there might be an indication of a possible relationship between them and specific processes, but this again varies slightly among disciplines. Affect, for instance, appears more frequently in relational and mental clauses in literature essays but it is more clearly linked to relational processes in geography texts and, especially, to mental processes in history essays where mental processes frequently encode affect in their meaning (see examples 24 and 25). History texts also differ from literature and geography in the increased use of judgment linked to verbal processes, in this case verbal processes often introduce a projected clause that expresses some sort of judgment, as in (26).

24. *El texto que más me **gustó**MENTAL *fue el de Gurevich.* (H6)

    (The text that I liked most was the one from Gurevich)
25. *... en cambio a la otra le **interesa**MENTAL *el entretenimiento y la evasión del presente.* (H6)

    (... on the contrary, the other is interested in the entertainment and evasion of the present)
26. *... y menciona*VERBAL *que es necesario encontrar reglas de aceptabilidad.* (H1)

    (... and he mentions that it is necessary to find rules of acceptability)

Even if further exploration is needed to be able to establish clearer links between types of processes and types of Attitude, with our analysis we have found two important connections: one between relational clauses and Attitude (mainly Appreciation) in history and geography essays, and another between mental clauses and Attitude (significantly Affect) in history essays. In a future stage of our investigation, it will be important to determine the proportion of identifying and attributive subtypes in relational clauses in order to know if one of those types triggers more use of appraisal. It will also be important to determine the subtypes of mental clauses, as well as the participant role that is the target of the attitudinal expression. Thus, instead of taking into account the structural units (nominal group, verbal group, etc.) as realizations of appraisal, it will be important to take into consideration the experiential function of the participant roles.

Conclusions

This study is the first approach to an analysis that attempts to explore the relationship between ideational and interpersonal meanings by considering both the Transitivity and the Appraisal systems and establishing a connection between them. It was done by analyzing texts from three different disciplines within the area of humanities: history, literature and geography. As we have seen, the analysis shows similarities in the use of elements in both systems and differences that could be explained by field and disciplinary discourse conventions as well as students' familiarity with them.

Even if it is extremely difficult to make some kind of generalization based on only a few texts, in terms of disciplinary discourse, our study showed a different use of process types that may be due to the different purpose of the texts in each discipline. These texts might receive the same name – essay – in the academic setting of humanities studies, but results point to the fact that they can be considered different genres as they seem to realize and emphasize different meanings. A higher number of certain process types in each discipline may be related to preferences in the functional meanings deployed in student texts such as arguing and criticizing in history, narrating and describing in literature, and reporting and classifying in geography. In this sense, however, a deeper analysis is needed to determine the genre(s) they are exemplars of with more detail. At the same time, the choice of process types can also be related to differences in disciplinary preference for certain academic conventions, such as the use of verbal processes and the frequency of attribution, which appears to be more common in history than in geography and literature.

On the other hand, the field of study of each discipline and the participants students refer to in their texts could also be related to differences found in the types of attitudinal meanings. The increase of expressions of judgment in geography and literature and of affect in history, for example, point towards differences in the kind of values expressed by students in different fields. At the same time, the higher presence of inscribed attitude in texts written by freshmen students (as compared to the senior students of literature) can signal the development of students' evaluative resources. In that regard, the analyses of published texts in different disciplines is needed to better understand how experts use these resources and thus have a better understanding of disciplinary discourses and of students' development and familiarity with them.

This study has also allowed us to explore the interaction of Transitivity and Appraisal in academic texts written in Spanish. Given the relatively few studies that consider student discourse in this language, the study is also a step towards a better understanding of how these systems work and the resources involved for their realization in a language other than English. Both systems have proven to be applicable to this study of academic discourse in Spanish. We have previously mentioned a universal potential of the Appraisal model and this assumption was confirmed by our analysis. However, it would be important to expand the analysis to include not only more texts but to consider all the possibilities that this study has shown it terms of its scope. Given the differences found in the polarity and types of evaluation, it might be interesting to explore the link between Appraisal and Transitivity – not only in terms of process types but also in terms of the participants, thus establishing a clearer picture of the relationship between the kind of experience and knowledge each discipline builds and the position that is taken towards specific parts of it.

Summing up, the analysis of these fifteen texts – five of each discipline – has allowed us to approach the interaction of two metafunctions and two systems in student writing. This has given us a brief glimpse at how university students construe the world in their respective disciplines and position themselves towards it at the beginning of their academic life. However, we need to consider more texts and different genres to have a better picture of how meanings are construed in each discipline. Further studies, currently in development, will allow us to see more closely the interactions at play in the discourse of the humanities.

About the authors

Natalia Ignatieva has a PhD in Theoretical Linguistics and an MA in Applied Linguistics. She is currently working at the National School of Languages, Linguistics and Translation (National Autonomous University of Mexico). She is a lecturer in linguistics, psycholinguistics, and second language acquisition at the postgraduate program in linguistics. As a researcher she works at the Department of Applied Linguistics and she is a member of the National Research System (National Counsel for Science and Technology of Mexico). Her research interests include second language acquisition, pedagogic grammar, systemic functional linguistics and discourse analysis and she has published widely in these areas.

Daniel Rodríguez-Vergara is a full time researcher at the Applied Linguistics Department of the National School of Languages, Linguistics and Translation of the National Autonomous University of Mexico (UNAM). He obtained a PhD in Linguistics, an MA in Applied Linguistics at UNAM, and a BA in Modern Languages at the Meritorious Autonomous University of Puebla. His main academic interests have been in the fields of systemic functional linguistics (SFL), discourse analysis, academic writing in L2, and translation studies. Within SFL he has studied logico-semantic relations, transitivity, appraisal, thematic structure, etc. He has also developed research within Rhetorical Structure Theory and English for Specific Purposes.

Victoria Zamudio Jasso has a PhD in Linguistics and an MA in Applied Linguistics from the National Autonomous University of Mexico (UNAM). She currently works as a full-time associate professor in the Applied Linguistics Department of the National School of Languages, Linguistics and Translation at the UNAM. Recently, she has developed and taught courses on the pedagogy of writing, ESP and academic discourse analysis at the undergraduate and graduate programs in Applied Linguistics. Her main academic and research interests include the use of evaluative language (including work within the appraisal framework), the analysis of academic discourse, (focusing mainly on the analysis of student texts), the development of academic literacies and the teaching of writing and reading for academic purposes.

Notes

1. URL: http://www.lenguajeacademico.info/
2. This fragment is meant to illustrate the coding of processes in the analysis, it does not have any expression of ATTITUDE.

Acknowledgement

The project *Verbal typology and attitude evaluation in the academic writing of the humanities: A systemic functional study* (IN401716) is carried out thanks to a grant from the National Autonomous University of Mexico.

References

Banks, D. (2008). *The Development of Scientific Writing: Linguistic Features and Historical Context*. London: Equinox.

Chen, L. (2005) Transitivity in media texts: Negative verbal process sub-functions and narrator bias. *International Review of Applied Linguistics in Language Teaching*, **43**, 33–51. https://doi.org/10.1515/iral.2005.43.1.33

Chen, L. (2007) Analysing attitude: Positive verbal process sub-functions and media bias. *RASK, International Journal of Language and Communication*, **25**, 25–55.

Cope, B. & Kalantzis, M. (1993). Introduction: How a genre approach to literacy can transform the way writing is taught. In B. Cope & M. Kalantzis (eds.), *The Powers of Literacy: A Genre Approach to Teaching Writing* (pp. 1–23). London: Routledge. https://doi.org/10.4324/9780203149812

Halliday, M. A. K. (1968). Notes on transitivity and theme in English. *Journal of Linguistics*, **4**, 179–215.

Halliday, M. A. K. (1976). *System and Function in Language*. London: Oxford University Press.

Halliday, M. A. K. (1978). *Language as Social Semiotic: The Social Interpretation of Language and Meaning.* London: Arnold.

Halliday, M. A. K. (1985). *Spoken and Written Language*. Geelong: Deakin University Press.

Halliday, M.A.K. (1994). *An Introduction to Functional Grammar* (2nd edition). London: Arnold.

Halliday, M. A. K. & Matthiessen, C. M. I. M. (2014). *Halliday's Introduction to Functional Grammar.* London: Routledge.

Hood, S. (2004) *Appraising Research: Taking a Stance in Academic Writing*. Unpublished doctoral dissertation. University of Technology.

Hood, S. (2010). *Appraising Research: Evaluation in Academic Writing*. London: Palgrave Macmillan.

Hyland, K. (1999). Academic attribution: Citation and the construction of disciplinary knowledge. *Applied Linguistics,* **20**, 341–67. https://doi.org/10.1093/applin/20.3.341

Ignatieva, N. (2011). Verbal processes in student academic writing in Spanish from a systemic functional perspective. *Lenguaje*, **39**, 447–467. https://doi.org/10.25100/lenguaje.v39i2.4939

Ignatieva, N. (2016). Reflexiones sobre los procesos verbales en el marco sistémico. In N. Ignatieva & D. Rodríguez-Vergara (eds.), *Lingüística Sistémico Funcional en México: Aplicaciones e Implicaciones* (pp. 35–48). Mexico: UNAM. https://doi.org/10.19130/iifl.adel.5.1.2017.1423

Ignatieva, N. & Zamudio, V. (2012). Perspectiva funcional de los procesos verbales en los escritos estudiantiles de literatura e historia en español. *DELTA*, **28**, 561–579. https://doi.org/10.1590/s0102-44502012000300007

Ignatieva, N. & Rodríguez-Vergara, D. (2015). Verbal processes in academic language in Spanish: Exploring discourse genres within the systemic functional framework. *Functional Linguistics*, **2**, 1–10. https://doi.org/10.1186/s40554-015-0014-9

Ignatieva, N. & Colombi, C. (eds.) (2014). *El Lenguaje Académico en México y los Estados Unidos: Un Análisis Sistémico Funcional*. Mexico: UNAM. https://doi.org/10.1353/hpn.2016.0122

Lavid, J. (2008). The grammar of emotion in English and Spanish: A systemic-functional approach. In C. Jones & E. Ventola (eds.), *From Language to Multimodality: New Developments in the Study of Ideational Meaning* (pp. 67–85). London: Equinox.

Macías, T. (2018). *Estudio ideacional e interpersonal de la expresión de Actitud en la escritura académica desde la lingüística sistémico-funcional*. Unpublished masters dissertation. Universidad Nacional Autónoma de México. https://doi.org/10.19053/0121053x.4910

Martin, J. R. (1985). *Factual Writing: Exploring and Challenging Social Reality*. Oxford: Oxford University Press.

Martin, J. R. (1992). *English Text: System and Structure*. Philadelphia: John Benjamins.

Martin, J. R. & Rose, D. (2003). *Working with Discourse: Meaning Beyond the Clause*. London: Continuum.

Martin, J. R. & Rose, D. (2008). *Genre Relations: Mapping Culture*. London: Equinox.

Martin, J. R., & White, P. R. R. (2005). *The Language of Evaluation*. New York: Palgrave Macmillan.

Martínez, V. (2016). Una aproximación al discurso económico en textos periodísticos. In N. Ignatieva & D. Rodríguez-Vergara (eds.), *Lingüística Sistémico Funcional en México: Aplicaciones e Implicaciones* (pp. 79–98). Mexico: Universidad Nacional Autónoma de México. https://doi.org/10.19130/iifl.adel.5.1.2017.1423

Matthiessen, C. M. I. M. (1995). *Lexicogrammatical Cartography: English Systems*. Tokyo: International Language Sciences.

Matthiessen, C. M. I. M. (1999). The system of Transitivity: An exploratory study of text-based profiles. *Functions of Language*, **6**, 1–51. https://doi.org/10.1075/fol.6.1.02mat

Matthiessen, C. M. I. M. (2006). Frequency profiles of some basic grammatical systems: An interim report. In G. Thompson & S. Hunston (eds.), *System and Corpus: Exploring Connections* (pp. 103–142). London: Equinox.

Matthiessen, C. M. I. M. (2018). Transitivity in systemic functional linguistics: Achievements and challenges. In S. R. Scotta & L. Barbara (eds.), *Estudos de Transitividade em Linguística Sistêmico-Funcional* (pp. 14–108). Santa Maria: PPGL Editores.

Matthiessen, C. M. I. M., Teruya, K. & Lam, M. (2010). *Key Terms in Systemic Functional Linguistics*. London: Continuum.

Moss, G. & Mizuno, J. (2015). Las voces del texto. In N. Barletta & D. Chamorro (eds.), *El Texto Escolar y el Aprendizaje: Enredos y Desenredos*, 2nd Edition (pp. 89–117). Barranquilla: Editorial Universidad del Norte. https://doi.org/10.4067/s0718-09342015000200006

Navarro, F. (2014). Gradación y compromiso en escritura académica estudiantil de humanidades: Análisis contrastivo desde la Teoría de la Valoración. *Estudios de Lingüística Aplicada*, **60**, 9–33.

Perales-Escudero, M. D. (2018). Writer–reader interaction in economics abstracts in English and Spanish: Implications for teaching and translation. *MEXTESOL Journal*, **42**, 1–16.

Rodríguez-Vergara & Contijoch (2016). Transitividad y valoración de la actitud en ensayos de geografía: Un análisis sistémico-funcional. *Signos Lingüísticos*, **23**, 8–29.

Scotta, S. R. & Barbara, L. (eds.) (2018a). *Estudos Sistêmico-Funcionais no Âmbito do Projeto SAL*. Santa Maria: PPGL Editores.

Scotta, S. R. & Barbara, L. (eds.) (2018b). *Estudos de Transitividade em Linguística Sistêmico-Funcional*. Santa Maria: PPGL Editores.

Thompson, G. (1996). *Introducing Functional Grammar*. London: Arnold.

Thompson, G. & Hunston, S. (2000). Evaluation: An introduction. In S. Hunston & G. Thompson (eds.), *Evaluation in Text: Authorial Stance and the Construction of Discourse* (pp. 1–27). Oxford: Oxford University Press. https://doi.org/10.1177/14614456020040041104

Zamudio Jasso, V. (2016). La expresión de opiniones y puntos de vista en textos académicos estudiantiles sobre literatura. *Lenguaje*, **44**, 35–39. https://doi.org/10.25100/lenguaje.v44i1.4629

Zamudio Jasso, V. (2017). *El Estudiante Ante el Texto: Caracterización de los Recursos de Posicionamiento del Estudiante-Escritor*. Unpublished doctoral dissertation. Universidad Nacional Autónoma de México. https://doi.org/10.2307/3537356

7 Scaffolding the wave: Supporting student teachers in professional academic writing through LCT and SFL

Anna-Vera Meidell Sigsgaard and
Susanne Karen Jacobsen
Copenhagen University College, Copenhagen,
Denmark

Introduction

Supporting tertiary students in developing academic writing skills appears to be a universal need, an assumption supported by the presence of learning and writing centers found at colleges and universities worldwide (see for example Coffin & Donohue, 2012; Lillis, Harrington, Lea, & Mitchell, 2015). This is also the case in undergraduate teacher-education programs which require students to write papers connecting theories of learning and teaching to educational practice, presenting accumulated curriculum knowledge for evaluation (Lillis, 2001; Lillis et al., 2015; Schmidt, 2001; Swales & Feak, 2005). Scaffolding students in developing their understanding of curriculum content, by providing them with simple yet powerful analytical tools focused on how meaning is made in texts, builds their awareness of what counts as legitimate knowledge in their field of study (Clarence, 2015; Humphrey & Dreyfus, 2012; Kirk, 2017; Mahboob, Dreyfus, Humphrey & Martin, 2010). This chapter explores the above claim, showcasing an example from a pre-service (undergraduate) teaching degree program in Denmark, while focusing on scaffolding pre-service student teachers' academic writing skills.

Similar to higher education students in other professional degree programs, pre-service teachers in Denmark exhibit difficulty writing about practice in a theoretically-informed way (Nielsen, Henningsen, Laursen, &

Paulsen, 2006). Providing academic literacy support in "academic language centers" is only partially helpful in developing students' academic writing skills (Griffin, 1982). Incorporating writing support within the disciplines, on the other hand, is an effective way of supporting students' academic writing at all levels of study (see for example Coffin & Donohue, 2012; Lillis et al., 2015; Macken-Horarik, 2006; Rose & Martin, 2012).

The work reported on in this chapter is situated, more specifically, in an obligatory second-language education module, providing a unique opportunity to support students' written academic language development, while at the same time modelling and reflecting the kind of scaffolding work students will be expected to provide for their future pupils once they become practicing teachers. Based on our analyses of high- and low-achieving written exams from this module, we suggest a number of ways of scaffolding the students' writing. Our focus here is on the analysis section in these exams, as this in particular is the section of their exam where students demonstrate their ability to combine what they know (theoretical concepts) with what they see (educational materials and practice).

Context of the study – The *Teaching bilingual pupils* module

The work presented here is set in the context of a teaching degree program at one of the largest teacher-training institutions in Denmark. As part of the undergraduate teaching degree, students must successfully pass a number of obligatory so-called "competency area exams". One of these is a written-only exam, following the *Teaching bilingual pupils* module. This exam is a type of research paper based on a research question formulated by the students themselves. The research question takes its point of departure from a nationally set prompt, which requires students to present relevant theoretical knowledge from the module and apply it to analyze an aspect of pedagogical practice. Doing so in an academically appropriate register is therefore paramount.

The *Teaching bilingual pupils* module is meant to prepare students in accommodating the Danish public school's growing population of bilingual pupils in order to support both their second language and subject-knowledge development. Key in this module is the students' ability to integrate theory with practice; reflecting on their practice, applying a theoretical lens, as well as inform their practice with theory. In the teaching degree program, this module is placed in students' third semester, meaning the average student is still early in his or her teaching degree program without much academic writing experience. The ten page maximum, prescribed by the national prompt, calls for a longer paper than students have yet written at the tertiary level. At the same time, the module's curriculum content draws on fields of second language education, educational linguistics, sociology and cultural studies, covering a wide range of knowledge and competency objectives. As a result, this exam is associated with high levels of anxiety for many of our students.

The *Teaching bilingual pupils* exam is currently the only one in the teaching degree program which does not include an oral component, making students' ability to communicate appropriately in writing within the recognized professional academic genre particularly important. In this exam, students must analyze an educational situation, a teaching unit and/or teaching material(s) from one of their major subject areas, on the basis of relevant problematics of teaching second language pupils within the mainstream classroom. Furthermore, students must provide suggestions for pedagogic practice in order to accommodate bilingual pupils' learning in the relevant academic subject. In this, the exam for this module reflects a common type of undergraduate assignment in professional degree programs, in which students must display their understanding of the module's curriculum by reflecting on aspects of pedagogic practice (either actually experienced or hypothetical) and interpreting these in terms of relevant theoretical concepts and ideas (Nesi & Gardner, 2012). The exam paper usually follows a predictable structure: an introduction, a problem statement, a presentation of applied theory, a presentation of data, an analysis section, a conclusion, suggestions for pedagogic practice and a bibliography.

Theory overview

The theoretical framework in this chapter draws both on Legitimation Code Theory (LCT) and systemic functional linguistics (SFL). Together, these provide complementary perspectives for analyzing the analysis sections of the *Teaching bilingual pupils* exams. Both LCT and SFL provide extensive analytical tools useful in analyzing meaning as it is construed through text. Their mutual compatibility is ongoing and demonstrated in studies focusing on education at different levels and within various subjects (see for example Christie, 2016; Doran, 2017; Macnaught, Maton, Martin, & Matruglio, 2013b; J. L. Martin, 2013; James R. Martin & Maton, 2017).

To facilitate understanding, we have chosen to present each theory and analysis separately, first presenting the chosen concepts from LCT and the corresponding analysis, followed by the chosen elements from SFL and the Appraisal framework, each followed by corresponding analyses.

From Legitimation Code Theory the concept of *semantic gravity* refers to the relative context-dependence of meanings (Maton, 2014). Research suggest that academic writing exhibiting so-called *semantic waves* is perceived as more successful (Christie, 2016; Clarence & McKenna, 2017; Kirk, 2017; Szenes, Tilakaratna, & Maton, 2015). We explain semantic gravity and its application in the section of this chapter titled "Semantic gravity and semantic waves: identifying passages between theory and practice". Here we first explain the concepts, showing how they manifest in our data. We then use this analysis to identify those passages in the collected exams' analysis sections which are "between theory and practice" so to speak: passages in which students connect what they see (educational practice) with what they know (theoretical understandings), either generalizing from examples, or vice versa, exemplifying from theory. Our analysis in this section illustrates how a high-achieving exam compares to a below-average exam when seen from the perspective of semantic waves. This identifies passages of interest which we subsequently examine further.

In order to explore how students are more or less successful in their attempts to connect theory with data, the passages identified in the LCT analysis are subsequently explored by applying elements from SFL (Derewianka, 2012; Derewianka & Jones, 2012; Halliday & Matthiessen, 2014; Mulvad, 2009), including SFL's Appraisal framework (Martin & White, 2005; Martin & Rose, 2007; White, 2015), in the chapter's section titled "Using SFL to explore how language creates meaning in the middle range of the semantic gravity range". Here the focus is on elucidating some of the linguistic resources students utilize when doing the work of meaningfully connecting theory to practice or vice versa. As with the chapter's section on LCT, we present relevant SFL resources, explaining these with reference to how these manifest in our data, facilitating an understanding of the correlated SFL analyses. When discussing the meanings of these analyses, we also connect to the earlier LCT analyses as necessary. First, however, we present the context of the study and expand upon the procedure employed.

The study and procedure

In order to help current students understand the requirements for the *Teaching bilingual pupils* exam, examples of high achieving exams from the previous semester were collected from one class known as the *Teach First* class – 24 students total. All Teach First students already hold a master's degree from a different field (such as anthropology, science or economics) and hold a provisional position as teachers at a public school. Their Teach First status requires them to complete a BA in teaching, studying evenings while working as teachers during the day. Because Teach First students already hold a master's degree, they have had more opportunity to practice academic writing. This means they often do not have the same difficulties in meeting the professional academic writing requirements that regular degree program students tend to have. Of the 19 exams handed in, 10 were graded with the highest grade, and a further 8 received the second highest grade. Only one assignment received a grade below average. This class therefore presents a competent cohort from which to choose model texts.

The 10 highest achieving exams were analyzed first from the perspective of LCT's concept *semantic gravity*. These analyses identified passages in the students' texts where students were "doing the work" of connecting theory with educational practice successfully. This happens in particular in the analysis section of the exam. As a result, this section of the students' exams has become the focus of our study: *we explore how students successfully apply theoretical concepts to practice and interpret data using theory*. Having identified passages of interest, further analysis was done using resources from SFL, including aspects of lexico-grammar and Appraisal. The main section of our chapter, titled *Analyzing the exam's analysis sections using LCT and SFL* is thus divided in two, first presenting the relevant theory and concepts from LCT followed by an LCT analysis, then presenting relevant theory and concepts from SFL followed by an SFL analysis. For illustrative purposes, our analyses draw on one of the high achieving students, Tina's, exam. Any of the analyzed assignments could have been chosen, however, since they all exhibit similar characteristics.

The majority of teacher degree students do not, however, have the experience and training in academic writing that the Teach First students' exams display. To illustrate the pedagogical challenge, we also analyzed an exam submitted by one of our regular teaching degree program students, Oliver. His assignment was graded at below average, surprising the instructor, as he had generally attended classes, had always appeared interested in the content and had taken an active part in group work and class discussions. His exam, however, did not reflect this at all. The examples included from his exam in our analyses below can thus be seen as those of a student who is representative of the majority of our regular undergraduate students, exhibiting difficulties with the professional academic writing requirements of the teaching degree program.

As the submitted assignments were written in Danish, we have translated a passage from each of the sections from which we draw our analyses. In our translation, we have aspired to keep the same meaning in the same type of grammatical structures. For pedagogical reasons, we have chosen analytical resources which can easily be understood and adopted by students who do not necessarily have an extensive metalanguage about language. Keep in mind that the purpose of the exam – and the analysis section of the exam in particular – is for students to reflect on past, present and/or future events, positioning themselves coherently and professionally. We examine how students do this in concrete instances of the two exams in particular, that of Tina (high-achieving exam) and that of Oliver (below average exam). In the conclusion we suggest how insights from the combined LCT and SFL analyses can inform a scaffolded approach to supporting current and future students in becoming more proficient professional academic writers.

Semantic gravity and semantic waves: identifying passages between theory and practice

The dimension of Semantics from LCT provides tools for analyzing the analysis section of the chosen exams in terms of what *meanings* students are managing in their texts. Extending Basil Bernstein's model of "knowledge structures" and knowledge-building (Bernstein, 2000), Karl Maton describes LCT's dimension of *Semantics* as capturing issues of condensation of meaning and context-dependence (Maton, 2014). For this purpose, he introduces the concepts *semantic density* and *semantic gravity*. Semantic gravity has been shown to be a particularly useful analytical tool in training teachers (Macnaught, Maton, Martin, & Matruglio, 2013a), academic staff (Clarence, 2015), and teachers of English for Academic Purposes (Kirk, 2017), enhancing their work with students (e.g. Blackie, 2014; Brooke, 2017; Szenes et al., 2015). *Semantic gravity* refers to the context-dependence of a concept or an idea, represented for example by a term or an icon (i.e., words or symbols/visuals) (Maton, 2014), and captures to what extent understanding the meaning of a concept depends on the context to make sense.

In other words, the more meaning is dependent on its context, the stronger the semantic gravity (SG+). In the context of the analyzed exams, stronger semantic gravity is associated with descriptions of teaching materials, cases, teaching plans, activity descriptions and/or excerpts of dialogue from the classroom and can include quotes from transcriptions and excerpts from materials, e.g., text and diagrams. Stronger semantic gravity is closely associated with the data which students draw upon in their exams.

Conversely, the less dependent meaning is on its context, the weaker the semantic gravity (SG-). Weaker semantic gravity in our data is seen when students directly name theories and models which they have learned about throughout the module, such as when, for example, students name concepts and terms from theories of (second) language and literacy development such as *message abundancy* (Gibbons, 2009) and/or when using terms from pedagogic models such as e.g. *The Teaching–Learning Cycle* (Rothery & Stevenson, 1995) or *Reading to Learn* (Martin & Rose, 2012).

Differences in semantic gravity can be plotted along a vertical continuum known as the semantic gravity continuum or the *semantic gravity scale*, with stronger semantic gravity (SG+), referring to practice, towards the bottom while weaker semantic gravity (SG-), referring to theory, is at the top of the semantic gravity scale. (Placing stronger semantic gravity at the bottom of the scale aligns with an intuitive understanding of gravity being stronger down rather than up.)

A prominent feature exhibited by successful academic writing is a series of so-called *semantic waves*: i.e. "recurrent movements are made between concrete particulars (such as an account of the 'critical incident') and more generalized and abstracted concepts" (Szenes, Tilakaratna & Maton 2015, p. 579). Szenes et al. explore this in the context of "critical reflection essays" in social work and "reflective journals" in business studies, while Kirk (2017) investigates reflective writing assignments across subjects. Kirk (2017) suggests that it is pushing descriptions and interpretations of personal experience "higher", for example through engagement with academic theory, which makes observations more generalizable; and that this, in fact, may be what is needed to access higher grades: "… students can [thus] genuinely transform their understanding of a critical incident or pattern of experience, enabling new understandings and the potential for new or revised future action" (Kirk, 2017, p. 4). Being able to connect observations from "practice" with theory by making semantic waves is important for a successful analysis section.

In the following section, we demonstrate how we applied the concept of semantic gravity to the analysis sections of the exams. In the subsequent section, we discuss what this analysis shows in terms of what is expected of students when interpreting practice with theory or, conversely, when connecting theory with examples of practice.

Semantic gravity analysis visualized in semantic profiles

For the purposes of our analyses, we follow Kirk (2017) in distinguishing three "sections" along the semantic gravity scale: the bottom (stronger semantic gravity, SG+), the top (weaker semantic gravity, SG-) and the middle section (SG0). Kirk suggests this middle section on the semantic gravity scale is associated with patterns and generalizations. This mid-level of the semantic gravity scale "represents meanings which generalize over specific episodes or illustrations but which are not entirely abstracted from a contextual base" (Kirk, 2017, p. 4). Dividing the semantic gravity scale into these three sections results in a heuristic for identifying and categorizing different forms of knowledge, without losing sight of the continuum.

The concept of semantic gravity also enables *profiling* of context dependent meaning-making over time in texts or, for example, in classroom practice, and can be a powerful way of making students aware of the characteristics of a successful analysis (Macnaught et al., 2013a; Meidell Sigsgaard, 2017). This is done by plotting the relative semantic gravity throughout a text, resulting in a profile (see Figure 7.1).

In order to create these profiles with our data, we divided an exam's analysis section into ranking clauses, assigning each a value corresponding to the bottom, middle or top sections of the semantic gravity scale. The three sections proved inadequate, however, since some clauses falling in the middle sections "seemed more theory-like" or "more context-dependent" without being extreme enough to warrant assignment in either the top or the bottom sections of the semantic gravity scale. Thus the middle-section was subdivided into three sub-sections resulting in a total of five sections along

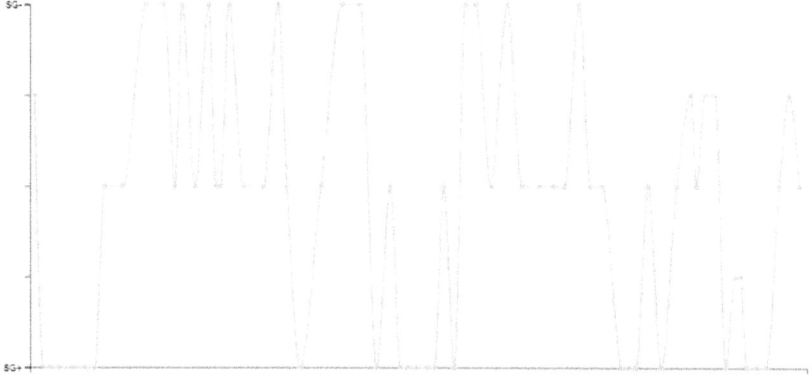

Figure 7.1 Semantic gravity profile of Tina's analysis section

the semantic gravity scale. Each clause was then assigned a value from 1 to 5, where 1 is at the bottom, exhibiting the strongest semantic gravity (SG+), and 5 is at the top, showing the weakest semantic gravity (SG-) (as seen in Figure 7.1). The following excerpt from Tina's analysis section shows a passage where Tina's text connects theory with practice through a series of semantic waves.

Text 1

Excerpt from Tina's analysis section, coded for semantic gravity. Bolded text are clauses coded 1 (strongest semantic gravity). Italicized text are clauses coded 5 (weakest semantic gravity). Remaining clauses are in the middle sections of the semantic gravity scale, coded 2, 3 and 4 (not distinguished here). Paragraphs and spacing reflect the student's layout. Words in square brackets have been added to help reading.

That the pupils are clever is thus far from enough. They also need to have the feeling of autonomy *and as Deci and Ryan emphasizes as the most important factor – the sense of belonging.*

Giving the pupils a basic understanding of the test procedures and of what it [the test] is used for in the explanation has thus contributed to strengthening their autonomy. The fact that they have had it thoroughly explained and have tried it themselves individually and in collaboration has strengthened their competence and sense of belonging.

This is according to Deci and Ryan contributory to strengthen the pupils' mental well-being, which must be seen as particularly important when the pupils in the future have many national tests ahead of them.

During the test several pupils were helped in their task-solving, perhaps more than what has been intended by the test instruction's standpoint.

But if you consider the DFNT [the voluntary national test] as a means of learning and a confidence creating factor preceding the DNT [the national test] rather than a precise guidepost for the DNT, it will according to Gibbons and Vygotskij not be professional [to do] otherwise. *Gibbons argues that learners at no point should be thrown into deep water, men always must have a solid ground in the process (Gibbons: 2016, 11). And Vygotskij argues that as long as the learner needs the teacher's presence, he is in his ZPD, and therefore actively learning.*

Original, Danish version

At eleverne er dygtige er altså langt fra nok. De skal også have følelsen af autonomi og som Deci og Ryan fremhæver som den vigtigste faktor – følelsen af at høre til.

At give eleverne en grundlæggende forståelse for afholdelsen af testen, samt hvad den skulle bruges til i gennemgangen har altså været medvirkende til at styrke deres autonomi. At de har fået den grundigt gennemgået og selv prøvet kræfter med den både individuelt og i samarbejde har styrket deres kompetence og følelsen af at høre til.

Dette er ifølge Deci og Ryan medvirkende til at styrke elevernes mentale velbefindende, hvilket må sandes særdeles vigtigt, når eleverne fremadrettet har mange nationale test foran sig.

Under selve testen blev flere elever hjulpet på vej i deres opgaveløsning, måske mere end hvad der har været intenderet fra prøveinstruksens side af. Men anser man DFNT som et læringsmiddel og en tryghedsskabende faktor forud for DNT for eleverne snarere end et præcist pejlemærke for DNT, vil det ifølge både Gibbons og Vygotskij ikke være professionelt forsvarligt andet. Gibbons argumenterer for, at elever på intet tidspunkt må smides ud på dybt vand men altid skal have et fast ståsted undervejs i processen (Gibbons: 2016, 11). Og Vygotskij argumenterer for, at så længe eleven har behov for lærerens tilstedeværelse er denne i ZNU og altså i gang med en aktiv læringsproces.

Tina's analysis section refers to theoretical concepts by using technical terms such as *the sense of belonging* and attributes these directly to relevant literature, *Deci and Ryan*, italicized in Text 1. She also refers directly to her observations in the excerpt *During the test several pupils were helped in their task-solving*, bolded in Text 1, and generalizes based on this observation in the following two clauses. Finally, she interprets her generalization by referencing Gibbons and Vygotsky, which represent relevant theory from the module. In this way Tina smoothly moves from the lowest section of the semantic gravity scale with the strongest semantic gravity, through generalization to the highest section of the semantic gravity scale with the weakest semantic gravity, creating a "wave up" through her text. This paragraph demonstrates her ability to clearly connect theory with practice, creating a semantic wave profile linking both extremes on the semantic gravity scale.

In contrast, applying semantic gravity analysis to Oliver's analysis section results in the semantic gravity profile displayed in Figure 7.2.

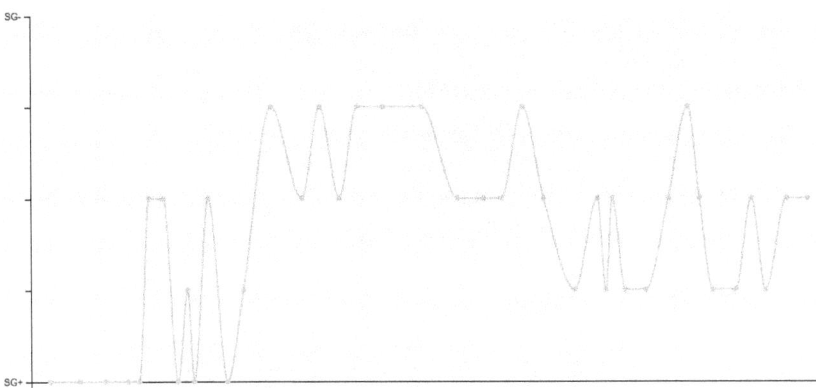

Figure 7.2 Semantic gravity profile of Oliver's analysis section

The following shows an excerpt of Oliver's analysis section.

Text 2

Excerpt from Oliver's analysis section, coded for semantic gravity. Bolded text are clauses coded 1 (strongest semantic gravity). Remaining clauses are in the middle sections of the semantic gravity scale, coded 2, 3 and 4 (not distinguished here). Paragraphs and spacing reflect the student's layout. Words in square brackets have been added to help reading, and the original, Danish version is quoted below.

For my data regarding if the teaching learning cycle works in practice, I have chosen my point of departure in a video from a 7th grade where the teacher, Mie is scaffolding her teaching in the four phases. In the video we see a class which is about to work with a text they have not seen before. Mie first shows them a text, and she goes through the expert language in it. Then the deconstruction phase begins. It seems in the video as if she has good command of the class. **They are given a lot of tools** which they transform into knowledge, and thereafter a product. When you analyze the video, it seems as if it works as intended. **I have not tried TLC [Teaching Learning Cycle] yet**, so that is what I have for comparison.

Pupils with writing and reading difficulties and bilinguals have troubles when traditional writing and process-oriented pedagogy dominate. Here, the genre pedagogical approach in this leaflet is particularly valuable, as it holds splendid examples of scaffolding and makes sure that all pupils are included in the activities of the classroom community.

Genre pedagogy originates from Australia and is a method which is developed to promote marginalized pupils' reading levels in order to give these pupils better pre-requisites for academic learning. It arose through a blooming interest for rhetoric and puts an emphasis on being argumentative, informational or instructional.

Original, Danish version

Min empiri i forhold til om Teaching Learning Cycle også virker i praksis, har jeg valgt at tage udgangspunkt i en video fra 7. Klasse, hvor læreren, Mie, stilladserer sin undervisning ud fra de fire faser. I videoen ser vi en klasse, der skal til at arbejde med en tekst, de ikke har set før. Mie viser dem først en notits, og hun gennemgår ekspertsproget i den. Derefter starter fase to med dekonstrueringen. Det virker på videoen som om hun har helt fat i klassen. De får en masse redskaber, de så omdanner til viden, og derefter et produkt. Når man analysere videoen, virker det som om at det virker efter hensigten. Jeg har ikke endnu prøvet TLC i praksis selv, så det er hvad jeg har at holde mig til. Jeg har ikke endnu prøvet TLC i praksis selv, så det er hvad jeg har at holde mig til.

Elever med skrive- og læsevanskeligheder og tosprogede har det svært, når den traditionelle skriftlige fremstilling og den procesorienterede pædagogik dominerer. Her er den genrepædagogiske tilgang i dette hæfte særdeles værdifuld, da den rummer fremragende eksempler på stilladsering og sørger for, at alle elever er med i klassens aktiviteter i et inkluderende fællesskab.

Genrepædagogikken stammer fra Australien og er en metode, der er udviklet til at fremme marginaliserede elevers læsestandpunkt for herigennem at give disse elever en bedre forudsætning for faglig læring.

Den opstod gennem opblomstrende interesse for retorikken og lægger vægt på at være argumenterende, informerende eller instruerende.

Figure 7.2 illustrates the semantic gravity analysis of Oliver's analysis section, which is made up of 40 clauses (compared to Tina's 65 clauses). Oliver's analysis section (Text 2) starts with five clauses which are categorized as the strongest semantic gravity (coded 1). In these first five clauses, his text provides a summary of what he observed, writing, "*In the video we see a class which is about to work with a text they have not seen before. Mie first shows them a text, and she goes through the expert language in it*". Here he narrates what he sees on the video which he has chosen as data, creating a reference point for the rest of his analysis section.

Figure 7.2 shows how Oliver's analysis section remains in the middle-range of the semantic gravity scale after clause 14, making generalizations such as, "*Pupils with writing and reading difficulties and bilinguals have troubles when traditional writing and process-oriented pedagogy dominate.*"

Notably, none of the clauses in Oliver's analysis section are coded 5 (the weakest semantic gravity), as Oliver does not make any direct references to theory or literature. Nor does his analysis section return to the lowest end of the semantic gravity scale, with the strongest semantic gravity after the initial five clauses. In other words, Oliver's analysis section is characterized by generalizations, connecting these neither to theory nor to his data.

Differences in semantic gravity as enacted in Tina's successful exam as compared to Oliver's below average exam

The *Teaching bilingual pupils* exam requires students to analyze and reflect on a concrete educational situation, a teaching unit and/or teaching materials from one of their major subject areas, similar to the reflective writing explored by Szenes et al. and Kirk reported on above. This could be a case-description from one of their practicum placements in a school or a concrete example of a planned or implemented lesson plan to which students apply relevant theory from the module's curriculum. Not surprisingly, the high-achieving exams analyzed show similar profiles, including a series of *semantic waves* which work to connect the data the student is analyzing with theoretical terms, most often by way of generalizing or extrapolating patterns based on the data in the middle-range of the scale. As seen in Tina's case (Figure 7.1), the profiles do not often jump between the top and the bottom without including a clause or two in the middle ranges. While Oliver's analysis section also exhibits semantic gravity waves (Figure 7.2), the difference is that the majority of his waves are all within the middle-section of the semantic gravity scale, leaving his analysis poorly (if at all) linked to either his data or to relevant theoretical concepts.

The semantic gravity analyses done on the collected exams help to spotlight those passages in the students' analysis sections where connections between what students have learned (theory about language/literacy development) is being connected with what they observe (in their chosen data). Comparing successful exams with below average exams' analysis sections highlights one way in which regular teaching-degree program students can be helped to write more successful analysis sections: successful analysis sections have a wider range in their semantic gravity profiles, incorporating meanings with a greater degree of context dependence and connecting these through clauses making generalizations to clauses with the least amount of context dependence where the semantic gravity is weakest. Generalizing without making connections to either concrete particulars or theoretical concepts leaves the analysis section opinionated and unsubstantiated.

The fact that both high-achieving and average exams frequently make meanings in the middle section of the semantic gravity scale warrants further exploration of the differences in how this is done. For this we turn to investigating some of the linguistic resources leveraged by students in the passages of the middle-range of the semantic gravity scale (coded 2, 3 and 4) to examine how students create meanings to connect theory with practice and how this can be done more or less successfully.

Using SFL to explore how language creates meaning in the middle range of the semantic gravity scale

To undertake a linguistic analysis of the analysis sections, and in particular passages in the middle range in the exams, we examine how students make meaning. According to Halliday and Matthiessen (2014, p. 30), the two basic functions of language are making sense of our experience and acting out our social relations. These functions are organized in order to establish cohesion and continuity. The language is thus mapping meanings in three dimensions, *an ideational,* which can be sub-divided into *an experiential* and *a logical, an interpersonal* and *a textual.* These are referred to as *metafunctions* (Halliday & Matthiessen, 2014). In the following, we provide a description of the lexico-grammatical resources from each of these three dimensions which are drawn on in our analysis. Together they establish the *register* of a given text. The register consists of three variables, *field, tenor and mode,* and can be described on continua moving from everyday-like to specialized, from informal and novice to formal and expert, and finally from spoken-like to written-like, respectively (Halliday and Matthiessen, 2014, p.33).

Reconstructing experience using lexico-grammatical resources within the ideational metafunction

From the perspective of the *ideational metafunction,* our interest is to see how the field of the exam's analysis sections unfolds: how students reconstruct their experiences and map their ideas, so to speak. How do the students impose linguistic order on their "experience of the endless variation and flow of events" (Halliday & Matthiessen, 2014, p. 213)? To explore this, we examine *processes* and *process types* as well as *participants* and *participant types* in the exams.

As evaluators of students' exams, we must understand how students interpret, experience and map their field, e.g., through their use of process types. When considering *processes* from a lexico-grammatical perspective, these can be sub-divided into the following types: *material, behavioural, mental, verbal, relational and existential* (Halliday & Matthiessen, 2014, p. 354). In students' analysis sections we would expect to find a relatively large number of *relational processes*, which act to link empirical observations/data with theory. To a lesser extent, we also expect to find *material processes,* as the purpose of the analysis section is also to explain to the reader what happened (e.g., in the classroom observed). Moreover, it is not unlikely that we would find mental processes with a modal meaning, such as *seems* or *appears,* as the analysis is where the student interprets the data. Finally, we also expect the analysis to be presented in the *present tense* as students in this section are expected to generalize from their concrete experiences.

In academic contexts, meaning is often packed and condensed (Gibbons, 2009, p. 50). This is seen when participants are realized by *embedded clauses, long nominal groups* and by the use of *nominalization*. Nominalization is a form of *grammatical metaphor* where a process-meaning from the *semantic stratum* is realized as a participant on the *lexico-grammatical stratum* (Halliday & Matthiessen, 2014; Mulvad, 2009). In the context of the exam's analysis section, nominalizations serve to generalize the content of the student's analysis as well as to "pack" long strings of action (i.e., what happened during data collection) into a relatively small linguistic space. This can be seen in how the participants are realized in the analysis section through determining *participant types* used: if they are *particular* or *general, everyday* or *technical,* or if they are *concrete* or *abstract* (Mulvad, 2009, p. 162), and create the appropriate *register* of the text. The whole idea is for the students to show their competence of generalizing, comparing and juxtaposing particular and concrete events; e.g., in the classroom, to relevant theories in order to elicit what is to be learned from them; in other words, to generalize and abstract from the specific situation. The students' choice of participant types can thus, for the examiners, be an indicator to see what general ideas and theories they elicit from the situations observed.

Determining textual patterns via Theme and Rheme

"Theme is the element that serves as the point of departure of the message; it is that which locates and orients the clause within its context. The speaker chooses the Theme as his or her point of departure to guide the addressee in developing an interpretation of the message; by making part of the message prominent as Theme, the speaker enables the addressee to process the message" (Halliday & Matthiessen, 2014, p. 89). *Theme,* in other words, is what the writer emphasizes by putting it first in the sentence. The rest is referred to as *Rheme* (ibid.). Examining *Theme/Rheme* structure in a text gives an indication of how the students structure their experiences. In the analysis section of an exam, the writer is expected to connect theory to empirical observation or vice versa, so one might expect a Theme/Rheme structure which reflects this, e.g., by using a theoretical concept in Theme and reference to data in Rheme or vice versa.

Capturing how students position themselves through Appraisal: Attitude, Engagement and Graduation

According to Martin and Rose, "Appraisal is concerned with evaluation – the kind of attitudes that are negotiated in a text, the strength of the feelings involved and the ways in which values are sourced and readers aligned" (2007, p. 25). It is through resources of *Appraisal* that writers position themselves in relation to the scene where theory meets the empirical observations. In order to position themselves as professionals or experts in the context of the assignment, the students must establish a convincing argument for the reader (the lecturers and evaluators), showing that the categories through which they choose to filter their empirical observations provide the field with new or at least relevant insights. Here, we are interested in three different sources of Appraisal: *Attitude, Engagement* and *Graduation.*

Attitude can be expressed in three different categories: Through feelings (*Affect*), through the judgment of human behavior (*Judgment*) and through the evaluation of the qualities of things (*Appreciation*) (White, 2015). In a successful analysis section of the exam, we would expect to find proportionally more attitudinal language expressed through *Appreciation,* as professionalism transpires through knowledge and consciousness about quality rather than about emotions and morality.

Graduation is an Appraisal resource which is used to amplify (*Force*) and to soften or sharpen (*Focus*) the attitude taken towards a given matter, expressing the writer's personal investment in the propositions being advanced in the text (White, 2015). How students employ resources of Force and Focus helps them to adjust attitude in more or less linguistically sophisticated ways. Again, what we would expect to find in an academic analysis, such as the one required in the exam, is that students position themselves in relation to their analysis, indicating to what extent they agree with the theoretical suggestion as to what would be ideal in a pedagogical situation (i.e., how things ought to be). The student's analysis section thus reflects their theoretical understandings when meeting examples of data.

The term *Engagement* refers to the sources of dialogistic positioning which the writer can take on in a text. It can be either *Monogloss* or *Heterogloss* (Martin & Rose, 2007; White, 2015). *Heteroglossia* is necessary in academic contexts, as it allows in the voices of experts. In this way, students promote their arguments, backed with quotes and references rather than as *bare assertion*. According to White (2015), the writer can attribute space for alternatives, making a statement "more or less contentious and agreed-upon, or otherwise, dialogistically problematic" (White, 2015, p.5). In other words, dialogistic positioning is about acknowledging alternative views versus taking on a particular perspective. The former can be referred to as *dialogistically expansive* and the latter *dialogistically contractive*. In the academic analysis, the writer cannot appear too opinionated and certain, but must rather put forward assumptions underpinned by theory and empirical data, and thus draw on *dialogically expansive* linguistic resources.

Exploring differences in linguistic resources employed in the middle section of the semantic gravity scale in successful and below average exams

At a quick glance, the difference between Tina's and Oliver's analysis sections is striking. Tina's analysis section covers 2.8 pages of a total of 8.8 pages (31%) of her exam, whereas Oliver's analysis section covers one page out of a total of 6.4 pages (15.7%). According to the guidelines provided, the paper must not exceed 10 pages of which the analysis section could be approximately 2 pages. Seen from a quantitative perspective only, Oliver's exam in general and his analysis section in particular are too short. It could be argued that his one-page analysis section is only half the expected length. Moreover, Oliver's analysis section aligns more with everyday, *common-sense* knowledge, where he positions himself as a student. Tina, on the other hand, uses her analysis section to present herself as more of an expert, already a professional positioning herself as a *legitimate knower* (Maton, 2014). These differences will be explored in the subsequent sections, drawing on description of the linguistic resources from SFL and Appraisal outlined above, in order to provide a qualitative perspective on the two exams to nuance the differences in length and scope referred to here.

Differences in processes and process types

Looking at Tina's analysis section through the lens of the ideational metafunction, a pattern emerges in her use of *processes*. Tina's analysis section reflects what can be expected here: to find patterns and/or generalize based on her observations, and to link these generalizations to theoretical concepts.

In total, Tina's analysis section has 97 processes of which 56 are relational. Her use of many relational processes illustrates for her reader (and evaluator) her ability to see her empirical observations through theoretical concepts, e.g.: *Giving the pupils a basic understanding of the test procedures and of what it is used for in the explanation **has** thus **contributed to strengthening** their autonomy; (Danish: At give eleverne en grundlæggende forståelse for afholdelsen af testen, samt hvad den skulle bruges til i gennemgangen **har** altså **været medvirkende til at styrke** deres autonomi)* and *But if one **considers** the DFNT as a means of learning and a confidence creating factor preceding the DNT rather than a precise guidepost for the DNT, it **will** according to Gibbons and Vygotsky not **be** professional [to do]otherwise. (Danish: Men **anser** man DFNT som et læringsmiddel og en tryghedsskabende faktor forud for DNT for eleverne snarere end et præcist pejlemærke for DNT, **vil** det ifølge både Gibbons og Vygotskij ikke **være** professionelt forsvarligt andet)*. Here, Tina also includes an instance of a mental process (*consider*). In doing this, Tina emerges as a competent author in her ability to take a position in her statements, but still allows for the reader to consider another perspective. While helpful in this case, too many mental processes potentially would damage the analysis section's purpose. Tina's analysis section comprises a total of 10 mental processes; a mere 10%, as compared to the nearly 58% of relational processes.

Oliver's text, on the other hand, features numerous material processes, e.g.: *Genre pedagogy **originates** from Australia* and *It **arose** through a blooming interest...* His analysis section includes a total of 61 processes of which 26 (42%) are material. For comparison, Oliver's analysis section only has 23 relational processes (37%). The abundance of material processes in Oliver's analysis section signals *a recount* rather than *an argument* or *an explanation,* particularly (as Oliver does), when used in the past tense (Martin & Rose, 2008; Mulvad, 2009).

Differences in participants and participant types

In Tina's analysis section the participants are made of long nominal groups, such as when she writes, *"But if one considers the DFNT as **a means of learning and a confidence creating factor preceding the DNT rather than a precise guidepost for the DNT**, it will..."* (bolded text denotes the nominal group). She includes extensive nominalizations, such as, *"**their competence and sense of belonging**"* and embedded clauses, i.e., *"**Giving the pupils a basic understanding of the test procedures and of what it is used for in the explanation** has thus contributed to strengthening their autonomy"*.

In her analysis, Tina juxtaposes her empirical observations with theoretical concepts, condensing complex observations dominated by stronger semantic gravity into manageable grammatical units (participants). In doing so, she weakens the semantic gravity and moves further away from the particular context of her study. She condenses all the scaffolding she provided during the practicum in her classroom which she is analyzing into one (albeit long) participant. This allows her to relate it to the theoretical concept (another participant), in a simple clause structure: participant ^ relational process ^ participant. This way of taking on an analytical perspective in one's practice is exactly what is required in this type of exam paper.

Though Oliver's analysis section also includes participants made up of long nominal groups (e.g. in the clause: ***Pupils with writing and reading difficulties and bilinguals** have troubles when **traditional writing and process-oriented pedagogy** dominate; Danish version: **Elever med skrive- og læsevanskeligheder og tosprogede** har det svært, når **den traditionelle skriftlige fremstilling og den procesorienterede pædagogik** dominerer.*), his analysis section distinctively lacks nominalizations, more commonly representing elements from his empirical observations. Moreover, no embedded clauses serve as participants in Oliver's analysis. This analysis shows that Oliver does not take an analytical perspective on his data in order to relate it to theoretical concepts. This is reflected in his semantic profile, which for the most part hovers in the middle layer of the semantic gravity scale (see Figure 7.2). So, despite Oliver's use of long nominal groups, the lack of nominalization leaves the impression that he cannot see patterns in his data nor generalize based on these patterns.

Focusing on *participant types* in Tina's and Oliver's analysis sections, more specifically on these three opposing pairs: *particular/general, concrete/abstract*, and *everyday/technical* (Mulvad, 2009, p. 162), we again see differences in the students' attempts to connect data with theory. Tina condenses her observations in embedded clauses and long nominal groups through the use of nominalizations, leaving her participants general and concrete at the same time (e.g. *a basic understanding of the test procedures and of what it is used for in the explanation*). Particular and concrete participants (*the pupils*) are linked via a relational process to an abstract and general participant (*their autonomy*). In this way Tina's analysis section meets the criterion of combining empirical observations or experiences with theoretical concepts. A significant number of Tina's participants are technical (i.e., *a confidence creating factor preceding the DNT; competence and sense of belonging;* and *basic understanding of the test procedures)* representing terms applicable to multiple contexts. This corresponds to weaker semantic gravity, and is a critical feature of an academic analysis section.

In contrast, Oliver's participant types reflect stronger semantic gravity: they are primarily general and concrete (*Pupils with writing and reading difficulties; bilinguals*; and *splendid examples of scaffolding*). Oliver also utilizes more general and abstract participant types associated with the middle range of the semantic gravity scale (e.g., *the genre pedagogical approach* and *method which is developed to promote marginalized pupils' reading levels in order to give these pupils better pre-requisites for academic learning*; Danish version: *... en metode, der er udviklet til at fremme marginaliserede elevers læsestandpunkt for herigennem at give disse elever en bedre forudsætning for faglig læring)*. Oliver does not, however, successfully combine the particular examples with relevant theory. Nor does he demonstrate an ability to combine concrete examples with abstract ideas. Neither does he generalize from his observations the way Tina does. His participant types leave his analysis section wavering in the middle range of the semantic gravity scale, neither connecting to his data nor to theoretical concepts.

Table 7.1 Theme and Rheme in clauses coded in the middle-range of the semantic gravity scale in Tina's analysis section. Original, Danish version below.

Theme	*Rheme*
Giving the pupils a basic understanding of the test procedures and of what it [the test] is used for in the explanation	has thus contributed to strengthening their autonomy.
The fact that they have had it thoroughly explained and have tried it themselves individually and in collaboration	has strengthened their competence and sense of belonging.
Danish original	
At give eleverne en grundlæggende forståelse for afholdelsen af testen, samt hvad den skulle bruges til i gennemgangen	har altså været medvirkende til at styrke deres autonomi.
At de har fået den grundigt gennemgået og selv prøvet kræfter med den både individuelt og i samarbejde	har styrket deres kompetence og følelsen af at høre til.

Differences in choices of Theme and Rheme

From the perspective of the textual metafunction we also detect differences in the two analysis sections. A prominent feature in Tina's writing is her usage of nominalizations to summarize her empirical observations in the Theme position, linking to theoretical concepts in the Rheme position. In doing so, meanings in Tina's text push up the semantic gravity scale towards weaker semantic gravity, as Kirk (2017) suggests is necessary (Table 7.1).

Conversely, Oliver's text recounts, providing only vague references to theory in both Theme and Rheme positions (see Table 7.2). Elsewhere in his analysis section, a similar pattern can be detected regarding his empirical observations: he merely recounts what happened, seen in both Theme and Rheme positions, supporting our initial analysis that Oliver's analysis section is unsuccessful in connecting "up" with relevant theory convincingly.

A first glance at the two exams give the impression that Tina's analysis section appears far more competent than Oliver's. This initial assumption is supported by the semantic gravity profiles for each analysis section and further nuanced by the SFL-informed analysis provided above. Tina's wider range on the semantic gravity scale is seen in her successfully linking her observations to theory. Her use of nominalizations, for example, condenses her observations into manageable units, making it possible for her to relate these to the selected theoretical lenses. At the same time, she uses

Table 7.2 Theme and Rheme in clauses coded in the middle-range of the semantic gravity scale in Oliver's analysis section. Original, Danish version below.

Theme	*Rheme*
Genre pedagogy	originates from Australia and is a method which is developed to promote marginalized pupils' reading levels in order to give these pupils better pre-requisites for academic learning.
It	arose through a blooming interest for rhetoric and puts an emphasis on being argumentative, informational or instructional
Danish original	
Genrepædagogikken	stammer fra Australien og er en metode, der er udviklet til at fremme marginaliserede elevers læsestandpunkt for herigennem at give disse elever en bedre forudsætning for faglig læring.
Den	opstod gennem opblomstrende interesse for retorikken og lægger vægt på at være argumenterende, informerende eller instruerende.

appropriate technical language to describe her observations as well as the theory in question. Oliver, in contrast, recounts and is unsuccessful in linking his empirical observations to the selected theory. His language choices do not make clear connections between theory and practice and leave his analysis section with an overabundance of (opinionated) generalizations in the middle section of the semantic gravity scale.

Differences in Appraisal resources

If the analysis section of the exam is considered an example of an *explanation*, (Martin & Rose, 2008; Mulvad, 2009, p. 142), *appreciation* is expected to be found rather than *affect* and *judgment* (White, 2015). In Tina's analysis section, we find several instances of appreciation (for example, *thoroughly explained*; *particularly important*; *a precise guidepost*; and *confidence creating factor*). Of these, the first three are graduated by *force* and *focus*. In Oliver's analysis section, we also find appreciation (for example, *particularly valuable*; *splendid examples*; *better pre-requisites*; and *a blooming interest*). Like Tina, Oliver utilizes force in his instances of appreciation. However, there is a striking difference in their two analysis sections: where Tina uses appreciation as a resource to position herself as capable in her profession, appreciating elements related to her analysis, Oliver's appreciation is aimed at genre pedagogy in general, making his analysis appear more common-sense, opinionated and unprofessional. If placed on the register continuum, Oliver's Appraisal resources are far more to the left than Tina's.

The same tendency can be found when examining the students' use of *judgment*. Tina writes that according to Gibbons and Vygotsky it would, "*not be professional to ...*". Her judgement is aimed at good and professional practice, attributing this judgment to theorists in the field rather than her own intuition. Oliver uses judgment to characterize pupils, such as when he writes about pupils who "*have troubles when traditional writing and process-oriented writing pedagogy dominate*". As it is, Oliver's is an unsubstantiated statement, which therefore appears postulating. Another interesting thing is Oliver's choice of the word *dominate*. In Danish, the word often collocates with human participants, so in this case when connected to *traditional writing and process-oriented writing pedagogy*, a non-human participant, Oliver passes a judgment on this type of pedagogy instead of, for example, using resources of appreciation to disqualify a certain pedagogical approach. The overall impression of his language is common-sense and everyday-like and as such, he positions himself as a novice, rather than a professional teacher.

An analysis of the two texts from the perspective of engagement (White, 2015), reveals that Tina establishes *heteroglossia* through the voices of theorists who serve as backup for the chosen perspective on her observations (*... it will according to Gibbons and Vygotsky ...*; Danish: *...vil det ifølge både Gibbons og Vygotskij...*; and *...as Deci and Ryan emphasize ...*; Danish: *...som Deci og Ryan fremhæver...*). She also uses the theoretical term "*sense of belonging*", which can be interpreted as an indirect way of letting in other voices than her own, establishing heteroglossia through what White (2015) terms *dialogistic engagement*. Additionally, she opens up for other perspectives through the use of modality (White, 2015, p.5): "*As a subject teacher it can be difficult to predict (...)*"; in Danish: "*Som faglærer kan det i hvert fald være svært at forudse hvilke (...)*". Finally, she involves the reader with her choice of the impersonal "one" (*But if one considers the DFNT...*). In Danish it reads: "*Men anser man DFNT ...*". In Danish, "man" can include the writer and the reader and can be used as generalization. In contrast, Oliver's analysis section exhibits more *monogloss*, not attributing ideas or concepts to any voices other than his own. Neither does he include previously established terminology. Most of his sentences are dominated by bare assertion (*Pupils with writing and reading difficulties and bilinguals* *have troubles ...; ... makes sure that <u>all</u> pupils are included*. Danish: *sørger for, at <u>alle</u> elever er med i klassens aktiviteter i et inkluderende fællesskab*), and as such his analysis is *dialogistically contractive* (White, 2015).

Conclusion: Scaffolding students' professional academic writing using LCT and SFL

When some students, i.e. the *Teach First* students, such as Tina, manage to produce highly proficient and successful academic writing, they may intuitively have picked up the patterns of good writing, decoding implicit expectations. As Tina said during class one evening: *"It is just something I have learned along the way; I just do it by intuition now."* We maintain that other, less experienced students would benefit from the shortcuts made by activities pointing their attention to successful writing as they are provided not only with examples, but also given a metalanguage to discuss the issues in question.

Within a Danish teacher-education context, where content knowledge is taught alongside the pedagogical knowledge, we as lecturers take on a double perspective on all teaching and learning activities. Given limited time to qualify tertiary students' competencies in relation to the field of *Teaching Bilingual Pupils* and at the same time supporting their development of writing skills calls for thorough planning and selection of content when designing the module. Providing students with the concept *semantic gravity* and the notion of *semantic waving* allows them to both analyze examples of teaching practice and materials as well identify crucial passages in model exams. In this way, the concepts *semantic gravity* and *semantic waves* provide an awareness and at the same time can help teach them how to bring theory and empirical observation together.

The linguistic analyses of the exam's analysis sections provided here have given us substantiation for how semantic waving is enacted through specific language choices, providing insights which can nuance students' introduction to semantic waves. While working with semantic gravity alone has been shown to be intuitive for students, it has also proved somehow insufficient (Meidell Sigsgaard, 2017, 2020). This chapter suggests that introducing students to the concepts of semantic gravity and semantic wave provides them with enough metalanguage to recognize more and less successful written analysis sections and how to identify passages where theory is being connected to data. Our analyses of the differences in the high-achieving and below average exams suggest several pedagogical implications for the tertiary setting. For example, in the results of the Appraisal analyses presented above, the lower achieving student could make significant improvements to his analysis section if he were taught how to make his analysis less assertive and less dialogistically contractive. Such students would also benefit from seeing how to expand the ranges of their semantic waves by, e.g., learning how to draw theoretical terminology and theorists into their analysis of empirical observations and to use instances of *mental processes* with a modal meaning (such as *seems, appears*). Additionally, a focus on making *appreciation* resources more technical, formal and written-like would move students' texts further "to the right" in the register continuum, making their analysis more academic-like.

Combining analytical tools from LCT with SFL, we have shown *how* texts employ resources from Appraisal, and various lexico-grammatical resources, to make successful connections between theory and data. We suggest that having knowledge about the functions of these linguistic resources enables us to design scaffolding for our students, while acknowledging that more work needs to be done both in terms of exploring which linguistic resources are employed to realize stronger, middle-range and weaker semantic gravity in written analysis sections, as well as developing methods for how to teach these. Current initiatives both with students of the *Teaching bilingual pupils* module and students writing their bachelor theses in education, however, suggests that presenting students with examples of the analyses such as those provided throughout this chapter gives them a point of departure for working with functional grammatical meanings in their own writing, while at the same time supporting their development in becoming more legitimate and professional knowers.

About the authors

Anna-Vera Meidell Sigsgaard is Associate Professor PhD, in Danish as a Second Language in the Department of Education at the University College of Copenhagen, Denmark. She teaches pre- and in-service teachers in the areas of second language education, literacy development, and language teaching pedagogy. She also teaches courses in academic writing for non-native English PhD students. Her research interests include exploring connections between language, knowledge and teaching/learning in the contexts of both elementary school and teacher education, as well as developing language-based (second language education) pedagogy in mainstream classes.

In collaboration with Susanne Karen Jacobsen, current work includes developing modules in teacher education to support student-teachers in writing academic texts.

Susanne Karen Jacobsen is Associate Professor in English as a Foreign Language and Danish as a Second Language in the Department of Education at University College of Copenhagen, Denmark. She teaches pre- and in-service teachers, primarily in the areas of English as a foreign language and second language education. She has written a resource book for teachers and contributed to numerous anthologies on language education, literacy and pedagogy. Most of her work draws on systemic functional linguistics and genre pedagogy. In collaboration with Anna-Vera Meidell Sigsgaard, her current work includes developing modules in teacher education to support student-teachers in writing academic texts.

References

Bernstein, B. (2000). *Pedagogy, Symbolic Control, and Identity: Theory, Research, Critique*. Rowman & Littlefield.

Blackie, M. A. L. (2014). Creating semantic waves: using Legitimation Code Theory as a tool to aid the teaching of chemistry. *Chemistry Education Research and Practice*, **15**, 462–469. https://doi.org/10.1039/c4rp00147h

Brooke, M. (2017). Using "Semantic Waves" to guide students through the research process: From adopting a stance to sound cohesive academic writing. *Asian Journal of the Scholarship of Teaching and Learning*, **7**, 37–66.

Christie, F. (2016). Secondary school English literacy studies: Cultivating a knower code. In K. Maton, S. Hood, & S. Shay (eds.), *Knowledge-building: Educational Studies in Legitimation Code Theory* (pp. 138–157). Abingdon: Routledge. https://doi.org/10.4324/9781315672342

Clarence, S. (2015). Exploring the nature of disciplinary teaching and learning using Legitimation Code Theory Semantics. *Teaching in Higher Education*, 1–15. https://doi.org/10.1080/13562517.2015.1115972

Clarence, S., & McKenna, S. (2017). Developing academic literacies through understanding the nature of disciplinary knowledge. *London Review of Education*, **15**. https://doi.org/10.18546/lre.15.1.04

Coffin, C., & Donohue, J. P. (2012). Academic Literacies and systemic functional linguistics: How do they relate? *Journal of English for Academic Purposes*, **11**, 64–75. https://doi.org/10.1016/j.jeap.2011.11.004

Derewianka, B. (2012). *A New Grammar Companion for Teachers* (2nd edition). Marrickville Metro, NSW: Primary English Teaching Association Australia.

Derewianka, B., & Jones, P. (2012). *Teaching Language in Context*. Melbourne, Australia: Oxford University Press.

Doran, Y. J. (2017). The role of mathematics in physics: Building knowledge and describing the empirical world. *Onomazein, 35*. https://doi.org/10.7764/onomazein.sfl.08

Gibbons, P. (2009). *English Learners, Academic Literacy, and Thinking: Learning in the Challenge Zone*. Portsmouth, NH: Heinemann.

Griffin, C. W. (1982). *Teaching Writing in All Disciplines. New Directions in Teaching and Learning, no. 12*. San Francisco: Jossey-Bass.

Halliday, M. A. K., & Matthiessen, C. (2014). *Halliday's Introduction to Functional Grammar* (4th edition). London: Routledge.

Humphrey, S., & Dreyfus, S. (2012). Exploring the interpretive genre in applied linguistics. *Indonesian Journal of SFL, 1*, 156–174.

Kirk, S. (2017). Waves of reflection: Seeing knowledges in academic writing. In J. Kemp (ed.), *EAP in a Rapidly Changing Landscape: Issues, Challenges and Solutions*. Proceedings of the 2015 BALEAP Conference. Reading: Garnet Publishing.

Lillis, T. M. (2001). *Student Writing: Access, Regulation, Desire*. London: Routledge.

Lillis, T. M., Harrington, K., Lea, M. R., & Mitchell, S. (eds.). (2015). *Working with Academic Literacies: Case Studies Towards Transformative Practice*. Fort Collins, Colorado: The WAC Clearinghouse/Parlor Press. https://doi.org/10.37514/per-b.2015.0674

Macken-Horarik, M. (2006). Knowledge through "know how": Systemic functional grammatics and the symbolic reading. *English Teaching: Practice and Critique, 5*, 102–121.

Macnaught, L., Maton, K., Martin, J. R., & Matruglio, E. (2013a). Jointly constructing semantic waves: Implications for teacher training. *Linguistics and Education, 24*, 50–63. https://doi.org/10.1016/j.linged.2012.11.008

Macnaught, L., Maton, K., Martin, J. R., & Matruglio, E. (2013b). Jointly constructing semantic waves: Implications for teacher training. *Education and Linguistics, Special Edition*, 1–23. https://doi.org/10.1016/j.linged.2012.11.008

Mahboob, A., Dreyfus, S., Humphrey, S., & Martin, J. R. (2010). Appliable linguistics and English language teaching: The scaffolding literacy in adult and tertairy environments (SLATE) project. In A. Mahboob & N. Knight (eds.), *Appliable Linguistics: Texts, Contexts and Meanings*. London: Continuum. https://doi.org/10.5040/9781474211758.ch-003

Martin, J. L. (2013). *On Notes and Knowers: The Representation, Evaluation and Legitimation of Jazz*. University of Adelaide.

Martin, J. R., & White, P. R. R. (2005). *The Language of Evaluation: Appraisal in English*. New York, NY: Palgrave.

Martin, J. R., & Maton, K. (2017). Systemic functional linguistics and legitimation code theory on education: Rethinking field and knowledge structure. *Onomazein*, **35**, 14–45. https://doi.org/10.7764/onomazein.sfl.02

Martin, J. R., & Rose, D. (2007). *Working With Discourse: Meaning Beyond the Clause* (2nd edition). London: Continuum.

Martin, J. R., & Rose, D. (2008). *Genre Relations: Mapping Culture*. London: Equinox.

Martin, J. R., & Rose, D. (2012). *Learning to Write, Reading to Learn : Genre, Knowledge and Pedagogy in the Sydney School*. Sheffield, UK: Equinox. https://doi.org/10.5433/2237-4876.2018v21n2p267

Maton, K. (2014). *Knowledge and Knowers – Towards a Realist Sociology of Education*. Abingdon: Routledge.

Meidell Sigsgaard, A.-V. (2017). *Teaching to Wave: Scaffolding Teaching Bilingual Students with Discourse Semantics and Semantic Waves*. Sydney, Australia: paper presented at the 2nd International Legitimation Code Theory Conference.

Meidell Sigsgaard, A.-V. (2020). Making waves in teacher education: Scaffolding in "teaching bilingual students." In C. Winberg, S. McKenna, & K. Wilmot (eds.), *Building Knowledge in Higher Education: Enhancing Teaching and Learning with Legitimation Code Theory*. London: Routledge. https://doi.org/10.4324/9781003028215

Mulvad, R. (2009). *Sprog i Skole – Læseudviklende Undervisning i Alle Fag*. København: Alinea.

Nesi, H., & Gardner, S. (2012). *Genres Across the Disciplines: Student Writing in Higher Education*. Cambridge: Cambridge University Press. https://doi.org/10.1017/9781009030199

Nielsen, B., Henningsen, C., Laursen, P. F., & Paulsen, J. (2006). *Teori og Praksis i Læreruddannelsen – En Interviewundersøgelse*. Copenhagen: CVU København & Nordsjælland.

Rose, D., & Martin, J. R. (2012). *Learning to Write, Reading to Learn: Genre, Knowledge and Depagogy in the Sydney School*. Sheffield, UK: Equinox.

Rothery, J., & Stevenson, M. (1995). *Writing a Book Review: A Unit of Work for Junior Secondary English (Write it Right, resourcers for literacy and learning)*. Sydney: Metropolitan East Disadvantaged Schools Program.

Schmidt, L.-H. (ed.). (2001). *Det Videnskabelige Perspektiv*. København: Akademisk Forlag.

Swales, J., & Feak, C. (2005). *Academic Writing for Graduate Students: Essential Tasks and Skills* (Second edition). Ann Arbor: University of Michigan Press. https://doi.org/10.1163/26659077-01802006

Szenes, E., Tilakaratna, N., & Maton, K. (2015). The knowledge practices of "critical" thinking. In M. Davies & R. Barnett (eds.), *Critical Thinking in Higher Education* (pp. 573–591). London: Palgrave Macmillan. https://doi.org/10.1057/9781137378057_34

White, P. R. R. (2015). Appraisal Theory. In K. Tracy, T. Sandel, & C. Ilie (eds.), *The International Encyclopedia of Language and Social Interaction*. Hoboken, NJ, USA: John Wiley & Sons, Inc.

8　Scaffolding argument writing in history: The evolution of an interdisciplinary collaboration

*Silvia Pessoa, Thomas D. Mitchell and
Aaron Jacobson*
Carnegie Mellon University in Qatar

"Through the collaboration, I learned the technical aspects – things like concede-counter – these things I had never heard of before. I just did them. You know, you read ten million books and everyone is doing it, so you just pick it up, like learning a language by ear. Through the collaboration with you, I feel more empowered to talk to students. Because of your backgrounds, I have had a greater introduction to the technical aspects of writing, and especially with second language writers." (Aaron Jacobson, History Professor)

Introduction

This chapter reports on a collaboration between two applied linguists (Silvia and Tom, the first two authors) and a novice history professor (Aaron, the third author) to scaffold student writing of the argument genre in a first-year history course. We[1] all teach at an English-medium branch campus of a US university in the Middle East where the majority of students have English as an additional language. Aaron arrived at the university in 2016 as a recent PhD graduate with no prior teaching experience. Prior to his arrival, Silvia and Tom had conducted extensive research on writing in the history course he was teaching: since 2013, in collaboration with an experienced history professor, we had analyzed student writing in the course, investigated its linguistic demands and student challenges, and delivered workshops to support student writing. When Aaron arrived (new to the country, the university, and the history course), we already had a deeply contextualized understanding of this course and the student population. Thus, this was a unique kind of collaboration where the language specialists had more contextualized knowledge than the disciplinary specialist. This chapter explores the evolution of our collaboration – how each party developed through recurrent interactions.

In history courses, particularly at the university level, students are often expected to display their learning by writing arguments about key issues, using primary and secondary sources (de Oliveira, 2011). The social purpose of the school history Argument genre is to argue "the case 'for' or 'against' a particular interpretation of the past and foreground the debatable nature of historical knowledge" (Coffin, 2006, p. 77). To write effective history arguments, students must incorporate complex interrelationships among ideas, evaluate information and perspectives, and attend to the possibility of multiple interpretations of historical events.

Thus, they must be taught "ways of knowing" in history (Wineburg, 1991) so that they do not view historical texts as necessarily factual, but rather as authored by humans for particular purposes and audiences in particular contexts; that is, students need to understand how historians consider the rhetorical nature of texts when they read in order to write effective arguments, because "writing [history arguments] is often inextricable from disciplinary ways of thinking and working with evidence" (Monte-Sano, de La Paz, & Felton, 2014, p. 543). Students must therefore use language to "do history" when they write. According to Schall-Leckrone and McQuillan (2012), "'Doing history' connotes processes historians use to construct knowledge, including sourcing, contextualizing, and corroborating" (p. 247). This requires students to control a range of linguistic resources, yet many students, particularly L2 writers, face challenges meeting the expectations of the argument genre (Schleppegrell, 2005).

Given these challenges, SFL-based research has emphasized the importance of making explicit the linguistic resources to write arguments. In Coffin's (2006) seminal work on school history genres, she describes the stages and linguistic resources of historical arguments. These stages include an optional background section to orient the reader to the historical context, a thesis that sets forth a central argument and introduces the overall structure, a supporting arguments stage, and a reinforcement of the thesis. Writers of effective arguments control particular interpersonal linguistic resources to acknowledge the tentativeness of historical interpretations, evaluate information, and guide the reader towards accepting their perspective. Coffin calls for studies that focus on collaborations between language experts and disciplinary teachers to make explicit the language of history genres.

While such collaborations are often productive, research has shown that they may be facilitated or inhibited by multiple external and internal factors (Jacobs, 2007; Pawan & Greene, 2017; Perry & Stuart, 2005; Zappa-Hollman, 2018). External factors, like institutional support and scheduling constraints, and internal factors, like group power dynamics, compatibility of personality types, teachers' experience, or teachers' beliefs about teaching and learning, can affect the results of the collaboration. Zappa-Hollman (2018) found that the most successful collaborations were ones where the relationship between parties was perceived to be reciprocal as everyone made professional gains. To this end, Nagle (2014) has suggested "building blocks for a teacher learning framework" that include "joint work as a collaborative process… an inquiry stance to understand the needs of English learners, and an integrated approach that merges disciplinary content and linguistic knowledge" (p. x).

Such an approach has been undertaken in studies across a variety of disciplines and educational contexts, including several collaborations in primary and secondary history classrooms. Studies have shown that history instructors often need support identifying the linguistic demands of history writing (e.g. de Oliveira, 2011; Schleppegrell, 2005). However, even when instructors are highly motivated to integrate language analysis and teaching into their curriculum, doing so successfully requires both significant time for their linguistic knowledge to develop and sustained support from language specialists (Schall-Lekrone & McQuillan, 2012; Schleppegrell & de Oliveira, 2006). Schall-Lekrone and colleagues have tracked teacher and student learning in secondary school history courses after teachers participated in a language-focused pre-service history methods course. They found that teachers made progress but still felt uneasy with the language knowledge from the methods course when attempting to incorporate it onto their teaching. Schall-Lekrone and Baron (2018) emphasize that "both novice and experienced teachers benefit from coaching in a classroom setting to actually implement pedagogical content and language knowledge" (p. 9) but acknowledge that the time needed to make their small-scale study successful is a large constraint.

Similar to other collaborations, ours was both enabled and constrained by external and internal factors. Our university's small size (around 400 total students housed in a single building) facilitated regular interactions. However, we were engaged in unfunded research; Aaron regularly taught between 60 and 90 students per semester; and he was not permanent faculty, but rather renewed with one-year contracts, which meant the collaboration evolved from semester to semester and he was limited in curricular changes he could implement, as initially he was not teaching his own syllabus.

Our collaboration was different from others reported in the research literature. First, most studies on teaching language in history classrooms focus on primary and secondary schools, while ours was in a first-year university course. Second, content teachers typically have deeper knowledge of the educational context and learners than the language specialists, but in this case the language specialists (initially) knew the course context (e.g., the students, course expectations for writing, the source texts), whereas the novice history professor did not. Given the particularities of this collaboration, we explore the following questions to understand how each party shaped the other:

1   How did the novice history professor's understanding of the language needed for "doing history" evolve over the three-year collaboration?
2   How did the language specialists use the novice history professor's feedback to make their language support materials more understandable to him and his students?

To answer these questions, we begin by providing contextual details about the history course and summarizing our related research conducted prior to Aaron's arrival. We briefly outline our collaboration's methodological underpinnings and data sources. Then, we explore the evolution of our collaboration in four stages. We conclude with reflections on our experience and implications for future collaborations.

The context: Research on the history course prior to a new professor's arrival

In 2009, Silvia began collecting student writing from the global histories class under study and conducted several interviews with the aforementioned experienced history professor (more than 15 years at our university) as part of a longitudinal study of academic writing development. Since 2013, Silvia and Tom have analyzed the writing of argumentative history essays as a part of an iterative collaboration with the experienced history professor in his course for first-year students. In this course, students are expected to write six short argumentative essays (approximately 300–500 words each) using one or two source texts and in response to one of several writing prompts. While the experienced professor's rubric explicitly values analysis and argument and discourages writing that is "narrative" and "chiefly descriptive," we initially noticed that it provided little instruction on how to use language to meet these expectations: the categories Argument and Evidence are worth 60% and include features such as "clearly stated thesis statement," "consistent organization," "explanation [...] of how evidence presented is relevant to the thesis," and "relevance of the argument to the [prompt]."

From 2013 to 2016, we conducted research that helped us make writing expectations more explicit to students. We analyzed student writing and interviewed the experienced professor to understand how his perceptions aligned with our analysis. Through our research and interactions with this experienced professor, we learned about history's "ways of knowing" (Wineburg, 1991) and how historical thinking relates to "doing history" when incorporating evidence for a claim in written arguments in this disciplinary context (De La Paz et al., 2012; Monte-Sano, 2010).

We have documented that many students who come to university with limited experience writing academic texts in English face challenges meeting these expectations for the argument genre. We have shown that students may respond with non-argument genres, like Historical Explanations or Descriptive Reports (Miller, Mitchell, & Pessoa, 2016), and are challenged by managing interpersonal resources effectively to maintain a consistent argumentative position (Miller, Mitchell, & Pessoa, 2014). We have also demonstrated that students may produce emergent arguments, effectively controlling some but not all of the genre's key resources (Pessoa, Mitchell, & Miller, 2017). To address these challenges, we have used our research findings to design writing workshops (Pessoa, Mitchell, & O'Reilly, 2019) and we have documented their effectiveness (Mitchell & Pessoa, 2017; Pessoa, Mitchell, & Miller, 2018).

Our analysis of student texts, development of scaffolding materials, and tracking of student writing development has been informed by the 3×3 toolkit (Dreyfus, Humphrey, Mahboob, & Martin, 2016). The 3×3 is a professional learning resource to assist instructors in describing key linguistic features of particular academic genres by considering contributions from the three metafunctions of language: ideational, interpersonal, and textual. The 3×3 describes the linguistic resources needed to meet genre expectations according to each of these metafunctions, from the level of the whole text, to its phases, to its sentences. We adapted the 3×3 to the Argument genre in history[2], drawing on Coffin's (2006) descriptions of the genre and attending to the particularities of the local classroom context (see Appendix 1).

Briefly, to meet the expectations for ideational meanings in this genre, writers need to provide a consistent answer to the prompt that is grounded in accurate and relevant evidence from the sources. They need to use specialized vocabulary to characterize an overarching claim and create a framework for analyzing the source text(s). For interpersonal meanings, writers need to answer the prompt with a defendable central claim that takes an argumentative position, rather than simply explain or report on historical events. This involves the control of external voices (e.g., the source text(s)) to demonstrate the relevance of evidence to the central claim and to acknowledge multiple perspectives. For textual meanings, writers need to preview the supporting arguments, follow this preview with supporting arguments, and conclude by reinforcing the thesis and supporting arguments.

Our 3×3 understanding of history arguments informed the writing workshops that we conducted in the history classes. Typically, we conducted two workshops. Workshop 1 emphasized the importance of responding to the prompt with an argumentative thesis, following the stages of argument, and staying consistent from beginning to end. We provided students with sample prompts and thesis statements to highlight the difference between argumentative and non-argumentative thesis statements. We made it explicit to the students that to write an argumentative thesis statement they need to make an interpretive or evaluative claim in response to the prompt about the source text(s), rather than just reproduce accepted historical information. We also showed examples from students who had ignored key language in responding to prompts that invite students to frame the thesis with an evaluation of degree, such as "*how compelling* do you find the author's argument?" We discussed how students who ignored the invitation to evaluate often wrote texts that were not arguments at all. We also focused on the disciplinary goal of writing an organized essay by illustrating an effectively organized sample essay with the stages clearly color-coded. When presenting the stages, we emphasized the importance of remaining consistent in the position being taken in the claim throughout the argument.

Workshop 2 focused on the interpersonal metafunction to emphasize the importance of bringing different voices into the argument and maintaining an argumentative stance. We drew on Martin and White's (2005) Engagement framework to help students effectively bring different voices into their arguments and align the reader to their positions. We highlighted how non-argumentative essays over-rely on single-voiced linguistic resources (monoglossic propositions in, e.g., non-modalized verbs in the past tense) which present information as factual. We contrasted this with the effective integration of multi-voiced linguistic resources (heteroglossic propositions) to present information as an interpretation that needs to be argued: for example, the incorporation of information from the source text(s) in terms of *expanding the dialog* by identifying the sources (e.g., *According to Hammurabi's Code*) and quoting from them, and then *narrowing the dialog* by explaining the quotes as they relate to the writer's argument (e.g., *this law shows that*) and thus bringing the reader closer to the writer's perspective. This mixing of expanding and contracting resources allows students to analyze their evidence and formulate *reasons* to explain *why* they chose certain quotes for evidence and to assert how the evidence supports their claims. We also introduced the students to the idea that effective arguments strategically align the reader to the writer's perspective, through the use of, for example, concede-counter moves (*although this… that*).

Design-based research methodology

In documenting our interdisciplinary collaboration to scaffold argumentative history writing, we employ a design-based research methodology (Anderson & Shattuck, 2012). Design-based research is a formative research method that involves collaborations between researchers and practitioners. This method focuses on the design and implementation of an intervention to examine its impact on learning and teaching in a real-world setting through mixed methods and techniques. Design-based research is an iterative process: data is collected, analyzed, and reflected upon to improve outcomes and more effectively develop future interventions, pedagogical practices, and theory.

In this chapter, we draw on multiple sources of data to document the iterative evolution of our collaboration:

1   interviews with the history professor that provide insights about his educational background, expectations for student writing, and periodic reflections about the workshops, student writing, and use of the rubric.
2   audio recordings of the workshops that demonstrate how the history professor increasingly moved from an observer to a co-teacher role.
3   the history professor's feedback on student writing.

We highlight recurrent themes in Aaron's developmental trajectory and show how the stages of this trajectory correspond with important changes to the language-focused scaffolding and assessment materials that we (re) developed.

The evolution of our collaboration

Stage 1: The arrival of a novice history professor who was enthusiastic but lacked confidence

During his first semester, Aaron taught two sections of the experienced professor's course (the experienced professor taught one section; all sections followed the same syllabus and schedule). Since we were already on the schedule to deliver a series of writing workshops in the experienced professor's class, we also delivered the workshops in Aaron's class. Immediately after the first writing workshop that we delivered in Aaron's class, he expressed extreme appreciation and enthusiasm for what we had done:

> I think it is so important what you guys are doing! Growing up, you know, I always got good grades and I just kept going along thinking everything was fine. That was until in one class sophomore year in college when I had this professor who just stopped everything a few weeks into the semester. He was like, "Nobody ever taught you guys to write?" And he just stopped everything and spent like three classes teaching us how to organize an essay and all that stuff that you guys are talking about. And I was like, "I can't believe nobody told me this before!" So, I think this is great. I wish someone had done for me what you guys are doing in here!

Aaron would tell this story to the students at the beginning of every subsequent workshop we delivered in his courses, which indicates both his belief in the importance of writing for students and his recognition of the need for writing support.

Throughout the semester, Aaron was extremely positive about the effects of the workshops, but he also expressed some anxiety about his ability to implement the language knowledge in his own teaching:

> I see you and Tom are experts, I'm more of a hack in this area [...] No one really ever trains you on anything, it's just like, "Oh good, you got a degree, go teach." I have your workshop stuff and I look at it

and stuff like that, but if you guys have any like resources on like how to help kids understand how to write and things like that… because I want to be better.

To reinforce the workshop content for Aaron, we showed him how we read the essays when we analyze them, providing more student examples of successful and less successful control of language resources for "doing history." At the end of the semester, even though he remained enthusiastic, Aaron confessed that some of the workshop material was confusing him and some students. Specifically, he was concerned that some of the metalanguage was overwhelming and the resources for maintaining an evaluative stance seemed difficult for students to manage. Nevertheless, he was eager to make time in the schedule for the workshops the following semester and we used his feedback to modify the materials to make the linguistic support more accessible to students.

Stage 2: Thinking and reading like a historian, but letting structure dominate writing

Prior to our delivery of the workshops in his class the second semester, Aaron invited us to observe his teaching on a day when he was to introduce the requirements and expectations for essay writing in the course. When we observed Aaron's writing-focused class, we noticed that he implemented several strong strategies that were particularly effective in showing students how to formulate their own interpretations of historical evidence. He provided them with a heuristic to use as an entryway to any historical document and heavily emphasized the need to interpret and infer. For example, when discussing how to make an argument about class hierarchy in ancient Babylonia based on Hammurabi's laws, he walked the students through the process of inference:

Okay, so we know there is a king and we know there are slaves, right? And this law says men have to pay this much for harming their equal and that much more for harming a freeman. What can we infer about the classes? Exactly! There must be at least one class between the freeman and the king, even though it has not been mentioned explicitly. And so when we write about this, we are not just telling the story of what we read. We could make a claim about the number of classes and support it with what is explicit and implicit in what we read.

Aaron also repeatedly told students to be alert to ways that the author's purpose shaped the text: "When we read we don't want to just take the author's word for it, you know? We want to think about why they might be writing it. We want to see if other people wrote about it the same way."

However, despite having told students that they need to avoid narrative and make an argument, Aaron provided students with a handout that was inconsistent with this message. Specifically, in trying to encourage clear structure, he provided students with a handout that used an example of a prompt and thesis that illustrated a Consequential Explanation rather than an Argument, as seen in Figure 8.1. This indicated that Aaron's control of the different history genres was still developing. He was modeling an Explanation genre while telling the students that he wanted an Argument.

We were concerned that this handout and our workshop content would send students conflicting messages. In our conversation with Aaron after class, we discussed this handout with him and learned that he felt that, faced with a very heavy marking load, structure was one of the most important things that the students needed to improve their writing:

> So they get lost, that's why I made up my little handout… I just said this is how to do it and we just did it. It was like, I don't know walking or riding a bike or something, like let's do this, okay now we did that. Now I'm going to hand you over to Silvia and Tom, they are going to

---

How to Write An Essay

The easiest way to create a thesis statement is to restate the question, but answer it…

Question: "What were the long-term effects of Greek and Roman agriculture?"

Thesis statement: "The long-term effects of Greek and Roman agriculture were…"

3-part argument: "the long-term effects were A, B and C…"

Paragraph 1 = Point A
Paragraph 2 = Point B
Paragraph 3 = Point C

Figure 8.1 The history professor's handout

teach you how to like ride a bike with no hands and stand up on the seat, things like that [...] even like last semester some of them will do the non-three points because they say it's not necessary. But then they just wander all over the place. I know you guys don't like structure.

By suggesting that we were opposed to structure, Aaron indicated that he had not fully grasped our explanation of the stages of argumentation in our workshop. Therefore, we had to persuade him that we agreed about the importance of structure, while also pointing out ways that an over-emphasis on structure could impede a student's rhetorical purpose even in an essay that mostly resembles the Argument genre. In this regard, Silvia told Aaron:

> Our students need structure and we teach them that. When we say that the five-paragraph essay is not the answer to everything, it doesn't mean that we don't believe in structure. We believe in structure; we believe in having a clear thesis, labels for claims, evidence like... "the social structure is essentially ruled by the social class system as clearly seen by the different kinds of benefits and punishments that people got depending on the rank." So what I want to see then is topics that are very clear and that go back to that. I want to see that very clearly in the topic sentence of this paragraph. The bottom line is that it has evidence and that evidence is presented in a way that is logical. I'm presenting A because I need to present A before I tell you about B and A & B so you can understand C. So we always try to explain to the students that there is a hierarchy and logic in their evidence. A takes me to B and A & B together take me to C because otherwise we get a list.

In other discussion with Aaron, we returned to the idea that different prompts can invite different genres, and he sent us prompts for our feedback in subsequent courses that he taught. Based on our multiple interactions with Aaron, we revised our scaffolding materials to integrate an emphasis on structure along with an emphasis on logical development of supporting claims in support of the thesis, as discussed in the next section.

Stage 3: Revision of workshop materials and creation of a new assessment rubric

By having invited us into his classroom to observe his teaching and engaging in honest critical reflection with us about his perceptions of our workshop delivery, Aaron created an opportunity for us to improve learning for students. This resulted in our making the scaffolding materials more accessible in two important ways: first, by keeping a focus on resources for creating strong structure without losing sight of other resources important for history arguments; second, by developing an assessment rubric that linked explicitly to the language resources discussed in the workshops and remained faithful to the original rubric.

In our revised materials, we emphasized not only restating the prompt's question, but also creating a particular characterization or evaluation of historical phenomena based on the student's own interpretation. We incorporated Aaron's "A + B + C" into our illustration of supporting claims (see Figure 8.2) and created a color-coded version of a full sample paper to illustrate the relationship between the thesis and supporting claims in the introduction, and in the corresponding supporting argument stages, to further emphasize structure (sample paper not shown).

To underscore the importance of crafting an interpretation or evaluation in response to the prompt, we presented students with multiple pairs of thesis statements. We asked students to compare each pair and decide which is more argumentative and more fully responds to the prompt (Pessoa *et al.*, 2019). Through group discussion, we also helped students see how they could bundle information into abstract nouns in the supporting claims (e.g., representation; mobility) and then unpack them with textual details and quotes as evidence in the supporting argument paragraphs.

Another important way that our interactions with Aaron shaped our revision to the materials was by integrating our focus on interpersonal language and argumentative reasoning with a strategy for creating effective paragraph structure. When we first delivered the workshops in his class and discussed the difference between single- and multi-voiced resources, Aaron enthusiastically repeated to the class that he did not want them to "just tell a story" in their essays. When we observed his class, he repeated this advice, but he did not go into detail or use examples to show the difference between re-telling information from the source text and transforming information for the purposes of an argument. Given his emphasis on structure, we decided to incorporate the PEEL heuristic (Point, Elaborate, Evidence, Link; see Figure 8.3) (Humphrey, Sharpe, & Cullen, 2015) into our materials, and to highlight for students how the interpersonal resources that are vital to argument could be integrated into a paragraph that develops according to this structure.

We were careful to explain that PEEL is not a rigid formula that would require them to produce four-sentence paragraphs, but rather is meant to

Which of these thesis statements is more argumentative and why?

Essay 1: The main view we get throughout the laws is that women held a much lower status in society than men, as seen in their lack of representation in the law, their limited mobility beyond the household, and their fewer rights in important matters such marriage and divorce.

Essay 2: The ancient Babylonia had three classes: free people from the upper class, free people from law state and slaves.

To write an argumentative thesis, you need to:

Step 1: comment on the source text with **_your own_** characterization/interpretation/evaluation/opinion

Step 2: preview your supporting claims (your A, B, & C).

For example:

Question: "What view do you **get** about the treatment of Babylonia women compared to men?"

Thesis statement: The main view we get throughout the laws is that women held a much lower status in society than men, as seen in their lack of representation in the law, their limited mobility beyond the household, and their fewer rights in important matters such marriage and divorce.

Step 1: Comment on the source text with your own evaluation.

Women held a much lower status in society than men.

Step 2: State your supporting claims for your evaluation.

Point A: lack of representation in the law

Point B: limited mobility beyond the household

Point C: fewer rights in important matters such marriage and divorce.

Figure 8.2 **Workshop materials for crafting argumentative thesis and supporting claims**

> One acronym that can help you remember how to develop effective paragraphs is PEEL:
>
> **P**oint Make a **point**, state your claim
>
> **E**laborate **Elaborate** your claim or expand on its meaning
>
> **E**vidence Provide **evidence** to support your claim
>
> **L**ink **Link** the evidence to your claim. Show how the evidence supports your claim.

Figure 8.3 Explanation of PEEL for students

help them avoid paragraphing problems that students often encounter, such as beginning a paragraph by presenting evidence or ending a paragraph with a quotation without explaining it or how it contributes to the argument. We provided students with several paragraphs, annotated to illustrate the components of PEEL and to demonstrate the potential for flexibility within the structure.

Having introduced interpersonal resources and PEEL, we then asked students to consider which types of these resources were used for the parts of the paragraphs previously identified in the PEEL examples (see Figure 8.4). Asking the students to comment on why particular language resources might be effective to create a Link, for example, allowed us to highlight the

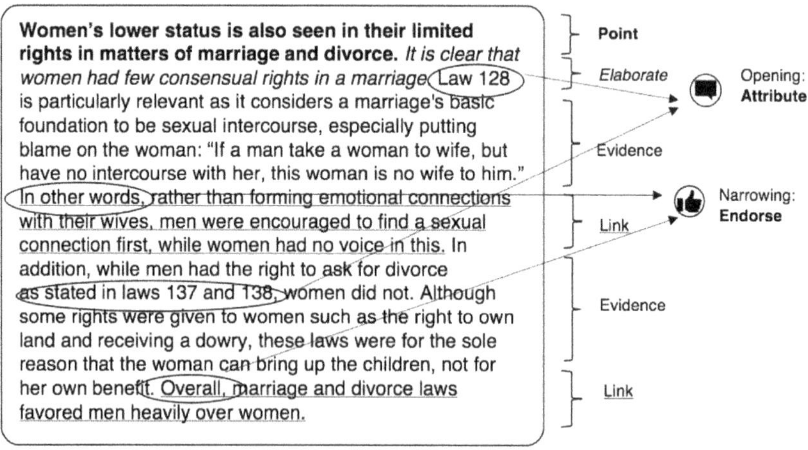

Figure 8.4 Integrating PEEL and Engagement resources in sample paragraphs

purposeful use of these resources in a way that also satisfied the professor's preference for focusing on structure.

Finally, we provided the students with several unannotated sample paragraphs (along with the thesis each was supporting). Students analyzed the paragraphs following a set of questions about their effectiveness in using PEEL and interpersonal resources. We then discussed their findings and co-constructed revisions to the less effective ones.

To further reinforce the conceptualization of history argument writing that we taught in the workshops, we developed an assessment rubric that was based on the 3×3 and similar rubrics (see Dreyfus, Humphrey, Mahboob, & Martin, 2016) and our own findings from research on writing in this course. Our process for rubric development was iterative and went through three major revisions, with each iteration aimed at becoming more user-friendly. Aaron piloted its first version in his third semester. By the fifth semester we had revised the rubric substantially based on Aaron's feedback. We incorporated it into the writing workshops by providing students with physical copies of the rubric during the workshops and ending each exercise by asking them to identify the categories of the rubric that related to what had just been covered.

The most recent iteration of the rubric (Figure 8.5) focuses the reader first on evaluating the essay as a whole text, then on the stages of argumentation, then on the argumentative development of the supporting paragraphs, and finally on the conventions of academic writing. In line with our workshop materials, the rubric spells out that an argumentative thesis asserts a characterization or evaluation of history with supporting claims that are previewed in the introduction. We highlight the use of PEEL for structuring paragraphs that focus on one claim and the use of linguistic resources to create logical flow (e.g., theme/rheme progression) and show logical connections (e.g., conjunctions for establishing cause and effect). The rubric also highlights the use of Engagement resources to develop an argumentative stance. While it captures less information from our 3×3 description of history arguments than previous iterations (e.g., the descriptions of Engagement resources are less extensive; less emphasis is placed on language for creating logical connections), this most recent rubric focuses the users' attention on the language resources that are most important for students to control at a level of detail that is manageable for both students and graders.

Purpose Analytical argumentative response **30%**	1. The essay provides a relevant answer to the prompt framed as an argumentative thesis with supporting claims. 2. The argumentative thesis asserts a characterization or evaluation of historical phenomena based on accurate interpretation of source text(s). 3. The argument is based on original analysis of the source text(s) and historical period and goes beyond reproducing information from the source text(s) by reorganizing the information to support the argument. 4. The essay incorporates evaluations consistently to develop the same position from beginning to end.
Structure Clear stages and use of key words to keep the reader on track **20%**	5. The introduction previews the supporting claims and these claims appear in the same order in the body. 6. The supporting claims are labeled using abstract nouns and discipline-specific vocabulary using the same/similar key words from the introduction. 7. The body paragraphs begin by stating a supporting claim and articulating how it supports the thesis. 8. The conclusion provides a consistent reinforcement of the thesis and main support by repeating key language from the essay.
Development Argumentative Support **40%**	9. Paragraphs follow PEEL (Point, Elaboration, Evidence, Link) and use connectors to create logical flow of information (e.g., *repetition of key words, this/that, old before new, transitions*) 10. Each paragraph focuses on a single supporting claim and uses words such as *because, since, so, thus, as a result of* to show the logical connections between ideas. 11. Paragraphs effectively integrate relevant and sufficient information or quotes from the source text(s) using "opening" phrases (*According to X, X argues that*) and show how the information supports the thesis and supporting claims using "narrowing" phrases (*this shows, this means*). 12. Paragraphs consistently support the argument while showing awareness of and/or refuting alternative perspectives or biases using language such as *although this/that, may, can, seem, possibly*.
Presentation Attention to academic conventions **10%**	13. The register (tone) is appropriate to the assignment (avoids conversational style). 14. The essay uses standard grammar, spelling, and punctuation. 15. The essay uses clear and concise language with appropriate word choice. 16. The essay uses consistent citations.

Figure 8.5 Current history argument rubric

Stage 4: Increased participation in workshops and level of comfort with the language of argument

Although we led the workshops, Aaron increasingly became a regular contributor. By the fourth semester, he would often interject, usually with the goal of reinforcing a point we had made. Because Aaron valued organization, he embraced PEEL and emphasized it frequently. There were times when Aaron referred to the "PEEL writing method" in a way that suggested it to be a formula, but overall he communicated its purposeful use beyond structure. In one workshop, Aaron interjected:

> How many of you know how to use the PEEL writing method? Let's look at an example of PEEL. Let's look at this as a mathematical equation. If I do A, B, and C, then I'm going to get an A. […] Your topic sentence should be guiding your reader, you know, you are guiding them through your arguments. You can't assume that your reader knows anything because they are not inside your mind, right? So that's the topic sentence, so make sure that you know how to do the topic sentence and that everything you write should be guiding your reader towards your thesis. You should always be reminding your reader about your thesis, okay, because you are guiding them through this […] because what a lot of people do is they give the evidence and then they just go, "There you go, reader," and that's, "No, no, no, no, no." You need to explain the evidence. You give your quote – I'm just saying, you are not going to leave the evidence by itself. You are going to explain the evidence and that would be your link. Link the evidence to your claim and show how the evidence supports your claim or your thesis, ok? Many of us, when we have our evidence, we get the points etc. but without that link, it is just narrative information, with the link you now supported your argumentative thesis and now you have got an argumentative essay.

Aaron connects the use of Link from PEEL to avoiding having an overly narrative essay. This shows that Aaron had an increasing understanding of the intricacies of argument that went beyond structure.

This increasing understanding also became evident with his comments about the tentative nature of history and the importance of modality for representing this tentativeness:

> One of the most depressing days of my life was when I was a history student and I learned that in history there is no such a thing as truth. Truth does not exist, history is just interpretation. I did my master's degree in Dublin. And then I learned that the Irish republican army they were heroes, they were fighting the evil British oppressors, but from a British perspective it is like they are terrorists […] from one side, they are called freedom fighters, and from the other they are called terrorists, who is right? so it all depends on your interpretation of the situation. That is why historians always use modality: possibly, potentially, may. Author 1 is absolutely right. Because at the beginning, I thought that historians are cowards and they did not want to say it, but at the end, the reality is who is to say, is this person… are they freedom fighters or are they terrorists? It always depends on the point of view and the interpretation that you take.

Because it connects his own experience of encounter with the epistemology of history to some of the metalanguage from the workshops (i.e., modality), Aaron's comment shows that he had developed a meta-awareness of the language needed to enact historical thinking.

Our analysis of Aaron's comments on students' writing using the rubric confirms his increasing understanding of the linguistic features of argument. For example, on one paper he wrote: "You have three separate theses in your thesis, rather than one thesis and three sub-claims." This reflects an understanding of the hierarchical relationship between thesis and supporting arguments that was not evident in the second semester when he was overly focused on structure. While Aaron continues to be adamant about the importance of structure, which is reflected in comments such as "Good topic sentences" and "Good use of PEEL!," he now also gives more specific comments that connect PEEL as an organizational tool to Engagement features of argumentative stance, evident in comments such as: "You don't have any direct quotes – you need to use the source you were given… it helps boost your arguments/thesis" and "Don't forget to link back to your thesis – you are leaving the conversation open here."

Conclusion

In this chapter, we presented the evolution of an interdisciplinary collaboration between language specialists and a disciplinary specialist to scaffold the argument genre in a first-year university history course. This was a unique collaboration as the language specialists were veterans to the context of the university with substantial institutional knowledge of the history course from years of research on it. In contrast, the history professor was new to the context of the country, the university, and the course, and also to teaching history. He began the collaboration with knowledge of ways of doing history but little meta-awareness of the linguistic resources needed to write history arguments.

In line with previous research on interdisciplinary collaborations (Pawan & Greene, 2017; Zappa-Hollman, 2018), this collaboration's effectiveness was enabled by external factors, such as the extended time of the collaboration over five semesters and the small size of the university that facilitated interaction through our proximity to each other; and internal factors, such as personality compatibility between the researchers, the enthusiasm of the disciplinary faculty, and his willingness to make changes to his practice. In our work in the course prior to Aaron's arrival, the experienced history professor was a generous collaborator when it came to providing access to his materials, his time for interviews, and the opportunity to deliver writing workshops in his class, but he was relatively resistant to change and did not participate in the workshops at all. Eventually, he made some minor adjustments to his writing prompts, but never sought out interactions with us or expressed interest in learning about our findings. On the other hand, Aaron, as a novice teacher, actively pursued the collaboration and explicitly recognized it as an opportunity to enhance his practice. Similar to what has been documented in other research with novice teachers (Perry & Stewart, 2005), initially he experienced anxiety and lacked confidence, but with time he developed an increasing understanding of the linguistic features of argument and adopted a more active role in the collaboration. We all approached the collaboration with an inquiry stance to best understand the needs of our students (Nagle, 2014); this shared mindset towards learning (Jacobs, 2007), and everyone's willingness to engage in recurrent reflection about the effectiveness of our materials and experiment with adjustments were instrumental to the collaboration's positive outcomes. Specifically, the collaboration led to professional development for both parties, and this has culminated in the three of us co-presenting at a liberal arts conference and co-authoring this chapter. We are currently measuring the impact of the revised materials and assessment rubrics on student learning.

As we write this chapter, Aaron is unfortunately leaving the university. Although Aaron's continued emphasis on the "PEEL writing method" reflects his initial intense focus on structure, his increasing participation as a co-teacher in the workshops and his feedback to students reveal a sophisticated understanding of the linguistic resources of history arguments that go beyond structure. With more time, we would have continued to work more closely with Aaron to develop further his facility with articulating to students the language resources embodied in the 3×3 that are needed to write like a historian, and develop strategies for efficiently integrating them into his feedback. More time would have also afforded us the opportunity to continue to learn from him new ways of presenting the linguistic resources to students. Although a great deal of time was invested on this project, it was unfunded; we all worked when we could find time beyond our normal teaching load on an *ad hoc* basis. If we were to begin the collaboration anew, we hope we would have recognized earlier the strong potential that stems from our compatible personality types and inquiry stance and leveraged these for a more in-depth approach. It would be ideal to engage in strategies to help the language specialists further develop their disciplinary knowledge and for the disciplinary specialist to further develop his language knowledge: for example, by reading and discussing both language-focused and history pedagogy-focused research (Schall-Leckrone & Barron, 2018) to devise ways to make adjustments to the curriculum; or by using the rubric together on student writing in calibration sessions to compare assessments.

Similar to other SFL-based interdisciplinary collaborations (e.g., Brisk, 2015; Humphrey, 2016), ours points to the importance of making metalanguage as accessible as is required by the context. Aaron's original understanding of history arguments and perception of student needs, reflected in his A+B+C+D = E (ESSAY) handout and his emphasis on organization, made us rethink our materials in ways that met him and the students where they were and offered appropriate scaffolding in their zone of proximal development. This led to a greater focus on structure and PEEL than previously implemented, but in ways that made the use of Engagement resources in argument clearer. Although in Aaron's mind and perhaps in some of the students' minds what we taught will be remembered as the "PEEL writing method," we are satisfied with this designation, knowing that first-year students, especially novice L2 writers, need a point of departure when learning to structure paragraphs. Additionally, our early versions of the grading rubric tried to fully capture our 3×3-based understanding of history arguments, but this comprehensiveness made them unwieldy in practice. With each iteration, we reduced the quantity of descriptions and their level of detail, making the rubric more usable for Aaron and more understandable and memorable for students. Through our work scaffolding writing across the curriculum, we know that the students are being exposed to genre flexibility and adaptability in later stages of their academic writing development at our university.

Although this collaboration is context-specific, there are certain take-aways that can apply to others who are interested in interdisciplinary collaborations. First, an enthusiastic collaborator can go a long way. Someone who believes in the benefits of working with language specialists and is willing to modify teaching practices without any top-down institutional requirement is key to the success of any collaboration. The fact that Aaron was a new faculty member perhaps increased his willingness to collaborate and experiment with new approaches. Second, time is crucial for developing an evolving understanding of the genres that need scaffolding. It is unlikely that language specialists will "get it right" the first time, as our understanding of disciplinary writing demands and student needs are not static; the more time we work with the same genre, the better materials we develop, as documented in similar SFL-oriented design-based research (see Moore, Schleppegrell, & Palincsar, 2018). Third, related to the time it takes to develop an evolving understanding of the genres that need scaffolding, we recommend engaging in design-based research to document the iterative process. In doing so, it is important to consistently reflect on the process, learn from successes and failures, and determine ways to increase the accessibility and usability of the materials. Fourth, it is important to create buy-in from disciplinary faculty. Although an enthusiastic collaborator motivated by an inquiry stance can go a long way, faculty should feel appreciated for their time commitment and knowledge, and this can be accomplished by co-presenting or co-authoring publications that showcase the collaboration. If funding sources are available, we recommend applying for grants with the disciplinary faculty as the co-principal investigators on the project. And finally, documenting and disseminating outcomes of the collaboration is crucial to gain institutional support, recruit more collaborators, and continue to enhance the teaching of disciplinary writing.

About the authors

Silvia Pessoa is Associate Teaching Professor of English at Carnegie Mellon University in Qatar where she teaches courses in academic reading and writing and sociolinguistics. She earned her Ph.D. in Second Language Acquisition from Carnegie Mellon University. Her research areas include academic writing development, second language writing, sociolinguistics, bilingualism, and immigration studies. Her research has been funded by the Qatar National Research Fund and has appeared in international journals such as the *Journal of Second Language Writing, Linguistics and Education*, and the *Journal of English for Academic Purposes*.

Thomas D. Mitchell is an Associate Teaching Professor of English at Carnegie Mellon University in Qatar where he teaches courses in academic reading and writing, style, professional writing, and discourse studies. He earned his Ph.D. in Rhetoric from Carnegie Mellon University. His research has appeared in international journals such as the *Journal of Second Language Writing, Linguistics and Education, Journal of English for Academic Purposes,* and *English for Specific Purposes.*

Aaron Jacobson is currently an independent scholar, who was previously a Visiting Assistant Professor of History at Carnegie Mellon University in Qatar, where he taught courses in global history, European history, and Latin American history. He earned his Ph.D. from the University of London. His research interests include refugee studies and forced migrations and his areas of expertise include Modern European history and Modern German history.

Notes

1   Since our collaboration involved two parties (the applied linguists and the history professor), the use of "we" will refer to Silvia and Tom, the applied linguists, and the use of "we all" will refer to all three authors.
2   For the full version of our 3×3 for history arguments, see Pessoa *et al.*, 2017.

References

Anderson, T., & Shattuck, J. (2012). Design-based research: A decade of progress in education research? *Educational Researcher*, **41**, 16–25. https://doi.org/10.3102/0013189x11428813

Brisk, M. E. (2015). *Engaging Students in Academic Literacies: Genre-based Pedagogy for K-5 Classrooms*. New York: Routledge. https://doi.org/10.4324/9781317816164

Coffin, C. (2006). *Historical Discourse: The Language of Time, Cause and Evaluation*. New York: Continuum.

De La Paz, S., Ferreti, R., Wissinger, D., Yee, L., &MacArthur, C. (2012). Adolescents' disciplinary, use of evidence, argumentative strategies, and organizational structure in writing about historical controversies. *Written Communication*, 29(4), 412e454. https://doi.org/10.1177/0741088312461591

de Oliveira, L. C. (2011). *Knowing and Writing School History: The Language of Students' Expository Writing and Teachers' Expectations*. Charlotte, NC: Information Age Publishing.

Dreyfus, S., Humphrey, S., Mahboob, A., & Martin, J. M. (2016). *Genre Pedagogy in Higher Education. The SLATE Project*. London: Palgrave Macmillan. https://doi.org/10.1007/978-1-137-31000-2_1

Humphrey, S. (2016). *Academic Literacies in the Middle Years: A Framework for Enhancing Teacher Knowledge and Student Achievement*. New York: Routledge. https://doi.org/10.4324/9781315625584

Humphrey, S., Sharpe, T. and Cullen, T. (2015). Peeling the PEEL: Integrating language and literacy in the middle years. *Literacy Learning*, **23**, 53–62.

Jacobs, C. (2007). Towards a critical understanding of the teaching of discipline-specific academic literacies: Making the tacit explicit. *Journal of Education*, **41**, 59–81.

Martin, J. R. & White, P. R. R. (2005). *The Language of Evaluation: Appraisal in English*. New York: Palgrave Macmillan.

Miller, R. T., Mitchell, T. D., & Pessoa, S. (2016). Impact of source texts and prompts on students' genre uptake. *Journal of Second Language Writing*, **31**, 11–24. https://doi.org/10.1016/j.jslw.2016.01.001

Miller, R. T., Mitchell, T. D., & Pessoa, S. (2014). Valued voices: Students' use of ENGAGEMENT in argumentative history writing. *Linguistics and Education*, **28**, 107–120. https://doi.org/10.1016/j.linged.2014.10.002

Mitchell, T. D & Pessoa, S. (2017). Scaffolding the writing development of the argumentative genre in history: The case of two novice writers. *Journal of English for Academic Purposes*, **30**, 26–37. https://doi.org/10.1016/j.jeap.2017.10.002

Moore, J., Schleppegrell, M. J., Sullivan Palincsar, A. (2018). Discovering disciplinary linguistic knowledge with English learners and their teachers: Applying systemic functional linguistics concepts through design-based research. *TESOL Quarterly*, **52**(4), 1022–1049. https://doi.org/10.1002/tesq.472

Monte-Sano, C. (2010). Disciplinary literacy in history: An exploration of the historical nature of adolescents' writing. *Journal of the Learning Sciences*, **19**, 539–568. https://doi.org/10.1080/10508406.2010.481014

Monte-Sano, C., De La Paz, S., & Felton, M. (2014). *Reading, Thinking, and Writing About History: Teaching Argument Writing to Diverse Learners in the Common Core Classroom, Grades 6–12*. New York: Teachers College Press.

Nagle, J. (2014). *English Learner Instruction Through Collaboration and Inquiry in Teacher Education*. Charlotte, NC: Information Age Publishing, Inc.

Pawan, F. & Greene, M. C. S. (2017). In trust, we collaborate: ESL and content-area teachers working together in content-based language instruction. In D. Brinton and M. A. Snow (eds.), *The Content-Based Classroom: New Perspectives on Integrating Language and Content* (pp. 323–337). Ann Arbor: University of Michigan Press. https://doi.org/10.3998/mpub.8198148

Perry, B. & Stewart, T. (2005). Insights into effective partnership in interdisciplinary team teaching. *System*, **33**, 563–573. https://doi.org/10.1016/j.system.2005.01.006

Pessoa, S., Mitchell, T. D., & Miller, R. T. (2018). Scaffolding the argument genre in a multilingual university history classroom: Tracking the writing development of novice and experienced writers. *English for Specific Purposes*, **50**, 81–96. https://doi.org/10.1016/j.esp.2017.12.002

Pessoa, S., Mitchell, T. D., & Miller, R. T. (2017). Emergent arguments: A functional approach to analyzing student challenges with the argument genre. *Journal of Second Language Writing*, **38**, 42–55. https://doi.org/10.1016/j.jslw.2017.10.013

Pessoa, S., Mitchell, T. D., & Reilly, B. (2019). Scaffolding the writing of argumentative essays in history: A functional approach. *The History Teacher*, **52**, 411–440.

Schall-Leckrone, L., & Barron, D. (2018). Apprenticing students and teachers into historical content, language, and thinking through genre pedagogy. In L. C. de Oliveira and K. M. Obenchain (eds.), *Teaching History and Social Studies to English Language Learners* (pp. 205–231). Cham: Palgrave Macmillan. https://doi.org/10.1007/978-3-319-63736-5_9

Schall-Leckrone, L., & McQuillan, P. J. (2012). Preparing history teachers to work with English learners through a focus on the academic language of historical analysis. *Journal of English for Academic Purposes*, **11**, 246–266. https://doi.org/10.1016/j.jeap.2012.05.001

Schleppegrell, M. J. (2005). Helping content area teachers work with academic language: Promoting English language learners' literacy in history. Santa Barbara, CA: UC Linguistic Minority Research Institute.

Schleppegrell, M. J. & de Oliveira, L. C. (2006). An integrated language and content approach for history teachers. *Journal of English for Academic Purposes*, **5**, 254–268. https://doi.org/10.1016/j.jeap.2006.08.003

Wineburg, S. S. (1991). On the reading of historical texts: Notes on the breach between school and the academy. *American Educational Research Journal*, **28**, 495–519. https://doi.org/10.3102/00028312028003495

Zappa-Hollman, S. (2018). Collaborations between language and content university instructors: Factors and indicators of positive partnerships. *International Journal of Bilingual Education and Bilingualism*, **21**(5), 591–606. https://doi.org/10.1080/13670050.2018.1491946

Appendix 1: 3×3 for analyzing arguments in history

	Whole text	*Paragraph*	*Sentences & Clause*
Ideational	i. The text is grounded in accurate and relevant knowledge from the source text. ii. The text is grounded in knowledge and language from the discipline. iii. Ideas are developed through discipline-specific topics and subtopics to form an analytical framework. iv. The answer to the prompt is consistent from beginning to end.	i. The text uses a clear analytical framework (overarching claim with sub-claims) to present information according to demands of prompt. ii. Related topics are grouped as distinct supporting claims. iii. Information related to one topic is expanded as the text integrates accurate, relevant and sufficient content from the source text. iv. Information is expanded within paragraphs in terms of general to specific, point to elaboration, evidence to interpretation; claim to evaluation v. Information is related in logical relationships to further a claim (e.g. cause, consequence, comparison) vi. Examples and quotes are logically integrated in the text to support claims.	i. Specialized/technical vocabulary is used to characterize an overarching claim. ii. Nominal expressions are used in the introduction and in the topic sentences (hyper Themes in SFL terminology) to create a taxonomy for the sub-claims. iii. Vocabulary is discipline-specific and formal. iv. Well-structured sentences, causal and constrasting conjuctions, and text connectives expand and link ideas logically.

(Continued.)

	Whole text	Paragraph	Sentences & Clause
Interpersonal	i. The text answers the prompt with a defendable overarching proposition that shows interpretations of history as tentative (not factual) and as something that has to be argued for. ii. The proposition is reinforced, justified, and defended to persuade the reader that a position is valid. iii. The text moves its points or positions forward across the stages using the source text as evidence for claims. iv. The text consistently guides the reader towards the overarching claim.	i. The text includes and controls external voices (e.g., the source text) to develop points, include evidence, and show how the evidence supports the claims. ii. Patterns of engagement develop the writer's stance within and across paragraphs to guide the reader towards the overarching claim. iii. Patterns of evaluation develop the writers' stance within and across paragraphs.	i. The text uses modality to set up or argue claims and to show interpretations of history as tentative. ii. The text uses expanding resources (Attribute) to bring in the source text. (e.g., *The author argues… According to the author*) iii. The text uses contracting resources such as: Endorsement: to show how the cited material supports the claims, and to draw and support conclusions (e.g., *This means/This shows that/This evidence is indicative of …*) Concede counter moves: to show awareness of a different perspective and bring the reader towards the writer's perspective (*although this… that*) Counter moves: to reveal an imagined position of the reader and align the reader to the writer (e.g., *even, just, only, although*) Justification: to provide reasons for claims (e.g., *this obstacle is important because…*) iv. Objective metaphors are used to negotiate opinions and recommendations (e.g., *It gives the impression* rather than *It makes you feel.*)

	Whole text	Paragraph	Sentences & Clause
Textual	i. The text previews the claims to be discussed in the introduction, includes supporting arguments in the body paragraphs, reiterates the points in the conclusion. ii. The text creates coherence by predicting, signposting, and scaffolding ideas.	i. The language and order of sub-claims in the body paragraphs matches the preview in the introduction. ii. Sub-claims are placed at the beginning of the paragraphs. iii. Paragraphs are developed in focus from general and abstract in "packed" topic sentences, to specific and concrete in "unpacked" sentences. iv. There is a logical flow of information within and across paragraphs through the use of cohesive resources (e.g., reference, substitution, repetition), internal conjunctions (e.g., theme/new, transitions), and consequential relationships (e.g., thus).	i. Nominal expressions and referring words are used to pack, signal or foreground information, and track ideas. ii. Choices of Theme predict the topic or focus of the sentence.

Note: Adapted from Humphrey et al. (2010) and Dreyfus et al. (2016).

Part III
Studies in translation

9 Translation as re-instantiation: An investigation of verbal projection

Hailing Yu
School of Foreign Languages and International Studies, Hunan University

Canzhong Wu
Department of Linguistics, Macquarie University

Introduction

There has been a series of studies that combine systemic functional linguistics (SFL) and translation studies (TS), such as application of "register" to translation quality assessment (House, 1997), consideration of appraisal in the process of translation (Munday, 2012), and use of metafunctions to distinguish translations and versions (Steiner, 1998). Being two of the most frequently discussed languages in SFL, English and Chinese provide a rich resource for scholars interested in translation studies (Huang, 2004; Zhang, 2002, 2013).

Although the Chinese language has a long history, Standard Written Chinese was not formally adopted until the early twentieth century, when pioneering Chinese academics were enthusiastically involved in a movement to create a "new" written language mainly through translating foreign (especially Western) literature and borrowing foreign linguistic features. Before the twentieth century, literary Chinese was used for almost all formal writing in China, as well as in Japan, Korea and Vietnam during various periods. It is the language that was used to record the wisdom of the culture over two thousand years, resulting in thousands of millions of texts, including *The Analects* and *Tao Te Ching*. However, literary Chinese differs in many respects from the Standard Written Chinese that we use today, which imposes a challenge when studying texts written before the 1920s, as there has been very little work done on describing literary Chinese from an SFL perspective.

While it is beyond the scope of this chapter to provide a comprehensive SFL description of literary Chinese, it is feasible to focus on a very special area, such as projection, by drawing on existing research in a range of different areas. There have been many studies on projection (e.g., Matthiessen & Teruya, 2013) in the field of SFL, but relatively few in the context of translation. In Xuan and Chen's (2020) review of studies on projection from 1977 to 2018, only 4 out of the 66 reviewed touch upon the issue of translation (e.g., Huang, 2014), which makes translation studies one of the under-explored areas in the area of projection. This chapter will focus on one type of projection, verbal projection, from the perspective of translation studies.

Taking the concept of translation as re-instantiation as the theoretical framework, this chapter will present a case study that investigates a Buddhist text written in literary Chinese and its four English translations, with a focus on verbal projection. The research questions are:

- What are the manifestations of verbal projection in the English translations of the text?
- What part of the systemic potential is instantiated in the translations?
- What contextual factors might have contributed to the translations as re-instantiation?

Translation as re-instantiation

The concept of translation as re-instantiation was first proposed by De Souza (2013) under the inspiration of Martin (2008a, 2008b, 2009). Later, Chang (2018) also applied this concept to his study of translation of a novel from English to Chinese.

According to De Souza, translation can be likened to a process of inter-lingual re-instantiation akin to intralingual re-instantiation as theorized by Martin (2006, 2008b). To be more specific, "[I]n intra- as in interlingual re-instantiation, a TT [translated text] reconstructs the meaning potential of a given ST [source text]. In the latter, this reconstruction is enabled by the translator's reading of the ST, which in turn is informed by his/her reper-toires in the two languages/cultures." (De Souza, 2013, pp. 580–581). This definition of translation as re-instantiation is related to the concepts of real-ization, instantiation and individuation.

Realization concerns the organization of language in strata at increasing levels of abstraction, each stratum realizing or recoding the previous one.

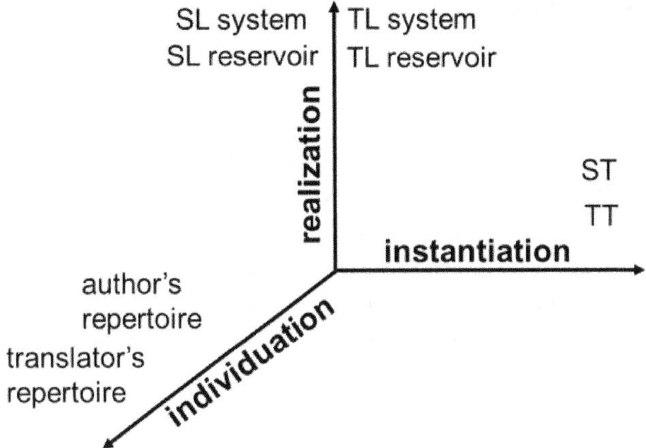

Figure 9.1 A three-dimensional model of translation as interlingual re-instantiation (adapted from De Souza 2013, p.581. ST: source text; TT: translated text)

Instantiation concerns the relation between language as an overall meaning potential and text as a concrete instance, where each instance instantiates systems from the language as a whole. Meanwhile, the text which is sourced on a previous one is conceived as a re-instantiation – a product of the homonymous process by which one instance reconstrues the meaning potential of a source instance (Martin, 2006). Individuation concerns "the relationship between the reservoir of meanings in a culture and the repertoire a given individual can mobilize" (Martin, 2006, p. 293). In the current study, although the reservoir of meanings is relatively stable between the language pair of literary Chinese and English, the translators as individuals may differ in their knowledge and command of the languages and thus their different understanding and interpretation of the same source text. Taking all these into consideration, De Souza proposes a three-dimensional model of translation as interlingual re-instantiation (Figure 9.1).

This model takes into account (i) the abstract language systems involved, that is, the source and target languages, through realization; (ii) the concrete uses of such systems in the forms of the two texts, the source text and the target text, through instantiation; and (iii) the individual users of such systems, in this case the translators as source text readers and target text writers, through individuation. The meaning potential of a language constitutes what Bernstein terms the "reservoir" of the language community, and each member of the community as an individual has her/his own set of strategies and analogic potential, which is referred to as their "repertoire" (Bernstein, 2000, p. 57).

In the process of re-instantiating the source text in a new language, there is always a tension between the constraints of the source text and the creativity of the individual translators. As Halliday (1992, p. 16) put it, translation is a "*guided* creation of meaning," since translating is a process guided by the source text. Matthiessen (2001, p. 64) maintains that translation is "not a passive reflection" of the source text, but rather "a creative act of reconstruing the meaning of the original" in the target text, which explains why the same source text can be variously re-instantiated in target texts (Chang 2018).

Verbal projection in literary Chinese and English

The concept of projection was first put forward by Halliday (1977) as a logico-semantic relation between clauses, along with expansion. Later, Halliday and Matthiessen (2014) defined it as a logico-semantic relation where "the secondary clause is projected through the primary clause, as a locution or idea" (p. 443).

The system of PROJECTION is provided in Figure 9.2. Projection is one of the two types of logico-semantic relation. It can be either direct quoting, or indirect reporting, and the projected clause can be either a minor or major clause. In terms of TAXIS, the projection can be either parataxis, where the projected clause is of equal status with the projecting one, or hypotaxis, where the projected clause cannot stand independently without the projecting one. In comparison with traditional views, this notion of projection provides a highly practical and systematic model for investigating the phenomenon of projection.

In the case of paratactic quoting, there are choices concerning the position of the projecting and projected clauses, and the position of the Sayer and the verbal process within the projecting clause. The projecting clause can be put in the beginning, at the end, or in the middle of the clause complex. If the projecting clause comes first, it has the structure of "Sayer + verbal Process"; if the projecting clause follows the projected clause or is inserted between the projected clause(s), Sayer of the projecting clause can be put either in front of or following the projecting verb, as in:

1   The Master asked, "What is your name?"
2   "What is your name," the Master asked.

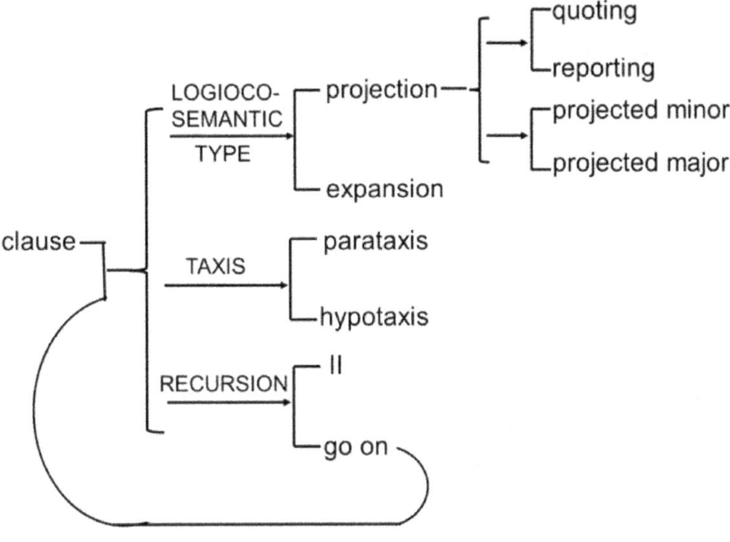

Figure 9.2 The system of PROJECTION (Halliday & Matthiessen 2014, p. 511)

> "What is your name," asked the Master.
>
> 3   "What is your name," the Master asked, "And where do you come from?"
>
> "What is your name," asked the Master, "And where do you come from?"

With regard to literary Chinese, the systemic choices are the same as in English in the grammar of verbal projection, but there is a difference in how these choices are realized structurally, as indicated in Dong (2008), Harbsmeier (1994) and Wang (1980) on literary Chinese. Similar to English, literary Chinese also has the tactic choices of parataxis and hypotaxis, and the projected clause can be either a minor or major clause. However, while there are three ways for the projecting clause to be positioned in paratactic quoting in English, there is only one way in literary Chinese: the projecting clause always comes before the projected one. It was not until the 1920s that Chinese writers started putting projecting clauses at the end, or in the middle of the clause complex, as a result of the influence of Western languages (Wang, 1980, p. 373). Within the projecting clause, there may be a projecting verb only, as the Sayer (which often is also the Subject) can be left implicit when it can be inferred from the co-text or context, as in:

(師) 問 曰 汝 從 何 來 欲 問 何 事
(shī) wèn yuē rǔ cóng hé lái yù wèn hé shì
(The Master) ask say (asked), "What do you come from? What do you want to know?"

In this example, the projecting clause is "(師)問曰" (shī wèn yuē, the Master ask say), and the following two clauses are projected. The projecting clause always precedes the projected clauses. As the Sayer in the projecting clause, "師" (the Master) can be omitted since the previous clause is "A student came to visit the Master." This clause builds a co-text for the following clause, where the omitted first word is the same as the last word in the previous clause.

It is worth noting that, in literary Chinese, there is strong tendency for some verbs to quote and some other verbs to report (Wang, 1980). For example, the verb "曰" (yuē, literally meaning "say") usually functions as a quotation marker, indicating that a quote follows (H. Yu & Guo, 2016).

Verbal projection in the *Platform Sutra* and its translations

The data of the study includes a Buddhist text written in literary Chinese, the *Platform Sutra*, and its four English translations[1]. *The Platform Sutra* is dedicated to Huineng (638–713), a Chan master living in the Tang dynasty in China. The text belongs to the genre of "records of sayings" (yǔlù, 語錄) and is a collection of Huineng's public sermons and dialogical interactions with students which are "heard and recorded by other students" (Welter, 2008, p. 48). Verbal projection, therefore, plays a dominant role in the text. There are sentences, paragraphs and even chapters that are projected locutions, which take up nearly 90% of the whole book.

The four translations to be investigated include the first English translation produced by the Chinese translator Wong Mou-lam in 1930, translations by two American translators Heng Yin (1977) and Thomas Cleary (1998) in the late 20th century, and translation by another Chinese translator, Cheng Kuan, in 2011. All of these translations are based on the same Chinese version adopted in this study. The selection criterion is heterogeneity in terms of publishing time and translators' cultural and religious background (Wong and Cleary are lay people, while Heng and Cheng are Buddhists).

In this section, we investigate how the source text instantiates the verbal projection system of literary Chinese, and how the different translations re-instantiate the verbal projection of the source text in English. We first look at TAXIS on the level of clause complex, that is, whether the verbal projection takes the form of parataxis or hypotaxis, then the combination of the verb of saying and Sayer on the level of clause, and finally the choice of projecting verbs on the level of verbal group.

Taxis: paratactic quoting and hypotactic reporting

Although theoretically speaking, locutions can be either quoted or reported in literary Chinese, quoting generally enjoys much higher probability than reporting. This explains why out of the 155 cases of verbal projection in the *Platform Sutra*, only 1 locution is reported. The other 154 are all quoted.

The prevalence of paratactic quoting in the source text is largely retained in the translations by Heng, Cleary and Cheng (see Table 9.1), but not in Wong's translation, where there are 17 cases in which the original quoting is changed into reporting.

How verbal projections of the source text are re-instantiated in the translations is illustrated in the following examples:

Example 1
    ST: （師）次 問 上 人 攻 何 事業 (T2008_.48.0358a20)3
              (shī) cì wèn shàng rén gōng hé shì yè
    Wong: ...the Patriarch *asked him what line of work he was taking up* (1930, p. 52).
    Heng: The Master ... and *asked, "Superior One, what work do you do?"* (1977, p. 331)
    Cleary: The Master ..., then *asked, "What work do you do?"* (1998, p. 59)
    Cheng: The Master then *asked him, "What work are you specialized in?"* (2011, p. 127)

In Example 1, while translations by Heng, Cleary and Cheng all choose to re-instantiate the original paratactic quoting as paratactic quoting in

Table 9.1 Verbal projection in the source text and translations

	ST	**Wong**	**Heng**	**Cleary**	**Cheng**
Paratactic quoting	154	136	154	152	154
Hypotactic reporting	1	17	1	2	1
Total	**155**	**153²**	**155**	**154**	**155**

English, Wong's translation re-instantiates the quoting as reporting. In quoting, the projected clause retains all the interactive features of the clause as exchange, such as the interrogative mood, and the use of vocative in Heng's translation. The use of reported speech in Wong's translation, however, implies that the wording being reported may be quite different from the exact words used by the original speaker: what is being represented here is the sense, or gist of what was said.

Example 2

> ST: 師曰 善 哉 少 留 一宿 (T2008_.48.0357c17)
>   shī yuē shàn zāi shǎo liú yī sù
> Wong: *"Well said!"* exclaimed the Patriarch. *He then asked Yuen Kwok to delay his departure and spend a night there* (1930, p. 50).
> Heng: The Master exclaimed, *"Good indeed! Please stay for a night"* (1977, p. 320).
> Cleary: The Master said, *"Good! Stay here at least one night"* (1998, p. 57).
> Cheng: The Master said, *"Very well put. Now just stay and put up for a night"* (2011, p. 119).

Example 2 presents an interesting case where the original quoting is divided into two parts, one part quoted and the other part reported in Wong's translation. This illustrates Halliday and Matthiessen's (2014) idea that paratactic projection allows for a greater range of speech functions. The exclamation in the source text, "善哉" (shàn zhāi, "Good!"), can only be projected, but not reported. This example may be interpreted as evidence of the translator's awareness of the different functions of quoting and reporting.

Even when the original quoting is re-instantiated as quoting in English, Wong's translation sometimes also omits the projecting clause (2 cases) and retains the projected clause only. This is illustrated in Example 3.

Example 3

> ST: 曰 智 常 到 彼 凡 經 三 月 未 蒙 示 誨
>   (T2008_.48.0356b27–28)
>   yuē zhì cháng dào bǐ fán jīng sān yuè wèi méng shì huì
> Wong: "After staying there for three months without being given any instruction..." (1930, p. 43).
> Heng: *Chih Ch'ang said,* "After arriving there, three months passed and still I had received no instruction..." (1977, p. 292).

Table 9.2 Positioning of projecting clause in in the ST and translations

Position of projecting clause	**ST**	**Wong**	**Heng**	**Cleary**	**Cheng**
Before the projected clause	154	45	143	152	154
In the middle of the clause complex	–	50	2	–	–
After the projected clause	–	41	9	–	–
Total	**154**	**136**	**154**	**152**	**154**

Cleary: *Chih-ch'ang said*, "I was there for three months without having received any instruction..." (1998, p. 51).

Cheng: *Chi-Ch'ang then said*, "I had been there for three whole months without receiving any instructions..." (2011, p. 104).

Having a projected clause only is sometimes called free direct speech in stylistics and is considered a way to add variety to the style of the text.

In literary Chinese, paratactic quoting allows for one possible structure: the projecting clause always comes before the projected clause(s). In comparison, as discussed above, English has much more freedom, with the projecting clause being positioned before, in the middle of, or after the projected clause(s). This means that there exist different potential choices for the language users in the systemic potential in the two languages. Textually, it can be seen from Table 9.2 that in the source text, all the projecting clauses are before the projected clause(s). As for the translations, while those by Cleary and Cheng follow the exact pattern of the source text, the translation by Wong shows the greatest variety in the structure of the clause complex. In Wong's translation, nearly equal numbers of projecting clauses are put before, in the middle of and after the projected clause(s).

Examples where the projecting clause is put between or after the projected clause(s) in Wong's translation include:

Example 4

ST: 曰 念 法 華 經 已 及 三 千 部 (T2008_.48.0355b10–11)
yuē niàn fǎ huá jīng yǐ jí sān qiān bù

Wong: "Recite the Saddharma Pundarika Sutra," *replied Fat Tat*, "I have read the whole text three thousand times" (1930, p. 37)

Example 5

ST: 師 曰 汝 何處 未 明 (T2008_.48.0356c28)
       shī yuē rǔ hé chù wèi míng

Wong: "Which part of it do you not understand?" *asked the Patri-arch* (1930, p. 45).

Structure of the projecting clause

Within the projecting clause, the Sayer, if present, can only appear before the projecting verb in literary Chinese. In English, however, the Sayer can be either before or after the reporting verb if the projecting clause is not in the beginning of the clause complex.

Textually, the source text displays the structure of "Sayer + projecting verb" in all its 154 verbal projections. While this structure is retained in the translations by Cleary, Cheng and Heng, it only constitutes one (and less preferred) choice in Wong's translation, where the structure of "Projecting verb + Sayer" is preferred (Table 9.3).

This feature of Wong's translation can be illustrated through the examples above, provided here again for easy reference:

Example 6

ST: 曰 念 法 華 經 已及三 千 部 (T2008_.48.0355b10–11)
       yuē niàn fǎ huá jīng yǐ jí sān qiān bù

Wong: "Recite the Saddharma Pundarika Sutra," *replied Fat Tat,* "I have read the whole text three thousand times" (1930, p. 37)

Example 7

ST: 師 曰 汝 何 處 未 明 (T2008_.48.0356c28)
       shī yuē rǔ hé chù wèi míng

Wong: "Which part of it do you not understand?" *asked the Patri-arch* (1930, p. 45).

Table 9.3 Sequencing of Sayer and projecting verb in the ST and translations

	ST	Wong	Heng	Cleary	Cheng
Sayer + projecting verb	154	61	153	152	154
Projecting verb + Sayer	-	75	1	-	-
Total	**154**	**136**	**154**	**152**	**154**

Choice of projecting verbs

On the rank of verbal group, a significant feature of verbal projection in the source text is its repetitive use of the projecting verbs "曰" (yuē, "say") and"云" (yún, "say"). Of the 155 cases of verbal projection identified in the source text, 121 use the verbs "曰" (yuē) and"云" (yún), which account for more than 78% of the total projecting verbs used. "曰" (yuē) and"云" (yún), generally meaning "say," can be traced to the Oracle Bone Script in late 2 BCE. Of the two, as noted above, "曰" (yuē) has a strong tendency to quote rather than report (Wang, 2000).

Rendering of "曰" (yuē) and"云" (yún) in the English translations are summarized in Table 9.4.

As can be seen from Table 9.4, Wong's translation distinguishes itself from the others in that it uses a wider variety of verbs to translate the original "曰" (yuē) and "云" (yún). The unmarked reporting verb "say," which is the literal translation of "曰" (yuē) and "云" (yún), dominates in the English translations by Heng, Cleary and Cheng, although sometimes

Table 9.4 Projecting verbs "曰"/"云" and their translations

ST		Wong		Heng		Cleary		Cheng	
曰 (yuē)	100	reply	33	say	80	say	105	say	66
云(yún)	12	ask	25	reply	24	ask	3	ask	12
		say	22	ask	5	reply	3	reply	15
		remark	6	exclaim	1	omitted	1	demand	7
		retort	5	continue	1			remark	3
		rejoin	3	answer	1			rejoin	3
		commend	2					return	2
		reprove	2					observe	2
		tell	2					pronounce	2
		explain	2					speak	1
		observe	2						
		concur	1						
		exclaim	1						
		demand	1						
		declare	1						
		address	1						
		add	1						
		omitted	2						
Total	**112**		**112**		**112**		**112**		**112**

these translations also use verbs of saying with more specific meaning, such as "exclaim" and "demand". In comparison, "say" is used only 22 times in Wong's translation, where the verbs "reply" and "ask" are used more frequently. Wong's tendency to re-instantiate the unmarked projecting verb by using a more specific verb in English can be illustrated through the following examples:

Example 8

ST: 師 曰 如 是如 是 (T2008_.48.0357c12–13)
       shī yuē rú shì rú shì
Wong: "That is so, that is so," *concurred* the Patriarch (1930, p. 49).
Heng: The Master *said*, "So it is; so it is" (1977, p. 318).
Cleary: The Master *said*, "That is so, that is so" (1998, p. 57).
Cheng: The Master *said*, "Quite so, quite so" (2011, p. 20).

Example 9

ST: 簡 曰 明 喻 智 慧 暗喻煩 惱 (T2008_.48.0359c29)
       Jiǎn yuē míng yù zhì huì àn yù fán nǎo
Wong: "Light signifies wisdom," *explained* Sit Kan, "and darkness signifies Klesa (mental intoxicants or defilement)" (1930, p. 63).
Heng: Hsieh Chien *said*, "Light represents wisdom and darkness represents affliction" (1977, p. 374).
Cleary: Pi Chien *said*, "Light symbolizes wisdom, darkness symbolizes affliction" (1998, p. 69).
Cheng: Jien *said*, "The Brightness is a metaphor for Wisdom, and the Darkness a metaphor for Annoyances" (2011, p. 145).

In both Examples 8 and 9, while Wong uses two projecting verbs "*concur*" and "*explain*," which convey more information on the way of saying, the other three translators choose to re-instantiate the original projection by using the unmarked "*say*" in English.

In summary, of the four English translations of the *Platform Sutra*, three re-instantiate the source text by choosing similar/equivalent ways of realization in a new language system. Only one translation, i.e., the translation by Wong Mou-lam, re-instantiates the source text by fully exploring the systemic potential provided by the new language. For instance, Wong transformed some of the direct quotations into indirect reports. He moved the projecting clause around in the clause complex and switched the positions of the Sayer and projecting verb in the projecting clause, which are not permitted in the source language. Wong also adopted a larger variety of projecting verbs to render the monotonous "曰" (yuē) and "云" (yún) in the source text.

Interpretation of the re-instantiation in context

A text cannot be separated from its context. The relation between text and context is dynamic in that context is realized in text and text can reveal context (Butt, Fahey, Feez, Spinks, & Yallop, 2006). Similarly, in the field of translation studies, context is indispensable in the discussion of the translator's choices, as "there is always a context in which the translation takes place, always a history from which a text emerges and into which a text is transposed" (Lefevere & Bassnett, 1990, p. 11).

Taking into consideration De Souza's model of translation as re-instantiation, one may say that Wong's translation is the only one where the translator's individuation plays a significant role. Does this imply that Wong has a wider repertoire of the English language than the other translators? This probability is low, as Wong is the only translator who had never lived in an English-speaking culture. Among the translators, Heng Yin and Thomas Cleary are Americans, and Cheng Kuan is a Buddhist master who spent many years living and preaching in the U.S. It then follows that we may have to find other possible interpretations for the phenomenon, not from the perspective of individuation only, but from the broader context of translation, that is, the related social, cultural and ideological environment of the translating activity.

Wong started translating the *Platform Sutra* in 1928 and his translation was published by Yu Ching Press of Shanghai in 1930. During the late 19th and early 20th century, Chinese society, or more accurately, Chinese intellectuals, were caught in a mental dilemma. On the one hand, the defeats of the Chinese army by foreign powers since the First Opium War (1839–1842) made it apparent that China was lagging far behind the West in terms of military and economic development. On the other hand, the deep-rooted culturalism that regarded China as the nation of advanced civilization still dominated some people's minds. The desire to preserve cultural identity became even stronger when the inpouring of Western culture and Christianity was seen as a conspiracy of the Western invasion. Against this background, many Chinese intellectuals turned to traditional Chinese culture to find ways to resist the trend of Westernization (Li, 2008, pp. 76–77). Moreover, the translation of Christian literature into Chinese inspired a desire in Chinese

Buddhists to take counter measures by spreading Chan Buddhism to the West (Guo, 2010).

This attitude can be clearly seen in the preface by Dih Ping Tsze, the person who initiated and supported Wong's translation. In his preface, Dih stated that

> "[S]o far as felicity in the form of material comfort is concerned, the occidentals are in a more favorable position than our Eastern people. But in spite of their favorable position, the Great Law reaches them at a later date than it reached us" (1930, p. I).

Dih even named the translation *Message from the East*, which conveys his belief that by translating the sutra, they were taking the responsibility to transmit Chan Buddhism to the West to save the people there, in the same way that Bodhidharma transmitted Buddhist ideas from India to China long ago.

Just as the country was facing foreign invasion, Chinese Buddhism at that time was also confronted with both criticism and persecution from outside. It was constantly attacked by Confucian scholars and Christian missionaries for being useless to society and unspiritual. The New Culture Movement in 1915, the May 4th Movement in 1919, and establishment of the Federation against Religion in 1922 further aggravated the difficulties faced by Chinese Buddhists. These criticisms and anti-religious movements also increased the government's aggression in appropriating Buddhist temple properties, which directly endangered the survival of Chinese Buddhism (X. Yu, 2004, pp. 56–62). Against this background, some revolutionary Buddhists began a campaign of Buddhism reform in 1912 in order to ensure its survival. The most influential figure is Taixu, the "Saint Paul of Chinese Buddhism" (Chan, 1969, p. 56). Unfortunately, Taixu's reform met resistance from conservatives and the turbulence of Chinese society at that time made it impossible to carry out his ideas, which led Taixu to turn to the West. As almost all the political powers with considerable influence within China had their western patrons, to get western recognition and support would presumably provide an alternative to the success of Buddhism reform in China. From 1928 to 1929, when Wong was translating the *Platform Sutra*, Taixu made his journey to visit Europe and the U.S., hoping to start communication between Chinese Buddhists and western scholars.

According to the literature, Wong was familiar with Taixu and took an active role in transmitting Chinese Buddhist ideas to the West (L. Yu, 1999, p. 282). Apart from the *Platform Sutra*, Wong also translated many other

Buddhist texts into English, such as *The Diamond Sutra*, *Amita Buddha Sutra*, *The Lotus of Wonderful Law Sutra*, and *The Avatamsaka Sutra* (Ko, 1996, pp. 10–11). He even founded the *Chinese Buddhist Journal* in 1931, which was the first English Buddhist journal ever established in China (Gao, 1990, p. 32).

Therefore, the main purpose of Wong's translation of the *Platform Sutra* was to gain recognition and support from the target readers, which was expected to satisfy both the spiritual need to preserve China's cultural advantage and the practical need to ensure the survival of Chinese Buddhism. This determined that acceptability, i.e., consideration of the expectations and preferences of the target readers, rather than adequacy, i.e., adherence to the style of the source text, was the "norm" of Wong's translation (Toury, 1980, p. 55). Verbal projection in the source text, which might seem rather monotonous, was re-instantiated in a translated text that fully exploits the systemic potential of the target language, and the translation became more "literary" and enjoyable.

By contrast, translations by Heng, Cleary and Cheng were produced at much later stages when Chan Buddhism already had recognition in the west through efforts by scholars like Suzuki (1935, 1965), Goddard (1932), Watts (1953), and Humphreys (1994). The aim of translation changed into transmitting the profound knowledge contained in the source text to the target readers. Reverence to Huineng as the founder of Chan Buddhism and the source text as a religious canon probably prevented the translators from exploiting the systemic potential provided by the target language. As a result, their translations as re-instantiations appeared to be more "faithful" to the source text.

Conclusion

By investigating ways to re-instantiate verbal projection of a Buddhist text, this study demonstrates that translators made different choices. While Heng, Cleary and Cheng generally re-present the verbal projection as it is in the target language, Wong chooses to employ his repertoire of English and re-instantiate the source text in a way that exhibits the systemic potential of the target language.

The study is significant in that it represents an attempt to expand the application of systemic functional linguistics to the translation of literary Chinese, on which very little work has been carried out. During the New Culture Movement in the early twentieth century in China, tens of thousands of English texts were translated by Chinese literati as a way to develop written vernacular Chinese. As translators ventured to introduce new ways of expression, the repertoire of the language was expanded, and Standard Written Chinese gradually took shape. Although Standard Written Chinese is the norm for writing in China nowadays, the encounter between literary Chinese and English continues, with classical Chinese texts translated into English. After all, almost all the Chinese texts were written in literary Chinese before the twentieth century, and any discussion of the translation of traditional Chinese text, whether it is poetry, philosophy or literature, would be inadequate without a proper understanding of literary Chinese, the language in which the texts were written.

About the authors

Hailing Yu obtained her PhD from Macquarie University, Australia, in 2017. She is currently professor in the School of Foreign Languages and International Studies, Hunan University, China. Her research interests cover systemic functional linguistics, translation studies, and multimodal adaptation of literary texts. She has publications in *Target*, *Lingua*, *Text & Talk*, and *Social Semiotics*. Her recent book entitled *Recreating the Images of Chan Master Huineng: A Systemic Functional Approach to Translations of the Platform Sutra* was published in 2019 by Equinox.

Canzhong Wu is a senior lecturer in the Department of Linguistics, Macquarie University, Australia. He has a wide range of research interests, including systemic functional linguistics, translation studies, text analysis, and corpus linguistics. His publications include books, book chapters and journal articles in these areas. Dr Wu has extensive knowledge and experience in corpus linguistics and computational linguistics. He has developed a range of SFL-based computational systems for facilitating text analysis and extracting linguistic patterns from a large body of texts, some of which have been used in various research and commercial projects by researchers and academics around the world.

Notes

1   The *Platform Sutra* has also been translated into Standard Written Chinese numerous times in history. In these intralingual

translations, projection of locution in the original text has generally been adapted to the features of projection in Standard Written Chinese, which is very similar to modern English (see Li, 2007).
2   There are two verbal projections being omitted in Wong's translation. One verbal projection has also been omitted in Cleary's translation.
3   Source text sentences are referred to by identifying their line numbers in the on-line database of TaishōShinshūDaizōkyō http://21dzk.l.u-tokyo.ac.jp/SAT/ddb-bdk-sat2.php?lang=en.

References

Bernstein, B. B. (2000). *Pedagogy, Symbolic Control, and Identity: Theory, Research, Critique*. London: Taylor & Francis.

Butt, D., Fahey, R., Feez, S., Spinks, S., & Yallop, C. (2006). *Using Functional Grammar: An Explorer's Guide*. Sydney: National Centre for English Language Teaching and Research, Macquarie University.

Chan, W.-t. (1969). *Religious Trends in Modern China* (2nd ed.). Michigan: The University of Michigan.

Chang, C. (2018). Modelling Translation as Re-instantiation. *Perspectives*, **26** (2), 166–179.

Cheng, K. (2011). *The Dharmic Treasure Altar-Sutra of the Sixth Patriarch*. Taipei: Vairocana Pulishing Co., Ltd.

Cleary, T. (1998). *The Sutra of Huineng, Grand Master of Zen: with Huineng's Commentary on the Diomand Sutra*. Boston & London: Shambhala Publications.

De Souza, L. M. F. (2013). Interlingual re-instantiation – a new systemic functional perspective on translation. *Text & Talk*, **33** (4–5), 575–594. https://doi.org/10.1515/text-2013-0026

Dih, P. T. (1930). Preface. In M.-L. Wong (ed.), *Sutra Spoken by the Sixth Patriarch, Wei Lang, on the High Seat of the Gem of Law (Message from the East)* (pp. I). Shanghai: Yu Ching Press.

Dong, X. (2008). Blending of Direct Discourse and Indirect Discourse in Actual Texts [实际语篇中直接引语与间接引语的混用现象]. *Science of Language*, **7** (4), 367–375.

Gao, Z. (1990). Pure Karma Buddhist Association of Shanghai in Chinese Republican Era [民国年间的上海佛教净业社]. *The Voice of Dharma*, **5**, 30–34.

Goddard, D. (1932). *A Buddhist Bible*. Vermont: Cosimo Classics.

Guo, X. (2010). Buddhist Activities in Shanghai and Other Places During the Chinese Republican Era [民国时期以上海为中心的佛教活动研究]. Retrieved from http://www.pusa123.com/pusa/xuefo/folife/2012/26187.html.

Halliday, M. A. K. (1977). Text as semantic choice in social contexts. In T. Van Dijk & J. S. Petöfi (eds.), *Grammars and Descriptions* (Vol. 176–225). Berlin: Walter de Gruyter.

Halliday, M. A. K. (1992). Language theory and translation practice. *Rivista internazionale di tecnica della traduzione,* 20, 15–25.

Halliday, M. A. K., & Matthiessen, C. M. I. M. (2014). *Halliday's Introduction to Functional Grammar*. London: Routledge.

Harbsmeier, C. (1994). Indirect speech in classical Chinese. In S. Gao & L. He (eds.), *Proceedings of the First International Conference on the Grammar of Classical Chinese* [第一届国际先秦汉语语法研讨会论文集] (pp. 420–478). Changsha: Yuelu Press.

Heng, Y. (1977). *The Sixth Patriarch's Dharma Jewel Platform Sutra*. San Francisco: Buddhist Text Translation Society.

House, J. (1997). *Translation Quality Assessment: A Model Revisited*. Tübingen: Gunter Narr Verlag.

Huang, G. (2004). A functional linguistics approach to translation studies. *Chinese Translators Journal*, **5**, 15–19.

Huang, G. (2014). Analyzing the reporting clause in translating Confucius's Lun Yu (The Analects). In Y. Fang & J. J. Webster (eds.), *Developing Systemic Functional Linguistics: Theory and Application* (pp. 256–270). London: Equinox.

Humphreys, C. (1994). *Zen comes West: The Present and Future of Zen Buddhism in Western Society*. London: Curzon Press.

Ko, P.-Y. (1996). The history of *The Sutra of Hui-Neng* in English versions translations. *The Dharmalakshana Buddhist Institute Buddhist Journal*, **IV**, 1–19.

Lefevere, A., & Bassnett, S. (1990). Introduction: Proust's Grandmother and the Thousand and One Nights. In S. Bassnett & L. André (eds.), *Translation, History and Culture* (pp. 1–13). London & New York: Pinter Publishers.

Li, E. S. (2007). *A Systemic Functional Grammar of Chinese*. London: Continuum.

Li, G. (2008). *Buddhism and Freedom* [佛法與自由]. Beijing: Religious Culture Publishing House.

Martin, J. R. (2006). Genre, ideology and intertextuality: A systemic functional perspective. *Linguistics & the Human Sciences*, **2** (2).

Martin, J. R. (2008a). Innocence: Realisation, instantiation and individuation in a Botswanan town. In N. Knight & A. Mahboob (eds.), *Questioning Linguistics* (pp. 27–54). Newcastle: Cambridge Scholars Publishing.

Martin, J. R. (2008b). Tenderness: Realisation and instantiation in a Botswanan town. In N. Norgaard (ed.), *Systemic Functional Linguistics in Use* (Vol. 29, pp. 30–62). Odense Odense working papers in language and communication.

Martin, J. R. (2009). Realisation, instantiation and individuation: Some thoughts on identity in youth justice conferencing. *DELTA*, **25**, 549–583. https://doi.org/10.1590/s0102-44502009000300002

Matthiessen, C. M. I. M. (2001). The environment of translation. In E. Steiner & C. Yallop (eds.), *Beyond Content: Exploring Translation and Multilingual Text Production* (pp. 41–124). Berlin: de Gruyter. https://doi.org/10.1515/9783110866193

Matthiessen, C. M. I. M., & Teruya, K. (2013). Projection in English: The environment of quoting. *Indian Journal of Applied Linguistics*, **39** (2), 50–81.

Munday, J. (2012). *Evaluation in Translation: Critical Points of Translator Decision-making*. London: Routledge.

Steiner, E. (1998). A register-based translation evaluation: An advertisement as a case in point. *Target*, **10** (2), 291–318.

Suzuki, D. T. (1935). *The Manual of Zen Buddhism*. Kyoto: Eastern Buddhist Society.

Suzuki, D. T. (1965). *The Training of the Zen Buddhist Monk*. New York: University Books.

Toury, G. (1980). *In Search of a Theory of Translation*. Tel Aviv: The Porter Institute for Poetics and Semiotics.

Wang, L. (1980) *History of Chinese Language [*汉语史稿*]*. Beijing: Zhonghu Book Company.

Wang, L. (Ed.) (2000) *Dictionary of Literary Chines*e [古汉语字典]. Beijing: Zhonghua Book Company.

Watts, A. (1953). *The Way of Zen*. New York: Penguin Books.

Welter, A. (2008). *The Linji Lu and the Creation of Chan Orthodoxy: The Development of Chan's Records of Sayings Literature*. London: Oxford University Press. https://doi.org/10.1093/acprof:oso/9780195329575.003.0003

Wong, M.-L. (1930). *Sutra Spoken by the Sixth Patriarch, Wei Lang, on the High Seat of the Gem of Law (Message from the East)*. Shanghai: Yu Ching Press.

Xuan, W. W., & Chen, S. (2020). Taking stock of accumulated knowledge in projection studies from systemic functional linguistics: A research synthesis. *Functional Linguistics*, **7** (1), 1–22.

Yu, H., & Guo, S. (2016). The master said, the master exclaimed: Reporting verbs and the image of Huineng in translations of the *Platform Sutra*. *Asian Pacific Translation and Intercultural Studies*, **3** (3), 1–13. https://doi.org/10 .1080/23306343.2016.1228148

Yu, L. (1999). *Biographies of Early Modern Chinese Buddhists, zhongguo jindai fomen renwuzhi, [*中国近代佛门人物志*]* (Vol. 5). Taipei: Torch of Wisdom Press.

Yu, X. (2004). *Buddhism, War, and Nationalism: Chinese Monks in the Struggle Against Japan 1931–1945.* (PhD), The University of Iowa, Iowa. https:// doi.org/10.4324/9780203959121

Zhang, M. (2002). Appraisal and the translator's attitude. *Foreign Languages and Their Teaching*, **160** (7), 15–18; 27.

Zhang, M. (2013). Stance and mediation in transediting news headlines as paratexts. *Perspectives*, **21** (3), 396–411. https://doi.org/10.1080/090767 6x.2012.691101

10 Building and enhancing intercultural communication in museum spaces through SFL and translation studies

Marina Manfredi
University of Bologna, Italy

Introduction

Today's museums are widely recognized as valuable spaces of cultural and social value. Rather than being regarded as an elite activity, access to art and culture, as well as science, is increasingly seen as a means of education and civic engagement which can enhance the quality of life at all levels of society. As Ng, Ware and Greenberg (2017) argue, museums are expected to create "meaningful experiences across lines of social difference" (p. 142). As a consequence, the concept of the inclusive museum has gathered pace, in that it should engage *all* members of society, "regardless of class, gender, age, race/ethnicity, or even *linguistic background*" (Garibay & Yalowitz, 2015, p. 2, emphasis added). However, despite more general key studies about museums and communication (e.g., Coxall, 1991; 1994; Hooper-Greenhill, 1991; 1994; McManus, 1989; 1991), language issues have been rarely addressed in museum studies (with exceptions such as Blunden, 2016; Koliou, 1997). Ferguson, MacLulich and Ravelli's guidelines (1995) are a notable example of collaboration between museum and language experts.

With the development of global tourism and the growth of international visitors on the one hand, and the impact of migration, which has produced multilingual societies, on the other hand, the need to address multilingual audiences in museum contexts has come to the fore. Yet, as Garibay and Yalowitz (2015) observe, museum professionals have been slow to identify strategies for such inclusion.

Due to their internationalization, museums should become major sites of intercultural and interlingual practice. In many countries, a significant amount of translation activity is being undertaken. Translation plays a vital role in providing multilingual visitors with essential information and enables them to learn about other cultures. Nevertheless, translation practices in museums are still a relatively under-researched area.

It is against this background that this chapter aims to explore the role of interlingual translation in museums from a linguistic and translational perspective. From the point of view of linguistics, this field remains largely underexplored, despite Ravelli's (1996; 2006) pioneering studies on museum texts in the framework of Systemic Functional Linguistics (henceforth SFL) and other sparse contributions (e.g., Purser, 2000)[1]. Within Translation Studies (henceforth TS), museum translation has received little attention so far, with a few notable exceptions (Guillot, 2014; Jiang, 2010; Liao, 2018; Neather, 2005; 2008; 2012a; 2012b; 2018; Sturge, 2007). The fruitful intersection between SFL and TS has been put forth by various scholars over the last three decades (e.g., Baker, 1992; Hatim & Mason, 1990; House, 1997; 2015; Kim & Matthiessen, 2017; Munday, 2012; Steiner & Yallop, 2001), even for teaching purposes (e.g., Kim, 2007; 2009; Manfredi, 2008; 2014), although not with respect to the museum context. By drawing on the resources of both disciplines, SFL and TS, the chapter aims to make a contribution to improving museum practices with a view to meeting the cultural and social challenges posed by the issues of multilingualism, accessibility and inclusion.

SFL theory has been advocated as "appliable linguistics" (see Matthiessen, 2012) and, in Halliday's (1984, p. 56) view, its major concern has been "social accountability." By offering a sociosemiotic model deeply embedded in the social and cultural situation, SFL can contribute to bridging the gap between theory and practice and engagement with society in the museum context. I argue that making interdisciplinary connections between SFL and TS and expanding their perspectives with insights provided by museum studies could help "re-imagine" the future of contemporary museums as multilingual, accessible and inclusive spaces addressed to *all* members of global society.

The purpose of this chapter is twofold: firstly, it aims to offer an illustration of the context in which interlingual museum translation takes place, with a general overview of the European situation and a more specific focus on the Italian setting. Secondly, it presents a proposal for a special training for museum translators, informed by SFL. Drawing on a study of museums in the city of Bologna, Italy, findings derived from interviews with museum professionals will be offered, accompanied by some concrete examples of museum texts translated from Italian into English that are used to illustrate how an SFL approach might be useful for analytical and translational purposes. The objective of this chapter is to show how the translation of a museum text may draw on a theory of language that enables expression not just of "content," but also is well-structured and considerate of the museum audience. The ultimate aim is to illustrate issues that can emerge in translation and recommend training for museum translators to address those issues.

Museums and translation: Setting the scene

According to the International Council of Museums (ICOM), a museum is "a non-profit, permanent institution in the service of society and its development, open to the public, which acquires, conserves, researches, communicates and exhibits the tangible and intangible heritage of humanity and its environment for the purposes of education, study and enjoyment," while museum professionals "include all staff of the museums and institutions qualifying as museums [...] and persons who, in a professional capacity, have as their main activity to provide services, knowledge and expertise for museums and the museum community" (ICOM, 2007, p. 3). As this definition shows, the importance of communication in its widest sense is on the agenda of museums nowadays. The main tools by which museums communicate with their often multilingual and multicultural audiences are language and translation. Yet, in key documents provided by ICOM, these issues are disregarded. For example, in Ruge (2008), a frame of reference for museum professions in Europe resulting from the collaboration of three European countries (i.e., France, Italy and Switzerland), activities of museum professionals are described, but museum translation is not represented.

Likewise, in *The Italian Chart for Museum Professions* (ICOM, 2008), the lack of awareness of linguistic and translational issues is clear if we search occurrences of the key words *lingua/e* ("language(s)") and *traduzione/tradurre/traduttore* ("translation/translate/translator"). Out of 21 occurrences of the word "language(s)," 19 collocate with *inglese* ("English") in the nominal group *conoscenza almeno della lingua inglese* ("knowledge of the English language at least"), which concerns one of the requirements for all jobs in the museum setting, from the Director to those responsible for the website. To the professional in charge of public relations, the knowledge of one of the other "languages" within the international professional community may be needed. However, only knowledge of language(s) is required, but not necessarily of translation skills. Finally, one occurrence of "languages" merely concerns the introduction of the label for "museum professionals" in English, French and Spanish, simply to explain that "this name is also used in other languages." The words "translation" and "translate" occur twice, albeit both in a figurative sense, while no occurrences of "translator" can be found. This seems evidence of the fact that the activity of translation is not deemed important in the professional world of museums.

Even when consulting the Website (http://www.aiti.org) of the Italian Association of Translation and Interpreters (Associazione Italiana Traduttori e Interpreti, AITI), selecting the region Emilia-Romagna, the category "museum translator" is not included. Such documentary evidence concerning the role of museum translation in Europe and Italy seems to confirm what Neather (2012b, p. 245) had observed from the perspective of TS: the "museum community" is not usually associated with translation. However, translation remains a major tool for spreading the European and Italian cultural heritage to international visitors and an increasingly multilingual society. Non-effective linguistic choices in a translated text may have negative consequences on the impact of the museum and the cultural inclusiveness it should convey. Linguistic and translation research can help improve both awareness of translation's important role and the practice of museum translation. It is hoped that this study will stimulate further theoretical research and professional attention to this crucial aspect of the contemporary museum industry.

Theoretical framework

The conceptual issues which are most relevant to this discussion are the notions of museum translation, museum text, accessibility, inclusion and translation expertise, which will be overviewed from the perspectives of TS, linguistics and museum studies.

The term "museum translation" can convey different meanings, including that of a whole exhibition. In this chapter, I use it with the common meaning adopted within TS, i.e., "the study of interlingual transmission of texts in museum exhibitions, with a set of source texts (STs) and target texts (TTs) as data" (Liao, 2018, p. 47). The label "museum text" can also be interpreted in different ways. Ravelli (2006, pp. 1–2) proposes two views, i.e. "texts in museums" and "museum as texts." The former refers to "the language produced by the institution, in written and spoken form, for the consumption of visitors, which contributes to interpretative practices within the institution," and the latter conveys "the way a whole institution, or an exhibition within it, makes meaning, communicating to and with its public"

(Ravelli, 2006, p. 1). In this chapter, I will use the first definition and will consider a "museum text" a verbal text expressed through the graphic[2] channel that is found in a museum. The verbal text is only one of the multi-layered components that contribute to meaning-making, since "every design element of an exhibition contributes to its meanings: from the use of sound, visuals, the floorplan and spacing of displays, [to] the lighting" (Ravelli, 1996, p. 369). Likewise, from a translation point of view, "the museum represents a particularly complex semiotic environment in which various systems of signification (verbal, visual, spatial) interact to produce meaning" (Neather, 2008, p. 218). A museum text is therefore a multimodal entity and comprehensive understanding would entail an analysis of other semiotic elements. However, since the primary goal of this chapter is to discuss a model that can help translators and practictioners make informed linguistic choices, the verbal text expressed through the graphic channel will be the main focus of attention.

Museum texts encompass a wide range of text-types, such as catalogues, leaflets, introductory and section panels, labels, websites, audio guides, interactive touchpads (Liao, 2018, p. 47), as well as guidebooks, brochures, audiovisual texts (through voice-over or subtitling) and, more recently, apps. Due to space constraints, this chapter is mainly concerned with text panels – taken from wall panels, which introduce visitors to a permanent or temporary exhibition – and exhibit labels, which describe single or multiple objects.

The term "accessibility" is defined in a variety of ways within different disciplines and contexts. In museum studies, it can be considered in terms of practical, physical, intellectual and cultural accessibility (Kjeldsen & Jensen, 2015, p. 92). Within TS, it has been almost exclusively viewed with respect to disabilities (see, e.g., Jiménez Hurtado & Soler Gallego, 2015; Neves, 2018; Soler Gallego & Jiménez Hurtado, 2013) rather than to language accessibility. From the perspective of linguistics, in Ravelli's (1996) pioneering study of accessible language to museum texts from an SFL perspective, accessibility does not presume a high level of reading knowledge (unlike a very academic textbook), "does not compromise the scientific integrity of the information needing to be conveyed" and entails a cohesive and coherent texture (Ravelli, 1996, p. 371). Ravelli also maintains that "a breakdown in any of these domains will cause problems for the reader, making it difficult to follow the text, to take it in, or to retrieve information from it" (Ravelli, 1996, p. 371). In this chapter, I adopt Ravelli's view.

Strictly linked to the concept of accessibility is the notion of "inclusion." In museum studies, the issue of inclusive museums has been prominent in the past decades, with the broad sense of encompassing race, ethnicity, class, gender, disability, etc. (see, e.g., Garibay & Yalowitz, 2015; Ng, Ware & Greenberg, 2017). The issue has not received much attention in TS, although Liao (2018, pp. 56–57) considers the "social-inclusive value" one of the five functions that museum texts should aim at. In her view, an "equal access to language" (Liao, 2018, p. 56) can be achieved through multilingual texts, not only addressed to international visitors, but also to members of a community who speak different languages.

From the point of view of translation, the notion of "expertise" is also an essential aspect. In his documentary study of translation expertise and professionalism in the Chinese museum community, Neather (2012b) observes different types of stakeholders who take part in the translation process, both "expert" and "non-expert." He found that in Guangzhou, Hong Kong and Macau museums, for example, translation can be carried out either within the museum community or by external professional translators and also academic institutions. Neather (2012b) – drawing on Bhatia (2004) from a monolingual perspective and on Jääskeläinen (2010) from a translational point of view – makes a distinction between "meta-textual," "meta-generic" and "meta-social" competence, which in the case of translation involves both the source language (SL) and the target language (TL). Bhatia (2004) categorized expertise in the context of genre production and proposed a classification into "textual," "generic" and "social" competence. Neather (2012b) argues that for a "meta-activity" such as translation, additional levels of "meta-competence" are needed, i.e. "meta-textual," "meta-generic" and "meta-social" (p. 250). According to Bhatia (2004, p. 130), "textual" competence is "the ability to construct grammatically correct and textually appropriate [...] stretches of language," a definition that is also valid for a translator's "meta-textual" competence (Neather 2012b, p. 251). The lack of "meta-textual" competence may lead to "awkward or incomprehensible translations" (Jääskeläinen, 2010, p. 221). In addition, a language expert may use inaccurate terminology and concepts, even translating into his/her mother tongue (Neather 2012b, p. 251), because s/he does not know the field but only the language. Bhatia's (2004, p. 130) "generic" competence refers to "the ability to construct and manipulate genres and their conventions for professional ends" (Neather 2012b, p. 250). Likewise, Neather (2012b) calls for a "meta-generic" competence for translators, i.e. the ability to produce TL genres through translation (p. 250). A translation professional may be highly competent but lack the "meta-generic" competence in dealing with museum genres and thus in producing an effective text in the TL which reflects the conventions in the target context. Finally, "social" competence is the "ability to use language more widely to participate effectively in a variety of social and institutional contexts to give expression to one's social identity" (Bhatia 2004, p.144). From a translation point of view, "meta-social" competence refers to "aspects such as the broader understanding of how such translations can be made to function effectively in the particular communicative and social context for which they are intended" (Neather 2012b, p. 251). Clearly, lacking "meta-social" competence may produce translations which are not functional for the cultural and social communities they are addressed to. Neather (2012b) remarks that "no one community has the full set of competences needed for fully effective museum translation" (p. 245). Such professional competence might be acquired through education and special training for museum translators.

SFL (Halliday & Matthiessen, 2014) can, on the one hand, offer a way of accomplishing accessibility and inclusion through the language of museum texts, and, on the other hand, provide a systematic approach to inform translation training with the purpose of creating a special profile of museum translator, cabable of coping with the multiple needs of museum translation, not limited to the mere propositional content. This study is grounded in SFL and TS, with some insights from museum studies. SFL offers the analytical toolkit to examine linguistic choices in museum texts according to the three metafunctions of language, i.e. textual, interpersonal and ideational; TS gives the conceptual framework to explore issues of translation theory, and museum studies provides a critical context for interpreting linguistic and translational choices in light of the role of museums in contemporary society. Over the last twenty-five years, a growing interest in a translation theory informed by Hallidayan linguistics has been shown both by SFL and TS scholars (see Kunz & Teich, 2017). However, museum translation from an SFL perspective has been largely neglected.

Within an SFL framework, Ravelli (2006) offers the most comprehensive study of museum texts, from a monolingual perspective, i.e., English. Drawing on Ravelli's work, Jiang (2010) proposes the application of a Translation Quality Assessment model grounded in SFL, to evaluate a given corpus of translated museum texts. This chapter partly draws on the SFL model for analysing monolingual museum texts put forward by Ravelli (1996; 2006) and applies it to translation, working with the Italian–English language pair. Ravelli's (2006, p. 9) analysis is based on three metafunctions – labelled as "organizational," "interactional" and "representational," which clearly reflect Halliday's (1994) textual, interpersonal and ideational metafunctions. I concur with Ravelli (2006, p. 15) that a text-based approach like the one proposed by SFL "addresses communication as a meaning-making resource, a creative potential, itself multifunctional and multipurposeful, and always socially situated."

Context and methodology

The study focuses on three public museums in the city of Bologna, Italy, namely MAMbo – Museo d'Arte Moderna di Bologna (Modern and Contemporary Art Museum), Museo Civico Archeologico (Archaeological Museum of Bologna) – which also hosts an important Egyptian collection – and Museo di Palazzo Poggi, University museum (composed of 14 museums of art and science). Within a current research project on museum translation, the three museums have been chosen as key cultural sites in the city and representative of different types of domain, since the objects which are exhibited vary and consist of works of contemporary art (paintings, sculptures, etc), archeological artefacts, scientific specimens and instruments. In all three museums, translation mainly occurs from Italian into English, which acts as a lingua franca.

The chapter combines a qualitative context-oriented methodology (see Saldanha & O'Brien, 2013) and a theoretical approach. Translation practices in these museum settings were examined through interviews with commissioners involved in the translation process. Findings from interviews are supported by personal observations drawn from museum visits preceding and following the interviews. Some linguistic examples taken from the museums under scrutiny offer the basis for discussing, from a theoretical and empirical point of view, how SFL could help museum translation and translators. However, since the purpose of the chapter is neither a text-focused descriptive case study nor a quantitative account of translation choices in museum texts, their quality is not the basis of the discussion.

Translation practices in Italian museums: The case of Bologna

This section will present an overview of findings derived from the interviews with museum professionals working for the museums in Bologna which I selected for the study, and from direct observation of graphic texts such as text panels and exhibit labels in the museums. Interviews focused on the importance of translation in today's museums, the translation agents who are involved, what they value in translation, the ideal translator, the translation process and finally their opinion on a special training for museum translators (the major questions are included in the Appendix at the end of this chapter).

Interviews and research participants

For the purpose of this research, five museum professionals were interviewed: four in two focus group interviews and one in an individual interview. Three semi-structured interviews were conducted in 2018, face to face. The research participants – indicated with the letters A, B, C, D and E – had different roles within the museum settings: one (A) responsible for the editorial sector of the museum, two (B, C) for the communication sector and two (D, E) for the technical coordination. Professionals who were interviewed are the commissioners of translations within their institutions and sometimes play the role of translators, although most frequently of revisers.

Translation practices: Findings from interviews

The major issues discussed with the interviewees will be illustrated in separate sub-sections below. For the sake of confidentiality, data will be globally presented, without any specific reference to the interviewed participant or the museum she worked for, since the final goal is to offer an overview of current translation practices and the value attached to the translation activity in museums.

The importance of translation in today's museums: The choice of the English language. All interviewees were fully aware of the importance of translation in today's museums, especially to meet the needs of the growing number of international visitors in the city of Bologna. Some noted with regret the general economic difficulties of museums, others reported time pressures. Although English is the main or exclusive TL in the three museums, two of the interviewees declared that, in a global society and with the constant growth of multilingual visitors, a wider range of languages would be desirable, e.g., French or Russian, in order to be more inclusive and also respectful of cultural identities. Regrettably, all interviewees agreed on the fact that developing multilingual resources is demanding and cost-prohibitive.

Who the translation agents are. In two of the museums, translation is contracted to external professional translators: since they are public museums under the city municipality, commissioners cannot choose *ad hoc* freelance translators and have to refer to translation agencies included in an official agreement. As noted in the section "Museums and translation: Setting the scene", the category of "museum translator" is not even encompassed within professional associations, thus they tend to seek translators who have already dealt with the special languages of art, archeology, and so on, even though that is not always possible. In another museum, translation is mainly handled internally, under the supervision of exhibition curators and/or the museum staff, by a variety of agents, namely museum professionals, academics, students who take part in internship or voluntary service programs. Even when museum professionals are involved in translating themselves, either for proper translation, revision or rewriting, their normal activities are not associated with translation.

Who the ideal translator is. The ideal translator, for some of the interviewees, would be a professional translator with a specific background in the domain field, who is in contact with native speakers of the TL who can be consulted. Unlike in the past, in most cases translators are in fact non-native speakers of the TL; this condition is not a great concern, since many of the interviewees reported past experiences with translators into the TL (i.e. English), who lacked the domain-knowledge and produced awkward translations. In one museum, the lack of financial resources and consequently of the opportunity to offer translated material leads museum professionals with a general knowledge of English to produce information sheets, for merely informative purposes.

All interviewees concurred that special training for museum translators would be extremely useful and appreciated.

What is valued in translation. All professionals who were interviewed put great emphasis on the quality of translated texts, in terms of accurate and reliable information and of terminological precision in the domain field. Although they realize that terminology is not the exclusive concern and that specific concepts which can pertain to philosophy or aesthetics also need to be interpreted, not all of them explicitly recognized the importance of fluency in translated texts. Two of the interviewees showed their concern for readability, especially in the cases when museum texts are written and translated by academics, who are used to academic writing in both the SL and the TL, but not to a more "popular" style which can engage a larger public. The same professionals pointed out a fundamental issue: Italian academic style is even more formal than English, so a first useful step would be intralingual translation in Italian, in order to produce a communicatively functional translation in the TL. They commented that a specialized text needs to be addressed from specialists to a general audience, and so an effort of simplification should be always made. One of the interviewees admitted that occasionally, when personally involved in translations, she prefers to produce an English ST and translate it into Italian, even though this requires a good proficiency and cannot be generalized. One of the museum professionals who was interviewed also highlighted the importance of cultural aspects of translation, reporting the case of an Italian translator living and working in the UK, almost perfectly bilingual, who had efficiently interpreted the linguistic and cultural aspects of a catalogue and had been able to adapt cultural references to the target audience.

The translation process. All interviewed participants asserted that translations invariably undergo extensive revision and that they take ample part in the process themselves, as field experts. Revision seems to occur at different levels and can consist at worst of complete rewriting, or at best of personal interaction with the translator. One of the interviewees insisted on the importance of "fidelity," in the sense of regular collaboration with the same translator(s) when possible. In general, catalogues and labels of the same exhibition tend to be commissioned to the same translator, who has gained expertise in that area and also for consistency. Interviewees declared that professional translators are respected in their role and for this reason guidelines or glossaries are not provided, even though, for example in the case of an artist, online information about biographical and artistic material is suggested.

My findings, albeit limited to a sample of museums and interviews, seem to confirm Neather's (2012b) results with respect to the Chinese context: even in the museums in Bologna, the translation activity is not performed by expert museum translators, a category of professionals which is still undervalued in our society.

Museum texts: Findings from interviews and direct observation

Translated material. In the three museums that were the object of my investigation, different text-types undergo a process of translation, almost exclusively into English. An exception is represented by editorial material, for which, on specific occasions, translation into other languages may be needed, even though the most common language remains English. One of the interviewees reported the interesting case of an Italian catalogue translated into three languages, i.e., Galician, Spanish and English, in collaboration with a museum in Galicia.

In one of the three museums, a wide variety of texts is translated, from institutional material to press releases, from catalogues to panels and labels. Catalogues represent a large part of the translation activity, since the institution is also the publisher of their exhibitions. In another museum, only the catalogue of a recent and successful exhibition is available in an Italian-English version. For this activity, only external professional translators are commissioned to do the work, with museum experts usually carrying out the revision process, most frequently challenging and time-consuming.

Observation revealed that, in general, exhibitions are supported by wall panels, which introduce visitors to the exhibition, and labels, which describe single or multiple objects. As regards permanent exhibitions, explicative text panels are translated in only two of the museums that I examined. Labels are normally translated in all museums, on some occasions through an abridged text; in one of the museums where all panels offer a bilingual version, only the most recent labels are translated. To compensate for the lack of translated panels in one of the museums – where a general information leaflet is available in Italian and English versions – in order to guide visitors throughout the exhibitions, take-away information sheets produced by the internal staff are provided, with all their limitations and language inaccuracies. Recently, English audio guides have been available. In two museums, subtitled audiovisual material is also included: in this case the translator needs to be external, given the specific technical constraints of the medium. A museum guidebook in book format is available in English only in one of the museums; in another, there used to be one, which is currently out of print.

As far as temporary exhibitions are concerned, it is usually the artist or chief curator who chooses the linguistic material to translate. For example, in a recent exhibition, artists chose one language, either Italian or English, and even an Italian dialect, for their work or part of it, without any explicative panel: interpretation needed to be supported by the work itself.

Within the museum text-types illustrated above, different registers can be found, even literary or institutional ones: the former are especially common in catalogues, the latter in panels or labels. Interestingly, the titles of contemporary works of art are not translated, since they are considered part of the creation itself, although this could be a source of problems for some visitors, who may miss part of the message. An interesting example could be taken from MAMbo Museum, where a label simply reads: "Mario Ceroli – *Girasole*, 1975 – *legno*/wood," without any translation provided for the word *girasole* ("sunflower") and thus leaving the interpretation of the original art piece to the visitor. In one of the museums, given the historical nature of many collections, Latin is widely employed even in translated texts, potentially causing problems of non-inclusiveness.

Complaints about the quality of translated museum texts (see, e.g., Neather, 2005) were reported by two of the interviewees, who admitted that the lack or poor quality of translated material has increasingly become an issue on social media.

As shown from the discussion of findings, the main concern of museum professionals who were interviewed is the quality and accuracy of museum texts, while some of them also recognized the importance of their communicative function, since they have to engage a great variety of visitors, with a different degree of expertise in the field, diverse cultural backgrounds and with English frequently used as a lingua franca. Professionals were fully aware that "a sense of frustration, cultural misunderstanding and exclusion" (Neather, 2005, p. 191) may derive from non-effective translation choices. The situation of translation and professionalism in contemporay museums should thus urge reflection and decisions at an institutional and, more broadly, political level. What linguists and translation scholars might do is to offer a theoretical and empirical contibution aimed at the creation of a new translator profile. A potentially valid theoretical approach useful for acquiring "generic," "textual" and "social" competence in translating museum texts will be the focus of the following section.

An SFL approach for museum translators

I argue that a specific training for museum translators informed by an SFL approach might help their meta-discursive competence. After a general illustration of the Hallidayan (1994) model, only selected aspects relevant to museum translation might be taught for translation purposes.

Meaning is typically understood in terms of representation, i.e. what the text is about. Yet, for an SFL scholar, this is only a partial view of the whole meaning of a communicative event. The type of interaction taking place and the way the text is organized also contribute to the global creation of meaning, since meanings operate simultaneously. In order to interpret a text at the level of experience, interactive event and textual organization, a translator should look into the clause as Representation, Exchange and Message, by analysing the three metafunctions of language. When translating a source text (ST) into a target text (TT), multi-layered meanings should be conveyed, not necessarily through the same language structures.

In discussing the three strands of meaning that any text entails, I will follow the same order of metafunctions as Halliday (1994) and Ravelli (2006), starting with textual/"organizational" meanings. As Ravelli (2006, p. 9) acknowledges, this is not an obvious place to start, since ideational meanings are usually the main (if not exclusive) interest. However, in museum texts, even though the technicality conveyed by ideational meanings is a key issue, the way the text is organized often poses problems to translators, and potentially to museum visitors if they face an ineffective TT. In the following sections, I will focus on the clause as Message, Exchange and Representation of both STs and TTs drawn from wall panels and labels found in the museums. The authentic examples will provide instances of both "good" and "poor" practices, which show the lack of a systematic approach to translation.

The clause as message

Any text is characterized as a message, realizing textual meanings, which Halliday (1978, p. 113) considers the "enabling" metafunction, without which ideational and interpersonal meanings would not be expressed. How a message is construed is crucial for museum translation, because it is closely related to language accessibility. Among the lexico-grammatical structures through which textual meanings are activated, particularly important for museum texts is the thematic structure of the clause, which determines the flow of meanings and influences the interpretation of the text. In her analysis of museum texts, Ravelli (2006) declares that "it is the issue of organizing texts which poses some of the more challenging communication issues for museums (p. 9)." I posit that this aspect can be even more challenging for a translator, especially when working with the Italian-English language pair, given that Italian grammar allows for a much more "creative" thematic structure than English.

The Theme of a clause, its point of departure (Halliday & Matthiessen, 2014, p. 89), is fundamental for museum texts. For example, as Ravelli (2006) notes, in a museum label there should be some correspondence between the Theme of the text and the object being illustrated. Moreover, in general, an English unmarked structure makes the text easier to follow, as in Table 10.1.

While the ST features a marked Thematic structure, with an Attribute (*Centrale*/"Central") in thematic position, followed by a Circumstance of

Table 10.1 Museum of Palazzo Poggi, Bologna: Panel, *Il museo di Diluvianum* ["The museum of Diluvianum"].

ST	TT
Centrale *nel dibattito scientifico della prima metà del '700 **fu** la discussione sui fossili. [...]*	Fossils **were at the centre** of scientific debate during the first half of the 18th century. […]

Place (*nel dibattito scientifico della prima metà del '700/*"in the scientific debate of the first half of the 18th century"), a relational Process (*fu/*"was") and a Carrier (*la discussione sui fossili/*"the debate on fossils"), the TT instantiates an unmarked thematic structure (Carrier^relational Process^Circumstance of place^Circumstance of time), which better places the focus on the objects displayed in the exhibition.

Cohesion is another extremely useful resource for the instantiation of textual meanings and the translator can employ it to make a TT clearer. We should keep in mind that a visitor of an exhibition is standing while reading a panel, probably not totally concentrating and using a language which could be a lingua franca. In the example of a museum text in Table 10.2, the translator made an effort to try to make the museum experience more inclusive, through the cohesive devices of repetition and synonymy.

The Italian text omits the Participant of the first clause, since the grammatical system allows this choice, and later employs a pronominal element

Table 10.2 MAMbo Museum, Bologna, Morandi Exhibition: Panel, *Morandi e l'arte dell'incisione* ["Morandi and the art of etching"].

ST	TT
*[Morandi] Aveva guardato a lungo e minuziosamente, le più difficili e oscure prove di Rembrandt di cui possedeva quattro incisioni originali [...] Naturalmente non **ne** imitò mai il gusto, la maniera o i soggetti; gli interessava invece la sua maestria indiscutibile, in questa pratica che richiede mano fermissima, occhio acuto e conoscenza tecnica. [...]*	**He** [Morandi] carefully and extendedly observed the most difficult and obscure works by Rembrandt of whom he owned four original etchings […] It goes without saying that **Morandi** never tried to imitate the style or subjects **of the Dutch master**; on the contrary he was interested in his indubitable mastery of this technique, which requires an extreme steady hand, a sharp eye and a deep technical know-how. […]

to refer to the Dutch artist, Rembrandt. In the TT, the translator adds the personal pronoun "he" at the beginning of the clause, then chooses to insert the proper name "Morandi" and finally to replace the pronoun *ne* ("of him," with the meaning of "his") with "of the Dutch master," an effective synonym which gives coherence to the text.

An important aspect that might compromise the accessibility of a text is its lexical density, in other words, how much ideational material is packed into a clause. Written texts tend to be more lexically dense than speech (Halliday, 1985). A typical resource that makes a text lexically dense is use of nominalization – clearly, the instantiation of textual meanings intersects here with the ideational metafunction. As Ravelli (2006, p. 61) remarks, "a text overloaded with nominalization is unlikely to be desirable in a museum context." Table 10.3 shows an instance where keeping nominalization in the TT makes it more complex to read, thus textually inappropriate.

Although from a grammatical point of view there is almost nothing "wrong" in the TT solutions of the example, in the social context of the exhibitions, they are unlikely to facilitate understanding, since "the ideational content [which] is densely packed in nominal constructions" (Halliday & Matthiessen 2014, p. 728) makes the text less straightforward and more "scientific." A more desirable translation might have been for example: "The amulets were powerful and effective due to various things, such as their shape or material. [...] They could have been more powerful thanks to portrayals and inscriptions."

Table 10.3 Archaeological Museum, Bologna, Egyptian collection: Label, *Amuleti* ["Amulets"].

ST	TT
Si chiamavano amuleti quegli oggetti che, portati sul corpo, venivano usati dagli Egiziani per proteggere i vivi e i morti dai più disparati pericoli. **La potenza e l'efficacia degli amuleti** *derivava da diversi fattori, il primo dei quali era dato dalla forma [...].* **Altro elemento di potere magico** *era costituito dal materiale con cui erano realizzati [...].* **La potenza degli amuleti** *poteva essere accresciuta* **dalla presenza di raffigurazioni e testi incisi.** *[...]*	The amulets are objects which were worn by the Egyptians to protect living and dead people from all kinds of dangers. **The power and effectiveness of the amulets** depended on various things, amongst which their shape. [...] **Their magical power** depended also on their material. [...] **The power of the amulets** could be increased **by their representations and inscriptions.** [...]

The clause as exchange

In museum research, the role of the visitor has become prominent in the past decades. In SFL, the dialogic interaction between addresser and addressee takes place at the level of the clause as exchange and is realized through interpersonal meanings, which Ravelli (2006, p. 70) labels "interactional." A typical resource for interpersonal meaning is Modality, which introduces negotiation into a text by recognizing the perspective of potential interlocutors. Modality can be instantiated in different ways in Italian and in English, as the example in Table 10.4 clearly shows.

In the ST, "probability" is instantiated by the verbal group *doveva essere* ("[it] should have been"); in the TT, it is conveyed by the modal adjunct "probably," maintaining the same function. This example demonstrates how SFL can offer a useful tool for avoiding the literal translation that museum texts frequently display.

As Ravelli (2006, p. 85) reminds us, one of the most typical resources for making a text closer to the reader is the use of a personal pronoun like "you." Table 10.5 provides an example, where an impersonal form is used in the ST.

Table 10.4 Museum of Palazzo Poggi, Bologna: Panel, *Sala di Davide* ["David's room"].

ST	TT
*La sala, che originariamente aveva l'accesso diretto al pianerottolo dell'ingresso principale, **doveva essere** destinata a funzioni di rappresentanza ufficiale. [...]*	The room, which was originally accessed from the landing of the main entrance, **was probably** used for ceremonial purposes. […]

Table 10.5 MAMbo Museum, Bologna: Panel, *Lo sguardo di Morandi tra Bologna e Grizzana* ["Morandi's gaze between Bologna and Grizzana"].

ST	TT
*In questa sala **è possibile** vedere alcuni paesaggi che Morandi dipinse ad olio e ad acquerello, disegnò e incise nei due luoghi in cui egli trascorse gran parte della sua vita, ovvero a Bologna e Grizzana. [...]*	In this room **can be seen** several landscapes that Morandi painted (in oils and watercolours), drew, and engraved in the two places in which he spent the greater part of his life, Bologna and Grizzana. […]

An analysis of the grammar of interpersonal meanings might have been useful to avoid the mistake in the translation, where "can be seen" is not preceded by a grammatical subject as required by English: a possible solution might have been to shift the impersonal *è possibile* ("it is possible") into a personal "you can see," preserving the same function of possibility, while construing less distance from the addressee, as is more typical of contemporary museum texts in English.

The clause as representation

The clause as representation construes experience, which is closer to the traditional notion of "content" and is realized by ideational (experiential and logical) meanings, which Ravelli (2006, p. 95) calls "representational." In a museum text, their realization includes the technical vocabulary – which represented a core issue for the museum professionals who were interviewed (see "What is valued in translation"). However, also the Transitivity structure, i.e. Processes, Participants and Circumstances through which reality is represented, plays an important role. In museum descriptions, special emphasis on the object which is illustrated could make the TT more accessible, as in the Table 10.6.

In the ST, the transitivity structure of the two clauses is Circumstance^ Process^ Participant, given the more flexible Italian system where elements of the thematic structure can be moved freely. In a museum text expressed in English, emphasis on the Participant can facilitate the reading experience. In the example above, the first Circumstance (*Lungo le pareti*/"Along the walls") has been transformed into a prepositional phrase which has

Table 10.6 Museum of Palazzo Poggi, Bologna: Panel, *Sala di Mosé* (1556) ["Moses' room"].

ST	TT
Lungo le pareti della sala scorre un fregio che contiene otto episodi della vita di Mosé. [...]	**The frieze along the walls of this room contains** episodes from the life of Moses. […]
Nel soffitto fastosamente decorato entro medaglioni sono raffigurate sei figure allegoriche riferibili ad altrettante discipline o linguaggi del sapere. [...]	**The lavishly decorated ceiling features medallions with** six allegorical figures symbolizing six disciplines or languages of knowledge. […]

Table 10.7 Museum of Palazzo Poggi, Bologna: Panel, *Il corno dell'unicorno o dente di narvalo* ["The unicorn's horn or narwhal tusk"].

ST	TT
*[...] Giuseppe Monti **riteneva che il corno proveniente dalla collezione di Ferdinando Cospi non potesse appartenere al mitico animale.** [...]*	[...] Giuseppe Monti **believed the tusk on display was part of Ferdinando Cospi's collection and did not belong to the mythological animal.** [...]

become part of a nominal group; in the second case the Circumstance (*Nel soffitto*/"In the ceiling") has become a Participant. Process type may also be considered; here material Processes in the ST (*scorre*/"runs" and *sono raffigurate*/"are represented") have been translated as relational Processes of a possessive kind in the TT ("contains" and "features"). These are more typical of descriptions and thus more straightforward for visitors.

In addition to making texts more readable, an accurate analysis within an SFL framework could also help translators avoid misinterpretation in the TT, as in the example in Table 10.7.

In the Italian text, at the level of logical meanings, the clause-complex is composed of a main clause (*Giuseppe Monti riteneva*/"Giuseppe Monti believed") followed by a projected clause introduced by *che*/"that." Within the latter, *il corno proveniente dalla collezione di Ferdinando Cospi* ("the tusk from Ferdinando Cospi's collection") is a nominal group, constructed with an embedded clause. In terms of transitivity structure, it can be analyzed as a Participant of a possessive attributive clause (Halliday & Matthiessen, 2014, p. 296), more specifically a Possessed, while *al mitico animale* ("to the mythical animal") functions as the Possessor. In other words, in Italian, the text says Monti believed that the tusk in the collection was not part of the animal. In the TT, "the tusk on display was part of Ferdinando Cospi's collection" conveys a different meaning.

A grammatical resource amply used in academic writing, as well as in museum texts with a more formal style, is grammatical metaphor. A useful strategy to simplify certain museum texts would be unpacking grammatical metaphors in favor of more congruent solutions. Let us consider the example in Table 10.8.

The ST features an abstract material Process (*viveva*/"lived"), with an inanimate Participant (*La Storia naturale*/"Natural history"), which has been more congruently transformed into a relational Process, with "Images and illustrations" as the Carrier. Although metaphorical language in museum

Table 10.8 Museum of Palazzo Poggi, Bologna: Panel, *Le tavolette di Ulisse Aldrovandi*/"Ulisse Aldrovandi's Woodblocks."

ST	TT
*La Storia naturale di Aldrovandi **viveva di** immagini e di raffigurazioni. [...]*	Images and illustrations **were** a fundamental part of Aldrovandi's Storia Naturale. […]

Table 10.9 An SFL framework for museum translators.

Aspect of the CLAUSE in focus	METAFUNCTION (meanings in focus)	Lexico-grammatical structures in focus
Message	Textual/Organizational	– Thematic structure – Cohesion – Lexical density
Exchange	Interpersonal/Interactional	– Modality – Use of personal pronouns
Representation	Ideational/Representational	– Technical vocabulary – Transitivity

texts may well be vivid, it might make a text less accessible and inclusive for a wide variety of English-speaking visitors.

These examples from museum exhibitions have not been provided with the purpose of assessing the quality of the translations. As a matter of fact, the examples showed both cases of effective solutions, which conveyed different types of meaning, and problematic choices in terms of realization of textual, interpersonal and ideational meanings. However, it is argued that a useful training for museum translation would include a systematic approach to translation which enables consistent and effective choices in order to guarantee language accessibility. Table 10.9 displays the most relevant linguistic aspects which should be tackled by museum translators.

Conclusions

In this chapter, I have reflected on current museum practices with respect to translation activity, taking the city of Bologna as a case in point. The contextual study, based on interviews with museum professionals and observation of translated texts, led to a theoretical and practical proposal which sees SFL as a useful tool for museum translator training, since it encompasses an ideal set of resources for dissecting texts in the SL and reproducing meaning(s) in the TL, within a wider socio-cultural context. One of the possible objections that might be raised is that the SFL model is excessively elaborated. Nevertheless, as Ravelli (2006, p. 16) clearly states, "communication itself is inherently complex, and to treat it otherwise, to treat it simplistically, is to fail to account for it at all." A limitation of this study is that the use of SFL is purely theoretical and has not been tested with museum visitors using the translations. It might also be claimed that the aspect of domain terminology has not been tackled. Obviously, training for museum translators should include the use of terminological resources such as specialized electronic corpora. Moreover, seminars on museum studies might help build bridges between disciplines. This proposal for an SFL approach to museum translation has put less emphasis on these points to focus on the grammatical choices of the translator.

More than a decade ago, Neather (2005, p. 195) remarked that "even in more 'museologically developed' nations, there remains a sometimes chronic lack of awareness of foreign language needs." The case of Bologna seems emblematic of such a "lack of awareness," but *not* at the level of museum professionals, who are fully aware of the importance of effective and accessible museum translation.

SFL might demonstrate its profound social commitment, which Halliday (1984) had pursued since the origins, in showing the value of interdisciplinary cooperation among experts from various fields towards the common goal of transforming museums into inclusive social agents that favor intercultural communication. More theoretical research is certainly needed and more empirical studies are undoubtedly called for. However, perhaps most importantly, experimenting with special training for museum translators is desirable, and this is the route I aim to explore in future projects.

About the author

Marina Manfredi is Lecturer and Researcher in English Language and Translation at the University of Bologna, Italy, in the Department of Modern Languages, Literatures and Cultures. She is also Director of the Language Centre at the same university. She teaches English Linguistics for undergraduate students and English Translation for postgraduates. Her main research interests lie in the field of Translation Studies and include Systemic Functional Linguistics and translation, translation teaching, postcolonial translation, metaphor translation, audiovisual translation, news translation, translation of popular science for press magazines, for the web and, most recently, museum translation. She has contributed to national and international conferences on these topics and has published various articles and three books.

Acknowledgements

I am extremely grateful to Federica Guidi, Annalisa Managlia, Marinella Marchesi, Martina Nunes and Francesca Rebecchi for their time and interest.

Notes

1   Some SFL scholars have focused on multimodality in museum texts (see, e.g., Pang, 2004; Ravelli, 2014; Ravelli & Heberle, 2016).
2   The term 'written' is not used here to avoid confusion with the notion of 'written' medium.

References

Baker, M. (1992). *In Other Words: A Coursebook on Translation*. London/New York: Routledge.

Bhatia, V. K. (2004). *Worlds of Written Discourse: A Genre-based View*. London: Continuum.

Blunden, J. (2016). *The language with displayed art(efacts): Linguistic and sociological perspectives on meaning, accessibility and knowledge-building in museum exhibitions*. PhD thesis. University of Technology Sydney.

Coxall, H. (1991). How language means: An alternative view of museum text. In G. Kavanagh (ed.), *Museum Languages: Objects and Texts* (pp. 85–100). Leicester, England: Leicester University Press.

Coxall, H. (1994). Museum text as mediated message. In E. Hooper-Greenhill (ed.), *The Educational Role of the Museum* (pp. 132–139). London: Routledge.

Ferguson, L., MacLulich, C., & Ravelli, L. (1995). *Meanings and Messages: Language Guidelines for Museum Exhibitions*. Sydney: Australian Museum.

Garibay, C., & Yalowitz, S. (2015). Redefining multilingualism in museums: A case for broadening our thinking. *Museums & Social Issues*, **10**(1), 2–7. https://doi.org/10.1179/1559689314z.00000000028

Guillot, M. N. (2014). Cross-cultural pragmatics and translation: The case of museum texts as interlingual representation. In J. House (ed.), *Translation: A Multidisciplinary Approach* (pp. 73–95). Basingstoke, England: Palgrave Macmillan. https://doi.org/10.1057/9781137025487_5

Halliday, M. A. K. (1978). *Language as Social Semiotic: The Social Interpretation of Language and Meaning*. London: Arnold.

Halliday, M. A. K. (1984). Linguistics in the university: The question of social accountability. In J. E. Copeland (ed.), *New Directions in Linguistics and Semiotics* (pp. 51–67). Amsterdam: John Benjamins Publishing Company.

Halliday, M. A. K. (1985). *Spoken and Written Language*. Australia: Deakin University Press.

Halliday, M. A. K. (1994). *An Introduction to Functional Grammar*. London: Arnold.

Halliday, M. A. K., revised by Matthiessen C. M. I. M. (2014). *Halliday's Introduction to Functional Grammar.* London: Routledge.

Hatim, B., & Mason, I. (1990). *Discourse and the Translator*. London/New York: Longman.

Hooper-Greenhill, E. (1991). A new communication model for museums. In G. Kavanagh (ed.), *Museum Languages: Objects and Texts* (pp. 49–61). Leicester, England: Leicester University Press.

Hooper-Greenhill, E. (1994). *Museums and their Visitors*. London: Routledge.

House, J. (1997). *Translation Quality Assessment: A Model Revisited.* Tübingen, Germany: Gunter Narr Verlag.

House, J. (2015). *Translation Quality Assessment. Past and Present*. London/ New York: Routledge.

ICOM (2007). *Statutes.* Retrieved October 15, 2018, from https://icom. museum/wp-content/uploads/2018/07/2017_ICOM_Statutes_EN_02.pdf

ICOM (2008). *Carta nazionale delle professioni museali.* Retrieved October 15, 2018, from http://www.beniculturali.it/mibac/multimedia/ UfficioStudi/documents/1261134207917_ ICOMcarta_nazionale_ versione_ definitiva_2008%5B1%5D.pdf

Jääskeläinen, R. (2010). Are all professionals experts? Definitions of expertise and reinterpretation of research evidence in process studies. In M. G. Shreve & E. Angelone (eds.), *Translation and Cognition* (pp. 213–227). Amsterdam: John Benjamins Publishing Company. https://doi.org/10.1075/ ata.xv.12jaa

Jiang, C. (2010). Quality assessment for the translation of museum texts: Application of a Systemic Functional model. *Perspectives:*

Studies in Translatology, **18**(2), 109–126. https://doi. org/10.1080/09076761003678734

Jiménez Hurtado, C., & Soler Gallego, S. (2015). Museum accessibility through translation: A corpus study of pictorial audio description. In J. Díaz Cintas & J. Neves (eds.), *Audiovisual Translation: Taking Stock* (pp. 277–298). Newcastle upon Tyne, England: Cambridge Scholars Publishing.

Kim, M. (2007). Using Systemic Functional text analysis for translator education. *The Interpreter and Translator Trainer*, **1**, 223–246. https://doi. org/10.1080/1750399x.2007.10798759

Kim, M. (2009). Meaning-oriented assessment of translations: SFL and its application for formative assessment. In C. V. Angelelli & H. E. Jacobson (eds), *Testing and Assessment in Translation and Interpreting Studies: A Call for Dialogue Between Research And Practice* (pp. 123–157). Amsterdam/Philadelphia: John Benjamins Publishing Company. https://doi. org/10.1075/ata.xiv.08kim

Kim, M., & Matthiessen, C. M. I. M. (2017). Ways to move forward in translation studies. In J. Munday, M. Zhang (eds.), *Discourse Analysis in Translation Studies* (pp. 11–26). Amsterdam/Philadelphia: John Benjamins Publishing Company. https://doi.org/10.1075/bct.94.01kim

Kjeldsen, A. K., & Jensen, M. N (2015). When words of wisdom are not wise: A study of accessibility in museum exhibition texts. *Nordisk Museologi*, **1**, 91–111. https://doi.org/10.5617/nm.3002

Koliou, A. (1997). Foreign languages and their role in access to museums. *Museum Management and Curatorship*, **16**(1), 71–76. https://doi. org/10.1080/09647779700601601

Kunz, K., & Teich, E. (2017). Translation studies. In T. Bartlett & G. O'Grady (eds.). *The Routledge Handbook of Systemic Functional Linguistics* (pp. 547–560). London: Routledge.

Liao, M-H. (2018). Museums and creative industries: The contribution of translation studies. *The Journal of Specialized Translation*, **29**, 45–62.

Manfredi, M. (2008). *Translating Text and Context: Translation Studies and Systemic Functional Linguistics, Vol. I, Translation Theory*. Bologna, Italy: Dupress.

Manfredi, M. (2014). *Translating Text and Context: Translation Studies and Systemic Functional Linguistics, Vol. II, From Theory to Practice*. Bologna, Italy: Asterisco Edizioni.

Matthiessen, C. M. I. M. (2012). Systemic Functional Linguistics as appliable linguistics: Social accountability and critical approaches. *D.E.L.T.A.*, **28**, 435–471. https://doi.org/10.1590/s0102-44502012000300002

McManus, P. M. (1989). Oh, yes, they do: How museum visitors read labels and interact with exhibit texts. *Curator*, **32**(2), 174–189. https://doi. org/10.1111/j.2151-6952.1989.tb00718.x

McManus, P. M. (1991). Making sense of exhibits. In G. Kavanagh (ed.), *Museum Languages: Objects and Texts* (pp. 35–46). Leicester, England: Leicester University Press.

Munday, J. (2012). *Evaluation in Translation*. London/New York: Routledge.

Neather, R. (2005). Translating the museum: On translation and (cross-)cultural presentation in contemporary China. In J. House, M. R. Martín Ruano & N. Baumgarten (eds.), *Translation and the Construction of Identity* (pp. 180–197). Seoul, Korea: IATIS.

Neather, R. (2008). Translating tea: On the semiotics of interlingual practice in the Hong Kong museum of tea ware. *META: Translators' Journal*, **53**(1), 218–240. https://doi.org/10.7202/017984ar

Neather, R. (2012a). Intertextuality, translation, and the semiotics of museum presentation: The case of bilingual texts in Chinese Museums. *Semiotica*, **192**, 197–218. https://doi.org/10.1515/sem-2012-0082

Neather, R. (2012b). "Non-expert" translators in a professional community. *The Translator*, **18**(2), 245–268.

Neather, R. (2018). Museums, material culture, and cultural representations. In S.-A. Harding & O. Carbonell Cortés (eds.). *The Routledge Handbook of Translation and Culture* (pp. 361–378). Abingdon, England: Routledge. https://doi.org/10.4324/9781315670898-20

Neves, J. (2018). Cultures of accessibility: Translation making cultural heritage in museums accessible to people of all abilities (pp. 415–430). In S.-A. Harding & O. Carbonell Cortés (eds.). *The Routledge Handbook of Translation and Culture*. Abingdon, England: Routledge. https://doi.org/10.4324/9781315670898-23

Ng, W., Ware, S. M., & Greenberg, A. (2017). Activating diversity and inclusion: A blueprint for museum educators as allies and change makers. *Journal of Museum Education*, **42**(2), 142–154. https://doi.org/10.1080/10598650.2017.1306664

Pang Kah Meng, A. (2004). Making history in *From Colony to Nation*: A multimodal analysis of a museum exhibition in Singapore. In K. O'Halloran (ed.), *Multimodal Discourse Analysis: Systemic Functional Perspectives* (pp. 28–54). London: Continuum.

Purser, E. R. (2000). Telling stories: Text analysis in a museum. In E. Ventola (ed.), *Discourse and Community: Doing Functional Linguistics* (pp. 169–198). Tübingen, Germany: Gunter Narr Verlag.

Ravelli, L. J. (1996). Making language accessible: Successful text writing for museum visitors. *Linguistics and Education*, **8**, 367–387. https://doi.org/10.1016/s0898-5898(96)90017-0

Ravelli, L. J. (2006). *Museum Texts: Communication Frameworks*. London: Routledge.

Ravelli, L. J. (2014). The objects of experience: Transforming visitor-object encounters in museums. *Visitor Studies*, **17**, 225–227. https://doi.org/10.4324/9781315417776-9

Ravelli, L., & Heberle, V. M. (2016). Bringing a museum of language to life: The use of multimodal resources for interactional engagement in the Museu da Língua Portuguesa, Brazil (pp. 521–546). *Revista Brasileira de Linguística Aplicada*, **16**(4), 521–546. https://doi.org/10.1590/1984-639820159920

Ruge, A. (ed.) (2008). *Museum Professions: A European Frame of Reference*. Berlin: ICOM. Retrieved July 15, 2019 from http://ictop.org/wp-content/uploads/2019/06/ICTOP-Museum-Profession_frame_of_reference_2008.pdf

Saldanha, G., & O'Brien, S. (2013). *Research Methodologies in Translation Studies*. London: Routledge.

Soler Gallego, S., & Jiménez Hurtado, C. (2013). Traducción accesible en el espacio museográfico multimodal: Las guías audiodescriptivas (pp. 181–200). *JoSTrans*, **20**. Retrieved October 15, 2018 from https://www.jostrans.org/issue20/art_jimenez.php

Steiner, E., & Yallop, C. (2001). *Exploring Translation and Multilingual Text Production: Beyond Content*. Berlin/New York: Mouton de Gruyter. https://doi.org/10.1515/9783110866193

Sturge, K. (2007). *Representing Others: Translation, Ethnography and the Museum*. Manchester, England: St. Jerome.

Appendix

Questions included in my interviews with museum professionals (2018)

1   What is the importance of translation in today's museums?
2   Who are the translation agents in your institution? Is the translation activity carried out within the museum you work for or outside? (if inside: Who takes care of it?; if outside: Do you rely on professional translators or academics? If you rely on professionals, on what kind of professional do you rely? (professional associations/translation agencies/freelance translators)
3   Who is the ideal translator?
4   What is valued in translation?
5   How is the translation process in your institution carried out? (Who is responsible for the activities related to translation such as rewriting, editing, etc.? Are guidelines or glossaries provided to translators?)
6   Which are the major text-types which are typically translated?
7   Would you be in favour of a special training for museum translators?

Index

3x3 learning resource 211, 221, 222
4th grade PE teaching 62–81
    adding language 63, 64, 67–71
    approaching generalizations 63, 64,
        73–75
    first experiences 63, 64, 65–67
    pedagogical considerations 64–65
    professional knowledge 63, 64,
        75–79, 81
    stretching language 63, 64, 71–73
    theoretical underpinnings 64–65

a priori identification/argumentation
    126, 129
abstract participant types/semantic
    gravity 191–192, 196
academic language 58–60
academic writing at university level
    117–233
    Appraisal studies 119–148
    scaffolding 177–205
    scaffolding/history 207–233
    Transitivity and Attitude 149–176
ACCESS test 16, 17
accessibility 261–262
Achugar, M. 49
acrobatic figures 62–63, 67–68, 71–73
    experimentation/presentation 73–74
    mind maps 75, 76, 80–81
    presentating/testing 67–71
    professional knowledge 75, 79
action
    4th grade PE teaching 63, 71
    language accompanying action 58,
        63, 64, 80
    language as action 58
    metalanguage 48–49
    progression in PE teaching sequence
        82

Register concepts as planning tool
    60, 61
actors/metalanguage 48–49
adding language to physical education
    63, 64, 67–71
addition/geometry 93–94, 104
adverbial adjuncts and modifiers 123,
    124, 125
adverbs and Appraisal models 122
Affect
    evaluation 153–154, 156, 158, 162,
        166–167, 169–170
    semantic gravity 192–193, 198–199
affirming propositions 123–124
"after that" expressions in PE 73
algebraic notation to denote geometrical
    generalizations 107–108
"and" conjunction 105, 106, 107
"and" as connector 41
"and if" conjunction 107
appears (mental process with modal
    meaning) 191
appliable linguistics 258
Appraisal
    argumentation 120–121, 126–128
    and argumentation in discourse
        120–121
    argumentative patterns 131–132
    discussion 135–138
    Engagement and argumentation
        132–134
    evaluative prosody 130–131
    methodology 128–130
    model 121–125
    results 130–134, 135
    semantic gravity 192–193, 198–200
    studies 119–148
    Transitivity and 150, 151–156, 158,
        161–167, 168

Appreciation
  semantic gravity 192–193,
    198–199
  Transitivity and Attitude 153, 154,
    156, 157, 162, 166–171
approaching generalizations/4th grade
  PE teaching 63, 64, 73–75
argumentation
  argumentative patterns 131–132
  in discourse 120–121
  Engagement and 132–134
  relevance/scaffolding/history
    210–211
  scaffolding/history 208, 211, 218,
    219, 220–224
ask/verbal projection 247–248
asking questions in physical education
  68, 69
assertions 131–132
Attitude
  semantic gravity 192–193
  systems 121
  see also Transitivity and Attitude
Attribute 124–125, 131, 138, 270–271
aunque textual operators 129

backings/Appraisal 126–128, 134–138
backwards (physical ed) 70–71
Bakhtinian notions of dialogism and
  intertextuality 122
balance in PE 66, 70–71, 75, 76
bare assertion/semantic gravity 193
Barron, D. 209
the base (4th grade PE teaching) 68,
  70–79, 81
behavioral process
  semantic gravity 191
  Transitivity and Attitude 151–152
"being" clauses 168
being processes to "tell" characters 37
belonging, sense of 199
Bernstein, B. 182, 239–240
best practice 13–32

from learners to teachers 27
  teacher changes 15
"between theory and practice" 180,
  182–183
Bhatia, V. K. 262
bilingualism
  best practice 13, 16–18, 19, 21
  metalanguage 33–53
  scaffolding 178–179
Bologna, Italy, museum translations
  257, 264–269
Brisk, M. E. 8
  best practice 13–32
Buddhism 249–251
building blocks for teacher learning
  frameworks 209
"but" conjunction 105, 106, 109
"but, if" conjunction 106–107
Butler, J. I. 55–56

Canzhong, W. 252
Carpenter, B. 49
Carriers/museum translations 270–271
Castro, M. 130, 135–136
"'cause then, if" conjunction 106
center of dilation 90, 91, 102
Chan Buddhism 249–250
Chang, C. 238
Chen, I.-A. 36
Chen, S. 238
Cheng, K. 242, 243, 245–249, 251
Cheung, L. M. E. 55, 56, 82
children's point of view 35
Chinese language translations
  237–256
Circumstance
  geometry 93–94, 101–102
  metalanguage 36, 38, 43–48
  museum translations 270–271,
    274–275
CLAE (*Corpus del Languaje
  Académico en Español*) 149,
    155–158

claim components/Appraisal models
128, 129, 134, 135, 136–137
claim/argumentation 126
class (geometry) 93, 96, 98
classification/description (theory)
55–56
clauses
"being"/"having" clauses 168
complexes and TAXIS terms
242–243
embedded clauses 191
impersonal clauses 125
as message/museum translations
270–272
positioning/verbal projection 245
shī wèn yuē projecting clause
241–242
structure/verbal projection 246
Theme/museum translations 270
in Transitivity and Attitude 161,
163
clearly stated thesis statements
210–211
Cleary, T. 242, 243, 245, 246,
247–248, 249, 251
CLIL (content and language integrated
learning) 56
Coffin, C. 208, 211
collaboration 207–233
context 210–213
design-based research 213–214
evolution of 214–224
commonsense knowledge 194
comparison (geometry) 93–94
comparison/one-point perspective
lessons 104
comprobar factual verbs 124
concede-counter moves 213
concentration (physical ed) 77
conclusions/Appraisal 126, 129, 133
concrete participant types/semantic
gravity 191–192, 196
concur/verbal projection 248

concurrence 123, 130–131
"condition" conjunction 105
conjunction 49, 93–94, 104–108, 109
connection, Transitivity and Attitude
149–176
connectors
Appraisal models 123
argumentation 127
metalanguage 38, 39–42, 46–47
consequence (geometry) 93–94, 104
consistent organizations 210–211
construction
language as construction 58, 63, 64,
80
mind maps 75, 76, 81
progression in PE teaching sequence
82
reconstruction 58, 60–61, 63–64,
80, 82
Register concepts as planning tool
60, 61
content and language integrated
learning (CLIL) 56
content of text *see* Field
context
collaboration 210–213
geometry 89–92
metalanguage 34–38
museum translations 264
physical education 58–60
profiling/semantic gravity 184
real-world mathematizing 87–116
re-instantiation 249–251
scaffolding 178–179, 207–208,
210–213
of situation 83
see also Field; Mode; Tenor
Contraction 122, 123, 134, 193
contrast
Appraisal models 122
geometry 93, 96–98, 100
*Corpus del Lenguaje Académico en
Español* (CLAE) 149, 155–158

Cospi, F. 275
counter connectors 127
countering 122, 123, 129, 138, 213
critical reflection essays 183
current history argument rubric 221,
      222

Danish
   Ministry of Education 57, 62, 83
   physical education 57, 68–70,
      77–79
   scaffolding 177–205
data components/Appraisal models
      126, 128, 134, 135, 136–137
de acuerdo con adverbial adjuncts 125
de hecho discourse markers 123
De Souza, L. M. F. 238, 239, 249
Deakin, L. 136
deber modals of epistemicity 124
decir reportative process 125
demand/verbal projection 247–248
demostrar factual verbs 124
denial 122, 123, 129, 138
density and semantic gravity 182
Derewianka, B. 57
   see also snail model
Descriptive Reports 211
design-based research in scaffolding/
      history 213–214
DFNT national scaffolding test of
      Denmark 185, 186–200
diagrams *see* geometry
dialogic contraction 123
dialogic space in corpus 131
dialogism and intertextuality 122
dialogistic engagement 199
dialogistic positioning/semantic gravity
      193
The Diamond Sutra 250–251
Dih, P. T. 250
dilation concepts 90, 91, 93, 102,
      108–111
direct quoting/projection 240

disabled people 25
disclaim subsystems 122, 130
discourse markers 123
discourse semantic analysis 150
discourse types 150
distance
   Appraisal models 125
   geometry 97, 98, 100–101
doesn't fall (physical ed) 71
   see also balance
"doing history" 208, 211
doing processes to "show" characters
      37
Dong, X. 241
Dragonfly Explanations 42–43
dynamic views of pictures 101–102

Earhart, M. 49
Eggins, S. 96, 97
ELA (English Language Arts) 37
elementary and secondary education
      11–116
   best practices 13–32
   geometry 87–116
   metalanguage 33–53
   physical education 55–86
ELLs (English language learners) 16,
      17
embedded clauses 191
empathetic autobiographies (EA) 20,
      21–22
emphatic first person 123
empirical identification/argumentation
      126, 127
en cuanto a textual operators 129
en primera instancia textual operators
      129
en relación con textual operators 129
endorsement 123, 124, 130–131
Engagement
   acknowledgement 124–125, 131,
      138
   and argumentation 132–134

discussion 135, 136
methodology 129, 130
models 121–125
PEEL heuristics 220
resources in academic discourse 119–148
results 131–132
scaffolding/history 212–213
semantic gravity 192, 199
Transitivity and 153
English for Academic Purposes in Spanish speaking countries 136
English Language Arts (ELA) 37
English language learners (ELLs) 16, 17
entertainment 124, 131, 138
equal access to language 261–262
es posible interpersonal metaphors 124
essays 149, 155, 166–167
critical reflection 183
how to 216
essential understandings 88
ethos 121
evaluation/choice (evaluating student choice) 55–56
evaluative identification/argumentation 126, 161
evaluative language 27
evaluative prosody/Appraisal 130–131
everyday participant types/semantic gravity 191–192, 196
evolution of collaboration in scaffolding/history 214–215
Exchange, museum translations 269–270, 273–274
exclaim/verbal projection 247–248
existential process
semantic gravity 191
Transitivity and Attitude 151–152
expanding dialog 212–213
Expansion 122, 124, 134
expansive, dialogistically/semantic gravity 193

expectancy relations, geometry 95–102
expenses of childcare 24
experiential function *see* Field
experiential meanings in ideational metafunctions 34
experimentation in 4th grade PE teaching 73
expert language 58–60
explanation
Appraisal/semantic gravity 198–199
historical 211
relevance of evidence/thesis construction 210–211
verbal projection 248
explicar reportative process 125
exploration (geometry) 92
exploring context/physical education 58–60
external factors in scaffolding/history 209

factual verbs, Appraisal models 124
Faculty of Arts 149
Field
4th grade PE teaching/theoretical underpinnings 64–65
content of text 14
functional approaches 58
maps of meaning in semantic gravity 190
as planning tool 60
rounding off physical education 83
figureheads in PE *see* acrobatic figures
finally expressions in PE 71
first expressions in PE 71, 73
Focus 193, 198–199
for example ("linking words") 20–21
Force 193, 198–199
Forey, G. 55, 56, 82
Freeman, J. 126, 129
French, R. 35

functional approach to PE 57–60
functional grammar 33–53
functional stages/Appraisal models 128

Galician museums 267–268
Garibay, C. 257
Gebhard, M. 36
general participant types/semantic
    gravity 191–192, 196
generalizations
    4th grade PE teaching 63, 64,
      73–75
    one-point conjunction analysis
      107–108
generative mode of geometrical
    interaction 108
generic competence 262, 269
genres
    Appraisal studies 128–129
    best practice 14–28
    metalanguage 35–36
    physical education 60, 77
    scaffolding 179, 187–188, 195–
      199, 208
    Transitivity and Attitude 155,
      167–172
    translation 242
geography 149, 155–159, 164–167
geometry 87–116
    conjunction 104–108
    context of study 89–92
    discussion 108–111
    expectancy relations 95–102
    findings 95–102
    goals of study 88–89
    nuclear relations 93, 94, 95–102
    research questions and methods
      93–94
    taxonomic relations 95–102
    vanishing points 93–105
Gibbons, – 185, 199
"go back and reread" strategies 46
Goddard, D. 251

Graduation systems 121, 153, 192
Graham, H. 36
grammatical metaphor 45, 191
Greenberg, A. 257
Greer, S. 36
Gunawan, W. 36

Hailing, Yu 252
Halliday, M. A. K. 14, 34, 45, 150,
    151–153, 168, 190
    museum translations 269, 270
    scaffolding 190
    social accountability of SFL theory
      258
    verbal projection 240, 244
handling 80
    see also action
Harbsmeier, C. 241
hasta contrast operators 122
"having" clauses 168
having eye contact (physical ed) 77
helping and supporting each other
    (physical ed) 77
Heng, Y. 242–244, 246, 247–248, 249,
    251
heteroglossic discourse
    in Appraisal 136–138
    in argumentation 133–134, 135
    semantic gravity 193, 199
heteroglossic flow 131
heteroglossic propositions 122
heuristics 218, 220–224
history 149, 155–159, 163–164
    of diagrams 88
    Explanations 211
    scaffolding 207–233
    specific attitude types 165
Hogdson-Drysdale, T. 15
hold (physical ed) 75, 76
"hook" (starting essays) 27
how language means 49–50
however ("linking words") 20–21
Huineng (Chan master) 242

Humphreys, C. 233, 251
hyper-Themes 127–128
hypotaxis 241, 243–246

ideal translators in museums 266
ideational meaning
    museum translations 274
    in semantic gravity 190, 191
ideational metafunctions 34, 94,
        150–151
"if" conjunction 105, 106–107
if–then statements 104–105, 108, 109
Ignatieva, N. 172–173
impersonal clauses 125
inclusion 261–262
incluso contrast operators 122
indirect reporting/projection 240
individuation 238–240
informative noun groups 24–25
instantiation/translation 237–256
institutional identification/
        argumentation 126
instructing and guiding (physical ed)
        68, 69
"interactional" labels 273
interactional metafunctions 263–264
intercultural communication in
        museums 257–282
interdisciplinary collaborations in
        historical scaffolding 207–233
internationalization of museums
        257–258
interpersonal mappings of meaning in
        semantic gravity 190
interpersonal metafunctions 34, 94,
        150–151, 212–213
interpersonal metaphors 124
interpretar/Transitivity and Attitude
        160
interpretation of diagrams 88
intertextuality 122
interviews, museum translations
        265–267

Introduction to Functional Grammar
        151–152
IRF patterns 59, 60
*The Italian Chart for Museum
        Professions* 259

Jääskeläinen, R. 262
Jacobsen, S. K. 201
Jacobson, A. 207
Jasso, V. Z. 173
Jiang, C. 263–264
joint construction of reports/
        professional knowledge 77–79
journals 183
Judgment 153–154, 162, 166–170,
        192–193, 198–199
justification/argumentation 126

keep the balance (physical ed) 71
    see also balance
King, M. L. 21
Kirk, S. 184, 197
knowledge
    4th grade PE teaching 63–65, 75–79
    scaffolding/history 207–208
    semantic gravity 194
    structures 182

L2 writers 208
Language & Meaning project 38
language accompanying action 58, 63,
        64, 80
language as action 58
language as construction 58, 63, 64, 80
language as reconstruction 58, 63, 64,
        80
language as reflection 58, 63, 64, 81
Language and Social Power 13
language use/PE teaching
    adding language 70–71
    approaching generalizations 74–75
    first experiences 67
    professional knowledge 76–77

theoretical underpinnings 64, 65
launch (geometry) 92, 94
learning objectives and roles/PE
    teaching 76–77
    adding language 70
    approaching generalizations 74
    first experiences 66
    theoretical underpinnings 64, 65
Lee, J. 136
Lee, S. 128
legitimate knower 194
Legitimation Code Theory (LCT) 4, 5,
    177–205
Lemke, J. 109, 110
lexical strings regarding one-point
    perspectives 93–101
lexicogrammatical analysis 150
lexico-grammatical stratum 191
Liao, M-H. 261–262
linear perspectives (geometry) 91, 96,
    99
linguistic background 257
"linking words" 20–21
literature 149, 155–158, 159
    Chinese and English, verbal
        projections 240–242
    specific attitude types 165, 166–167
    texts/process type tokens 164–165
    Westernization of China 249–250
logical mappings of meaning in
    semantic gravity 190
logical meanings in ideational
    metafunctions 34
logogenetic perspectives (geometry)
    102
logos 121
long nominal groups 191

McQuillan, P. J. 208
macro-Themes 127–128
making each other good 62–63, 66
    mind maps 75, 76, 81
    professional knowledge 77, 79

maps of meaning in semantic gravity
    190
Martin, J. R. 150, 167–168, 192, 238
    Appraisal model 119–148
    Engagement system 125
    scaffolding/history 212–213
mas contrast operators 122
matching up of elements in one-point
    perspective lessons 105
material process
    museum translations 267–268
    semantic gravity 191
    Transitivity and Attitude 151–152,
        156, 157, 167
material process/semantic gravity 191
material process/Transitivity and
    Attitude 151–152, 156, 157, 167
mathematical literacy of one-point
    perspective lessons 110
mathematizing from real-world
    contexts 87–116
Matthiessen, C. M. I. M. 45, 168, 190,
    240, 244, 258
meaning 33–53, 182
    experiential/ideational
        metafunctions 34
    museum translations 274
    "reservoir" of the language
        community 239–240
    semantic gravity scale 190–193
    sentence constituents in unfamiliar
        text 44–46
    see also metalanguage
mencionar/Transitivity and Attitude
    160
mental Process
    semantic gravity 191
    Transitivity and Attitude 151–152,
        156, 158, 160, 168
Menyuk, P. 36
message
    abundancy 183
    museum translations 269–272

Message from the East 250
metafunctions 150–151
   maps of meaning in semantic
      gravity 190
   museum translations 262–264,
      269–270
metalanguage 33–53
   classroom interactions 38–42
   data sources 42–43
   discussion 48–50
   findings 43–48
   functional grammar/reading support
      46–47
   geometry 94
   making sense of text 43
   meaningful sentence constituents
      44–46
   methods 38–43
   pedagogical contexts 34–38
   research context 38
   see also Systemic Functional
      Linguistics theory
metaphor 45, 124, 191
Miller, R. 127–128
mind maps 75, 76, 80–81
minor processes 45
Mizuno, J. 119
modal qualifiers/argumentation
   126–127
Modality 151
modals of deonticity/epistemicity/
   evidenctiality 124
Mode 14, 83
   functional approaches 58
   maps of meaning in semantic
      gravity 190
   as planning tool 60
   as progression 63
   rounding off physical education 83
   theoretical underpinnings 64–65
modifiers 24, 26, 123
monoglossic discourse 135–136, 193,
   199–200

Mood/Transitivity and Attitude 151
Moore, J. 37
Moss, G. 119
move (physical ed) 70–71
multilingual urban elementary school,
   Boston 13
Mulvad, Ruth 83
Museo d'Arte Moderna di Bologna
   (MAMbo) 264, 268–269, 271,
   273
museum translations
   Bologna, Italy case study 264–269
   clause as message 270–272
   context and methodology 264
   direct observations 267–269
   Exchange 269–270, 273–274
   findings from interviews 265–269
   interviews/research participants
      265
   Message 269–272
   Representation 269–270, 274–276
   setting the scene 259–260
   SFL approach 269–278
   theoretical framework 260–264
museums
   intercultural communication
      257–282
   Plimoth Plantation 20

nadie pronouns 122
Nagle, J. 209
name/metalanguage 36
"narrative" writing 210–211
narrowing dialog 212–213
National Council of Teachers of
   Mathematics 88
natural interest 35
naturalmente expressions 123–124
Navarro, F. 135–136
Neather, R. 262–263, 267
negative words for evaluative language
   27
Negroni, G. 123

New Culture Movement of 1915,
    China 250
next expressions in PE 71
Ng, W. 257
ni adverbs 122
ninguno pronouns 122
no adverbs 122
nominalization 191
nouns
    groups 24–25
    metalanguage 35, 49
    report writing 23
nuclear relations (geometry) 93, 94,
    95–102
nunca adverbs 122

obviamente expressions 123–124
Olbrechts-Tyteca, L. 120
one-point perspective lessons 90–96
    diagram/instructions provided
        91–92
    lexical strings 93–101
    mathematical literacy 110
    nuclear relations 101–102
    as qualifier 101
    research questions/methods 93–94
    summarizing 102–108
    taxonomic/expectancy/nuclear
        relations 95–96
one-point perspectives lessons 96,
    97–99, 100
opportunities for disabled people 25
organizational metafunctions 263–264
Oteíza, – 135–136

Palazzo Poggi, Bologna museum 270,
    271, 273, 274, 275, 276
Palincsar, A. S. 37
parataxis 241, 243–246
parecer modals of evidenctiality 124
part (geometry) 93, 96–99
Participant
    geometry 93–94, 101–102

metalanguage 36, 38, 39, 43–48, 49
museum translations 265, 271–272,
    274–276
semantic gravity 191, 195–196
Participant types/semantic gravity
    191–192, 195–196
particular participant types/semantic
    gravity 191–192, 196
pathos 121
pedagogical considerations in 4th grade
    PE teaching 64–65
pedagogical contexts/metalanguage
    34–38
pedagogy/process-oriented writing 199
PEEL heuristics 218, 220–224
pensar reportative process 125
Perelman, C. 120
pero contrast operators 122
personal pronouns, museum
    translations 273
perspective lines (geometry) 95–97,
    98–99
Pessoa, S. 127–128
physical education (PE) 55–86
    4th grade PE teaching 62–81
    and education and language 56–57
    exploring context 58–60
    functional approaches 57–60
    as planning tool 60–61
    principles to language-based
        teaching 62
    progression in teaching sequence
        81–82
    rounding off 82–83
    subjects' project 57
Piggybook 35
Place, Circumstance of 270–271
The Platform Sutra 242–249, 250–251
poder modals of deonticity/
    epistemicity 124
point of view 35
por lo tanto textual operators 129
por supuesto expressions 123–124

positioning of clause, verbal projection
245
positive words for evaluative language
27
PPP (presentation practice production)
model 58–60
precisamente adverbial modifiers 123
precision (physical ed) 75, 76
prepositional phrase 49
principles/sequence (sequencing
actions or ideas) 55–56
probablemente adverbial adjuncts 124
Process
geometry 93–94
geometry/nuclear relations
101–102
metalanguage 35, 36, 38, 39,
43–48, 49
museum translations 267, 270–271,
274–276
"process first" approaches 46
semantic gravity 191, 194–195
Transitivity and Attitude 151–152,
158, 159, 160, 163–164
writing pedagogy 199
Process types/semantic gravity 191,
194–195
proclamation 123, 130–131
professional development (PD) 15,
17–18
from learners to teachers 27
informative noun groups 24–25
report writing 23–25
theme/new information analysis 25
professional knowledge/4th grade PE
teaching 63, 75–79
professional and linguistic
progression/4th grade PE
teaching
adding language 71
approaching generalizations 75
first experiences 67
professional knowledge 77

profiling/semantic gravity 184–189
progression of content knowledge and
language 64, 65
see also professional and linguistic
progression
progression in PE teaching sequence
81–82
projection 237–256
pronouns
Appraisal models 122
museum translations 273
pronunciation 123, 129, 130–131
propositions 122–125

qualifiers
Appraisal models 126–127, 128,
134, 135, 136–137, 138
geometry/nuclear relations
101–102
qualitative context-oriented translation
methodology 264
quoting/parataxis 243–246
quoting/projection 240

Ravelli, L. J. 258, 261, 263–264, 270,
273, 274
reading a diagram 88
Reading to Learn 13, 183
realization/verbal projection 238–239,
248–249
reasoned conjectures (geometry) 104
rebuttals/Appraisal models 126–127,
128, 134, 135, 136–137
recalcar/Transitivity and Attitude 160
reconstruction
language as reconstruction 58, 63,
64, 80
progression in PE teaching sequence
82
Register concepts as planning tool
60, 61
rectification 123, 138
reflection

critical reflection essays 183
language as reflection 58, 63, 64,
      81
progression in PE teaching sequence
      82
reflective journals 183
Register concepts as planning tool
      60, 61
Register concepts 14, 57–60
   as planning tool 60–61
   principles to language-based
      teaching 62
   semantic gravity 191–192
   six lessons in PE 80
   translation studies 237
   see also Field; Mode; Tenor
re-instantiation (translation studies)
      237–256
relational Process
   museum translations 270–271
   semantic gravity 191
   Transitivity and Attitude 151–152,
      156, 157, 158, 167
relax (physical ed) 70–71
relevance of the argument 210–211
repetition (geometry) 93, 96, 98
reply/verbal projection 247–248
reportative process 125
reporting/hypotaxis 243–246
reporting/projection 240
Representation/museum translations
      269–270, 274–276
representational metafunctions
      263–264
research context
   metalanguage 38
   see also context
"reservoir" of the language community
      239–240
Rheme, semantic gravity 192,
      197–198
rhetoric/Appraisal models 124,
      126–127, 128

Rincon-Gallardo, S. 15
Rodríguez-Vergara, D. 173
Rose, D. 167–168, 192
Ruge, A. 259

SAL (*Systemics Across Languages*) 149
Sánchez, M. 130, 135–136
"say" verbal projection 242, 247–249
Sayer + projecting verb structure
      240–241, 246, 248–249
saying processes 34–35
   to "show" characters 37
scaffolding 24, 177–205
   context 178–179
   history 207–233
   physical education 80–81
   semantic gravity 182–189
   study and procedure 180–182
   theory overview 179–180
Schall-Leckrone, L. 208, 209
Schleppegrell, M. 3, 8
   best practice 13
   geometry 87
   metalanguage 33–53
   physical education 57–58
   scaffolding argument writing in
      history 208, 209, 227
school history genres 208
se ha dicho que impersonal clauses
      125
se peinsa que impersonal clauses 125
secondary education *see* elementary
      and secondary education
seems (mental process with modal
      meaning) 191
segregation of learner groups 59
semantic gravity 180, 181, 182–183
   difference in exam scores 189–190,
      193–200
   linguistic resources/middle range
      scale 193–200
   meaning/middle range scale
      190–193

visualized in semantic profiles
  184–189
semantic stratum 191
semantic waves 180, 182–183, 189
semiotic mediation 48–49
sense of belonging 199
sensing processes to "tell" characters
  37
sentence-level metalanguage 33–53
sentir/Transitivity and Attitude 160
sequence of actions 71
sequencing words 71
SFL *see* Systemic Functional
  Linguistics theory
shàn zhāi exclamation 244
shī wèn yuē projecting clause 241–242
sides in geometry 93
Sigsgaard, A.-V. 202
sino connector 122, 123
situation-independent language use
  74–75
Slater, T. 55–56
snail model 3
  physical education 57, 60, 61,
    62–82
  see also Field; Mode; Tenor
"so" conjunction 105, 106, 107
social accountability of SFL theory 258
social competence 262–263, 269
social-inclusion values 261–262
social-semiotic SFL analysis 83
Spanish 18, 21
  engagement resources in academic
    discourse 119–148
  Transitivity and Attitude 149–176
structure of clause, verbal projection
  246
sub-systems
  of disclaim 122
  physical education 58
subtopic graphic organizers 26
"such as" 20–21
summary

Engagement system 125
  geometry 92, 94, 102–108
  physical education 63, 70, 75–79,
    81
Suzuki, D. T. 251
Swales, J. 128
Sydney School research group
  152–153
symbolic notation of diagrams 88
Symons, C. 43, 50
synonyms (geometry) 93, 96, 98–99
Systemic Functional Linguistics (SFL)
    theory
  4th grade PE teaching/pedagogical
    considerations 64–65
  best practice 13–32
  framework for museum translators
    276
  functional approach to PE 57–58
  geometry 89, 94
  informed educational change 18, 19
  intercultural communication in
    museums 257–282
  metafunctions 150–151
  physical education 55–86
  Register concepts as planning tool
    60–61
  Russell Elementary School 16
  scaffolding 177–205
  and teaching/learning cycle 14–15
  translation as re-instantiation
    237–238
  see also metalanguage
Systemics Across Languages (*SAL*)
  149
Szenes, E. 183, 189

tampoco adverbs 122
Tao Te Ching 237
tax codes 24
TAXIS terms 240, 241, 242–243
taxonomic lexical relations in geometry
  93, 94

taxonomic relations, geometry 95–102
taxonomy, Transitivity and Attitude 167–168
Taylor, S. 36
Teach First classes 180–181
teacher changes, best practice 15
Teaching bilingual pupils module 178–179, 180–181, 189
teaching and learning cycle (TLC) 13, 14–18, 26, 183
technical participant types/semantic gravity 191–192, 196
tener modals of deonticity 124
Tenor 14, 83
    4th grade PE teaching 64–65
    functional approaches 58
    maps of meaning in semantic gravity 190
    as planning tool 60
textual competence 262, 269
textual mappings of meaning in semantic gravity 190
textual metafunction 34, 94, 150–151
textual operators/Appraisal models 129
textual patterns via Theme and Rheme 192
texture of text 97
Theme 20
    Appraisal models 127–128
    of clause/museum translations 270
    museum translations 270–271
    new information analysis 25
    and Process/co-patterning 35–36
    semantic gravity 192, 197–198
"then" conjunction 106–107
"then" expressions in PE 71, 73
theory inspired best practice 13–32
therefore ("linking words") 20–21
thing (metalanguage) 43–48
think-alouds 42–48
TLC (teaching and learning cycle) 13, 14–18, 26, 183
Tosi, C. 123

Toulmin, S. 120–121, 126–128
traditional writing and process-oriented writing pedagogy 199
Transitivity and Attitude 34, 149–176
    Appraisal system 152–153, 163–167
    discussion 167–171
    frequency of clauses in process 163
    geography texts/process type tokens 164–165
    history texts/process type tokens 163–164
    literature texts/process type tokens 164–165
    methodology 155–158
    percentage of evaluative/non-evaluative clauses 161
    polarity in expressions 162
    results 158–167
    SFL and metafunctions 150–151
    specific attitude types 165, 166–167
    system 151–152
    theoretical assumptions 150–155
    types of Attitude in text 162, 163
Translation Quality Assessment models grounded in SFL 263–264
translation studies 235–282
    intercultural communication in museums 257–282
    as re-instantiation 237–256
    translators in museums 266, 276
tratar/Transitivity and Attitude 160

U.S. National Council of Teachers of Mathematics 88

vanishing points (geometry) 93–105
verbal groups/Transitivity and Attitude 156
verbal Process
    semantic gravity 191
    Transitivity and Attitude 151–152, 160, 168

verbal projection 237–256
   choice of verb 247–249
   literary Chinese and English
     240–242
   Platform Sutra 242–249, 250–251
   positioning of clause 245
   in source text and translation 243
   structure of clause 246
*Verbal typology and evaluation
    in academic writing of the
    humanities: a systemic
    functional study* 149
verbs
   Appraisal models 124
   metalanguage 35, 49
video clubs 91–92
Vygotsky, – 35–36, 48–49, 185, 199

Walter, D. 49
Wang, L. 241
Ware, S. M. 257
warrant components/Appraisal models
    126, 127, 128, 129, 136–137
Washington, G. 21–22
Watts, A. 251
"ways of knowing" in history 208, 211
weight shift (physical ed) 75, 76
Westernization of China 249–250
"when" conjunction 105, 107

White, P. R. R. 150, 199–200
   Appraisal model 119–148
   Engagement system 125
   scaffolding/history 212–213
WIDA Consortium 17
Williams, G. 34–37
Wong M.-L. 242, 244–246–51, 247,
    249, 250–251
Write it Right 13
writing history arguments 208
Writing Project, The 13
written summaries
   physical education 63, 77–79
   see also summary
Wu, S. 136

Xuan, W. W. 238

Yalowitz, S. 257
yo sostengo que emphatic first person
    123
"you" personal pronouns 273
Yu Ching Press of Shanghai 1930
    249
yuē verb 242, 247–249
yǔlù (records of sayings) 242
yún verbs 247–249

Zappa-Hollman, S. 209

CPSIA information can be obtained
at www.ICGtesting.com
Printed in the USA
JSHW050347250621
16224JS00001B/12